FABLES

1001 NIGHTS of SNOWFALL

VERTIGO
DC COMICS

FAB

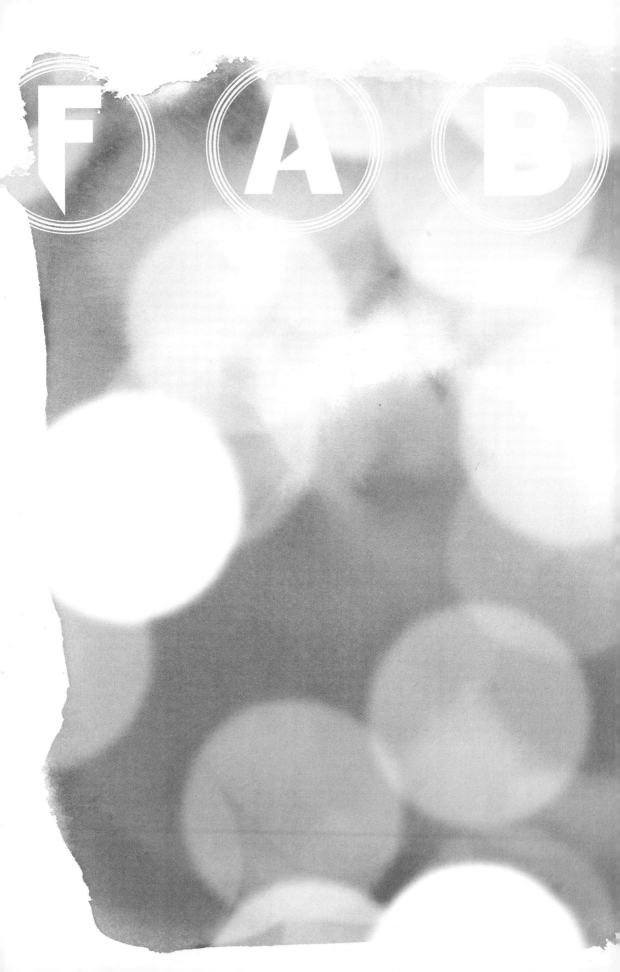

FABLES

1001 Nights of SNOWFALL

Written by Bill Willingham

Illustrated by

Esao Andrews

Brian Bolland

John Bolton

Mark Buckingham

James Jean

Michael Wm. Kaluta

Derek Kirk Kim

Tara McPherson

Jill Thompson

Charles Vess

Mark Wheatley

Lettered by Todd Klein

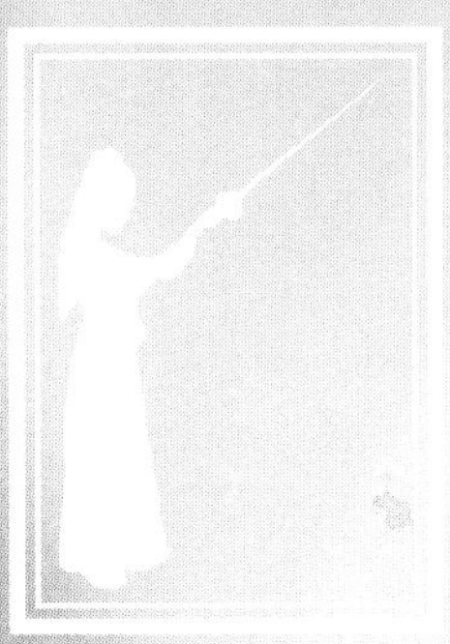

Karen Berger, Sr. VP-Executive Editor Shelly Bond, Editor Angela Rufino, Assistant Editor Louis Prandi, Art Director Paul Levitz, President & Publisher
Georg Brewer, VP-Design & DC Direct Creative Richard Bruning, Sr. VP-Creative Director Patrick Caldon, Exec. VP-Finance & Operations
Chris Caramalis, VP-Finance John Cunningham, VP-Marketing Terri Cunningham, VP-Managing Editor Stephanie Fierman, Sr. VP-Sales & Marketing
Alison Gill, VP-Manufacturing Hank Kanalz, VP-General Manager, WildStorm David McKillips, VP-Advertising & Custom Publishing
Lillian Laserson, Sr. VP & General Counsel Jim Lee, Editorial Director-WildStorm Paula Lowitt, Sr. VP-Business & Legal Affairs John Nee, VP-Business Development
Gregory Noveck, Sr. VP-Creative Affairs Cheryl Rubin, Sr. VP-Brand Management Jeff Trojan, VP-Business Development, DC Direct Bob Wayne, VP-Sales

Table of Contents

ALL STORIES WRITTEN BY BILL WILLINGHAM.
ALL STORIES LETTERED BY TODD KLEIN.

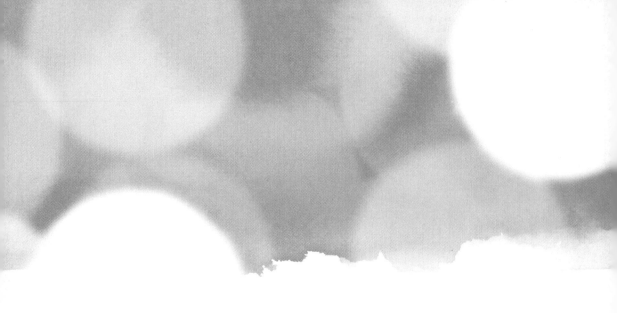

INTRODUCTION BY BILL WILLINGHAM

Welcome to the enchanted world of FABLES. For those of you who've read FABLES stories before, welcome back. I'm always glad to see you here. Grab a comfy seat and make yourself at home. We'll be starting the stories in a moment. But if you don't mind, I'd first like to have a quiet word or two with those who are visiting these lands for the first time.

FABLES has been, over the past four years, a monthly comic book series written by me and illustrated by many of the best artists working in the business, some of whom have also contributed to this book. I'm about to tell you everything you need to know about previous Fables stories so that you can get the most from this volume. Are you ready? Okay then, here we go.

FABLES is about the continuing modern day adventures of a group of characters who are already well known to you. Snow White? Prince Charming? The Big Bad Wolf? You've met them before, along with many others who've populated the beloved folklore and fairy tales of your youth. But now you're about to learn some of the things that have happened to them after (and sometimes before) the stories you already know. How did Snow White's marriage to Prince Charming turn out? What made the Big Bad Wolf so big and so bad? And so on.

In previous issues of FABLES we've learned that these immortal characters, who singly and collectively call themselves Fables, have long ago been chased out of their magical homelands by the armies of an evil warlord they knew only as The Adversary. Alone or in small groups, these refugees have eventually found their way here, to our very mundane and quite unmagical world. They established a secret underground colony for themselves in a small corner of New York City and named their community Fabletown. For centuries now they've been living among us while we were none the wiser. They dwell in their tiny community, keeping their secrets, squabbling, feuding, loving, prospering, failing and generally living their lives just like us. But they've also been biding their time against the day, someday in the near or far future, when they can once again marshal their strength, overthrow The Adversary and reclaim their lost homelands.

There. That's it. Since these are all new stories about characters you already know, you're not really new to FABLES after all. In that sense you get to start out as veterans like the rest of us. And since the stories in this book take place at least a century before the events depicted in the first issue of the regular FABLES comic book series, congratulations, you're already caught up. If, after reading these tales, you think you might enjoy a few more FABLES stories, I invite you to take a peek in the back pages of this book where you'll discover how to obtain some collections of those previous adventures which continue to this day.

In the meantime, welcome back to a world you knew once upon a time. We've certainly missed you.

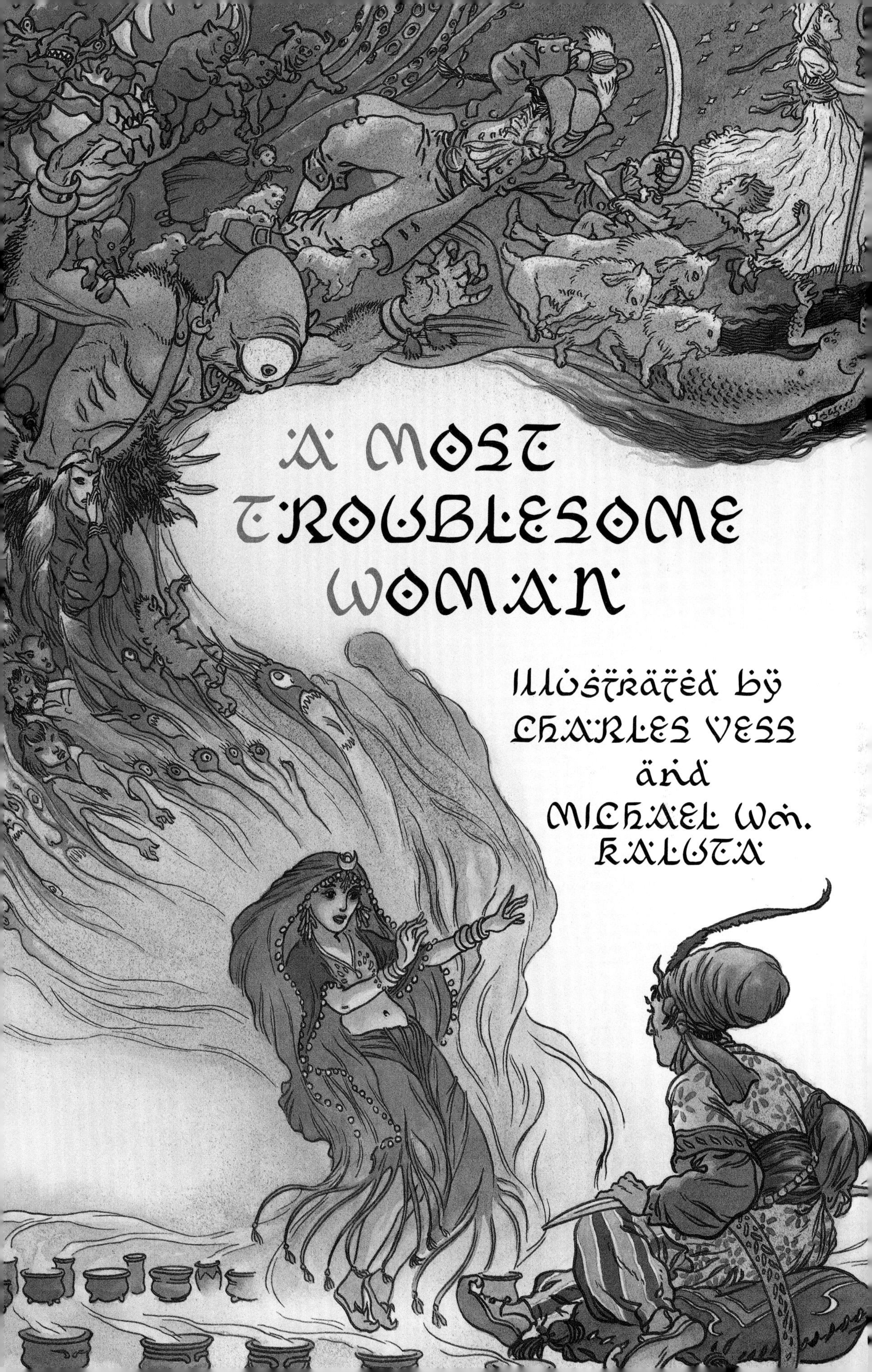
A MOST
TROUBLESOME
WOMAN
Illustrated by
CHARLES VESS
and
MICHAEL Wm.
KALUTA

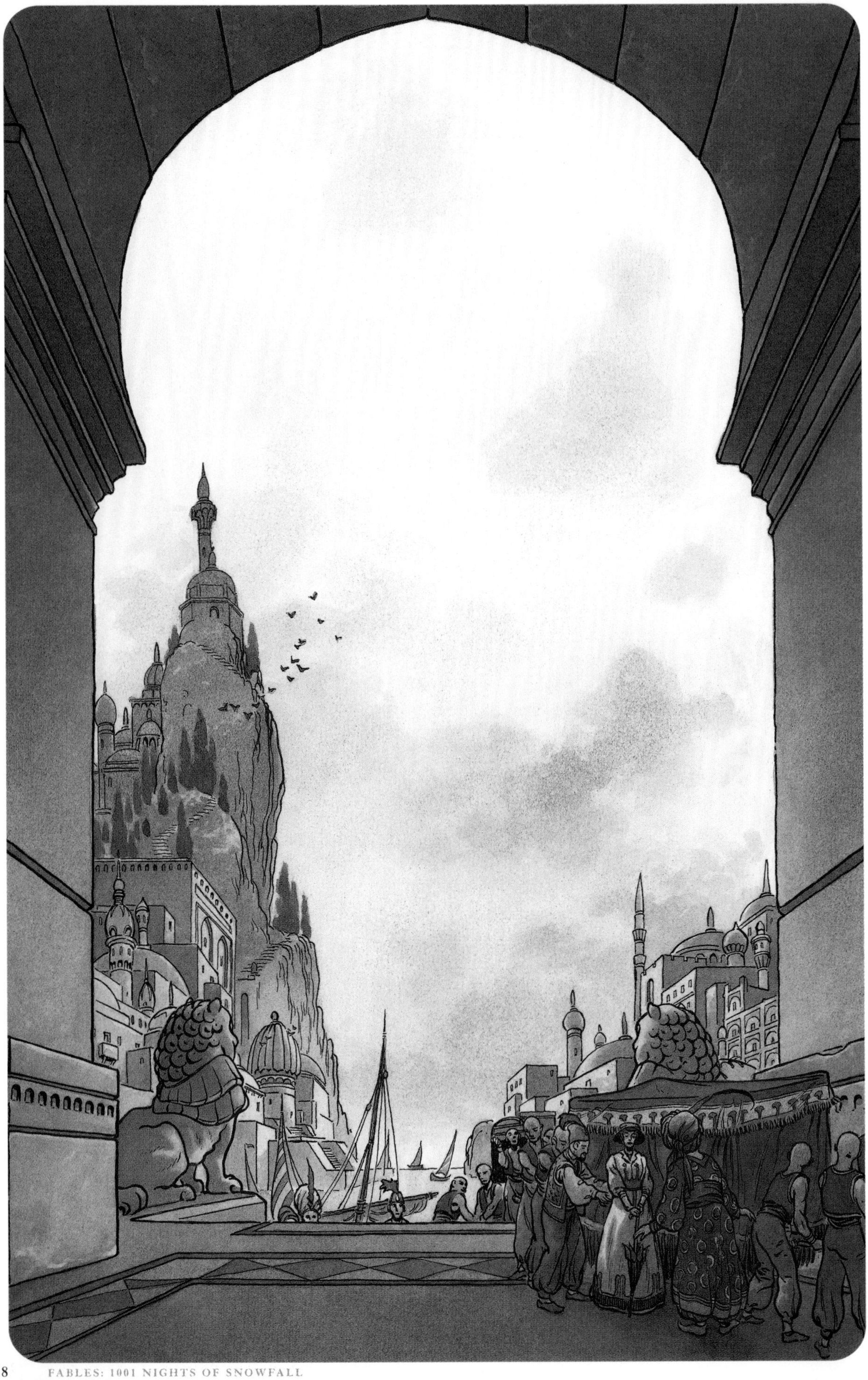

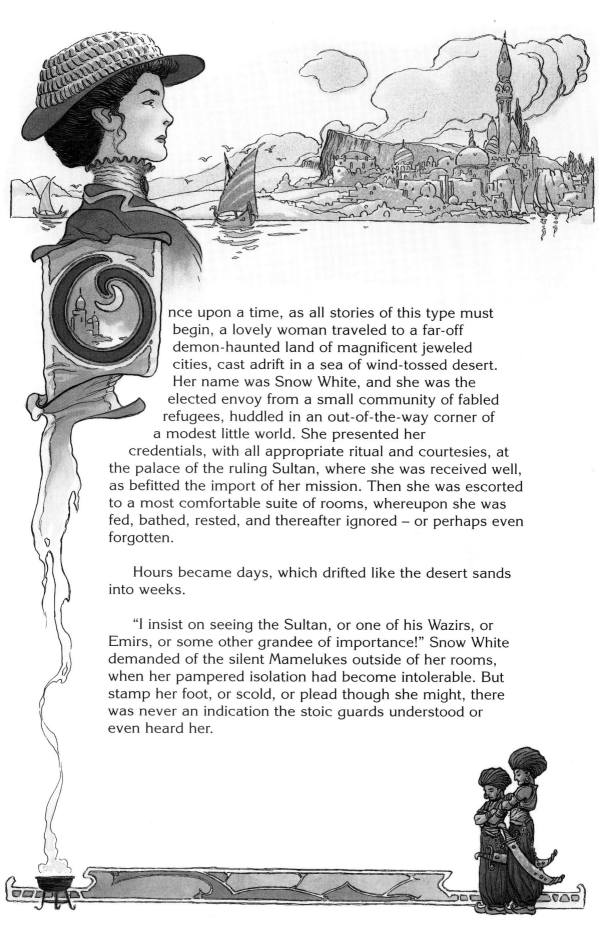

nce upon a time, as all stories of this type must begin, a lovely woman traveled to a far-off demon-haunted land of magnificent jeweled cities, cast adrift in a sea of wind-tossed desert. Her name was Snow White, and she was the elected envoy from a small community of fabled refugees, huddled in an out-of-the-way corner of a modest little world. She presented her credentials, with all appropriate ritual and courtesies, at the palace of the ruling Sultan, where she was received well, as befitted the import of her mission. Then she was escorted to a most comfortable suite of rooms, whereupon she was fed, bathed, rested, and thereafter ignored – or perhaps even forgotten.

Hours became days, which drifted like the desert sands into weeks.

"I insist on seeing the Sultan, or one of his Wazirs, or Emirs, or some other grandee of importance!" Snow White demanded of the silent Mamelukes outside of her rooms, when her pampered isolation had become intolerable. But stamp her foot, or scold, or plead though she might, there was never an indication the stoic guards understood or even heard her.

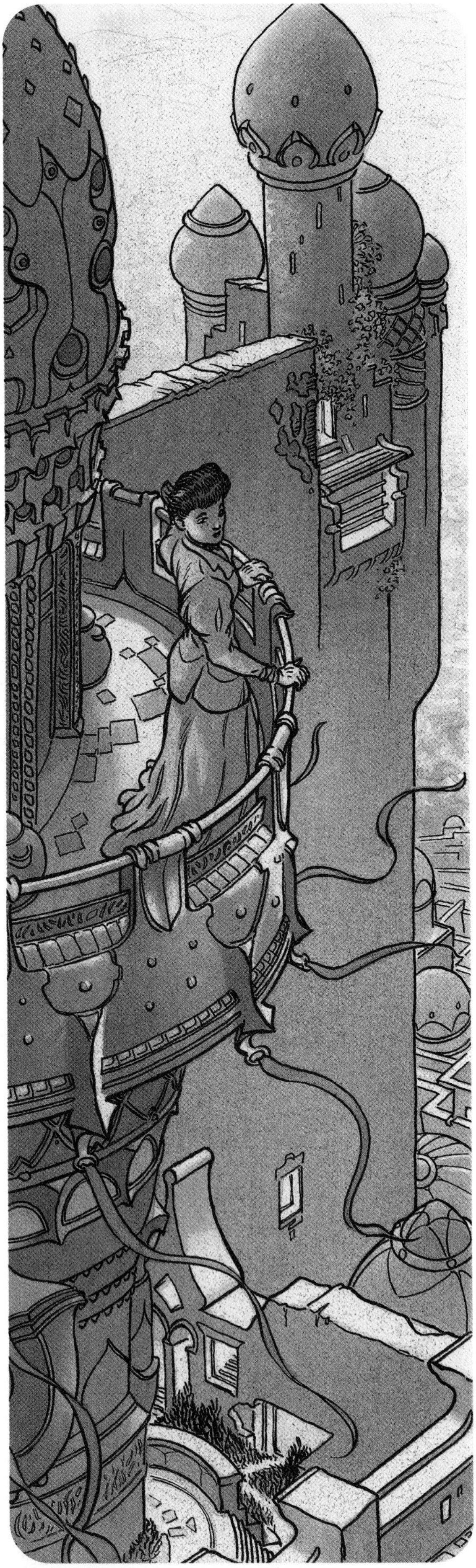

Her rooms were high in the palace, and though she enjoyed an open balcony overlooking the Sultan's walled pleasure gardens, it was too long a drop to the grounds below. And when she simply tried to walk out of her suite, the otherwise unmoving Mamelukes would politely, but firmly, block her way. It became clear to Snow that she was more prisoner than honored guest. So she changed her tactics and forgot courtly manners. When her meals arrived, she would overturn the trays of gold and argent, smash the fine china plates and crystal goblets, frightening the servants from her sight. When slave girls came to bathe her she would likewise chase them away, hurling foul foreign epithets at them, along with their priceless oils and perfumes.

Even so it was days later before the Sultan's most high Wazir finally came to call upon her.

"You are a most troublesome woman!" he said, after only minimal introductory courtesies were observed.

We don't know what to do with you. Our serenity is destroyed, leaving the palace in turmoil. You arrive here unveiled, wearing immodest foreign clothes, bringing no handsome gifts befitting the majesty of King Shahryar. And what sort of backward people would send a woman as their envoy? Do you intend to insult us? Why don't you go home?"

"I'm the ambassador from Fabletown, and you have the temerity to treat me so?" Snow nearly screamed in response. "If my mission weren't so dire, I'd gladly leave, forever turning my back on this misbegotten land, shaking the dust off my feet as I go. But I've been sent to warn you of a terrible threat to all the Arabian Fable worlds. The Adversary's unholy armies have already ravaged the European Fable worlds. Though he seems content to consolidate his gains for now, his hunger is insatiable. It will grow strong in him again, and when it does, it is manifestly evident that he will next turn his gaze this way.

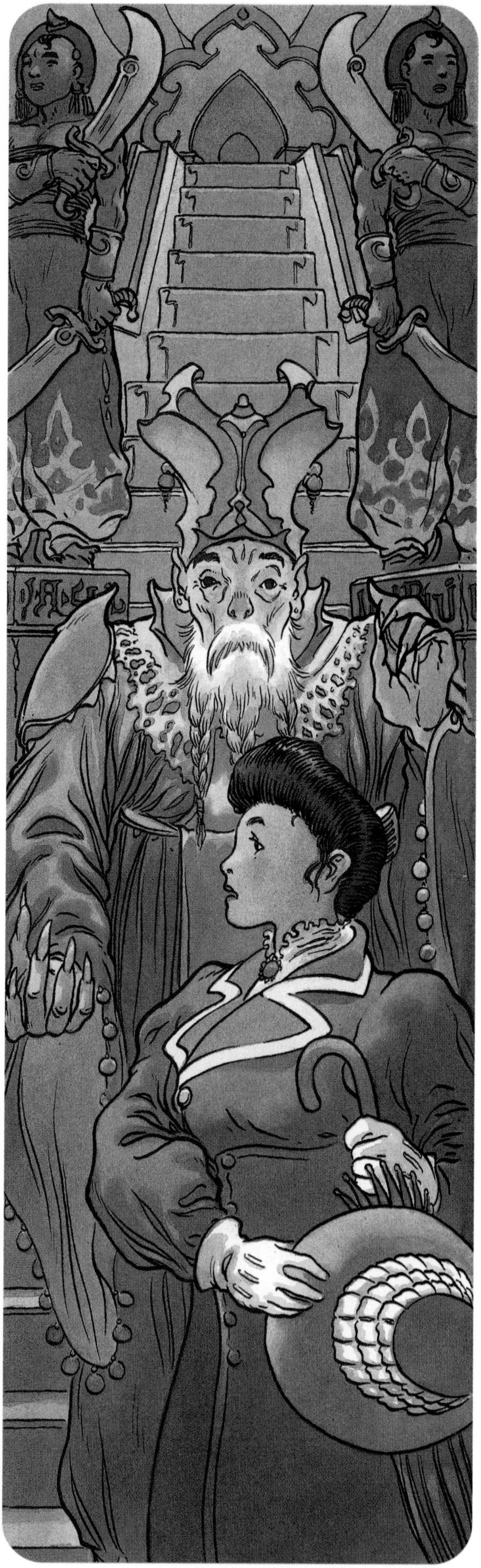

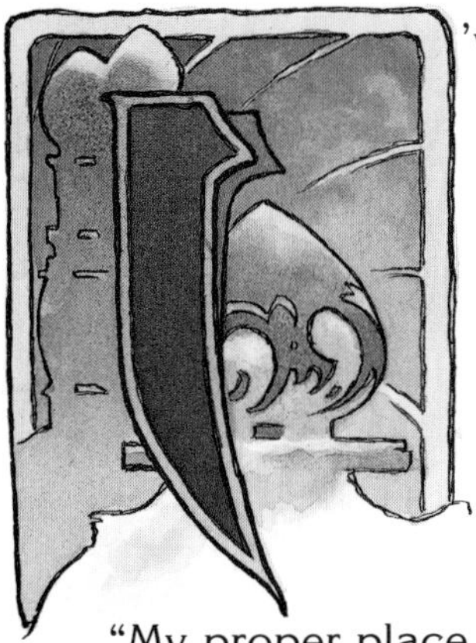

"I've come to offer an alliance between your kingdoms and our community-in-exile. With our hard-won centuries of experience fighting The Adversary coupled with your undiminished magical and military resources, we could..."

"Enough!" the Wazir interrupted. "I will not hear such things out of a woman's devil-painted mouth! Learn your place!"

"My proper place is in front of the Sultan's throne," Snow said. "My duty is to speak to him, just such entreaties as I've said to you."

And so the argument continued, back and forth between these two resolute forces, like the endless ebb and flow of sea tide, until finally a crafty look came into the Wazir's eyes. Twice he stroked his gray mustachios and then said, "Very well, woman. Your insistence has overpowered me, but on your own head be the consequences. If you truly wish it, I will arrange a private audience with the Sultan, tonight. In the meantime, assuming you've recovered your manners, I'll send my daughter's handmaidens to you, to bathe you and dress you in proper attire."

And with that, the Wazir quickly departed, leaving Snow to wonder at his abrupt change of heart.

That very afternoon the slave girls of the Wazir's house came unto Snow White and bathed and powdered and oiled her. Then they veiled and draped her in sumptuous garments of silk and gauze.

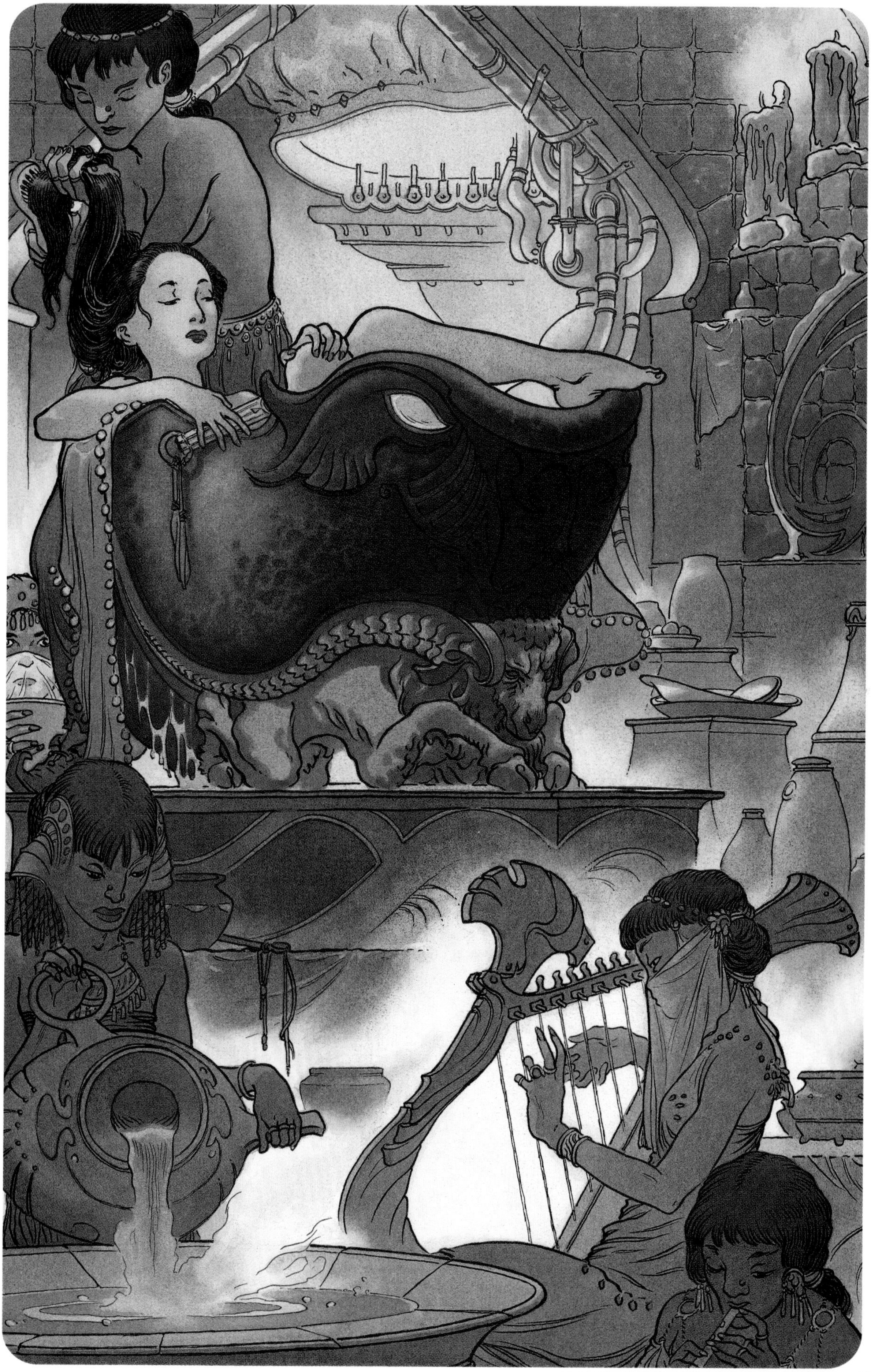

inally, they adorned her in gold and rubies without price, whereupon she was ushered with all pomp and ceremony before the Sultan, who marveled at the sight of her. "You are wondrous fair," he said, "a model of beauty and comeliness and symmetry and perfect loveliness! Your steps are the grace of a gazelle which pants for the cooling stream!"

Now Snow was a proper woman of demure manners and bridled inwardly at such public declarations from a stranger, even one whose suzerain encompassed thrice three times three dozen kingdoms, city states and satrapies. But she was also possessed of subtle cunning, otherwise she'd never have been dispatched on such a vital errand. Throughout the evening she feigned modest delight at the sultan's unceasing flattery and waited for her opportunity to plead her mission to him.

"I'm astonished that such a pearl beyond price could find its way here, from a land so distant," King Shahryar said, during their private dinner. There were wines from the far corners of the world and delicacies of sweet meats and ripe fruit, and slave girls came to meet them with instruments of music. "I'll be sorry to lose you so quickly."

"That won't be necessary, O King," Snow replied, "as I am prepared to stay as long as it takes to convince you."

"Convince me? Of what?"

"To help us. To ally yourself with Fabletown against The Adversary and his legions."

"Oh, I see," said the Sultan. "You're here with me alone in my private chambers strictly in your dubious role as ambassador from your tiny camp of refugees, is that it? Do you imagine this is how I normally receive foreign emissaries? Can you honestly believe that is why I've summoned you here this eventide?"

"Isn't it?"

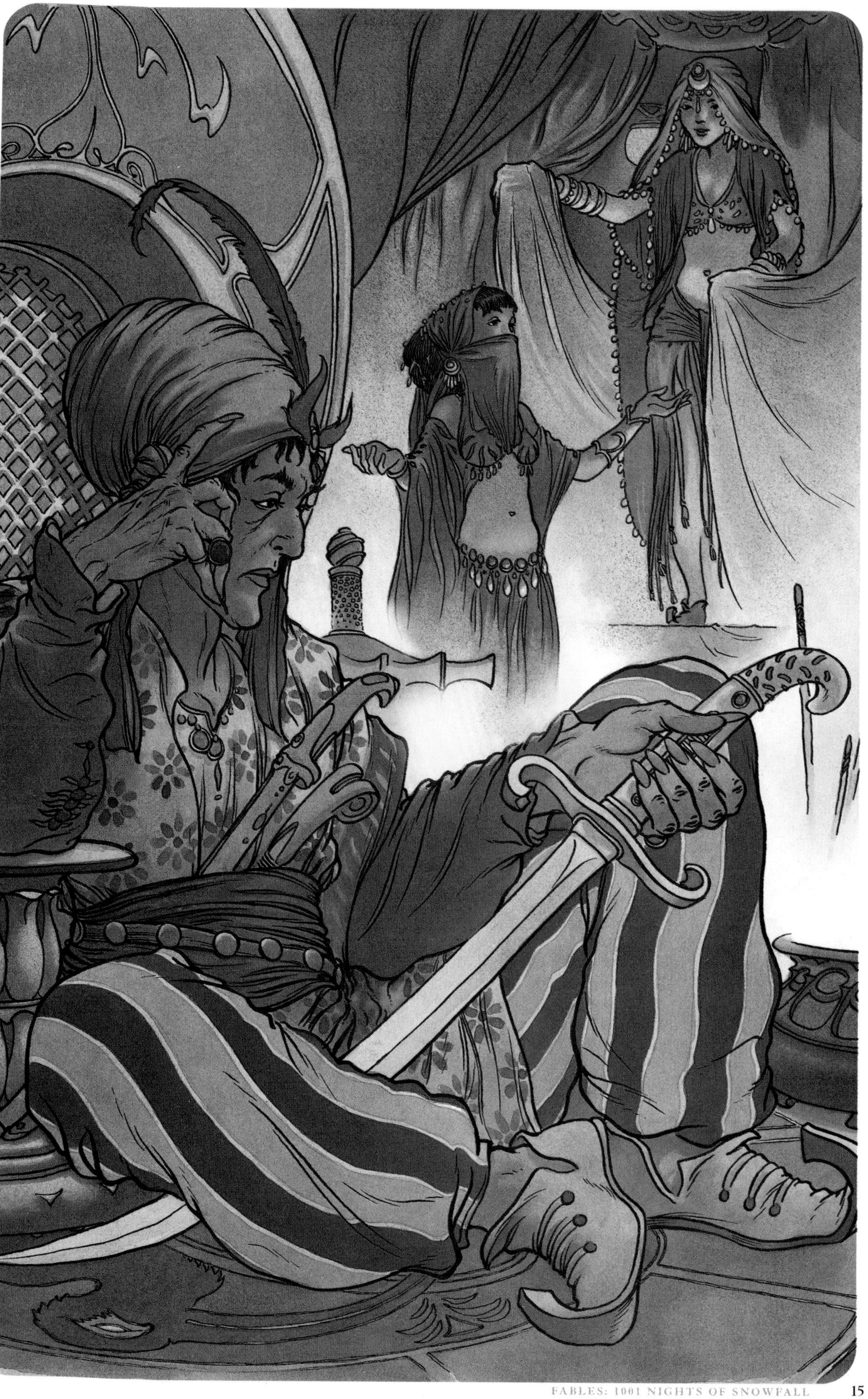

I have often thought myself the most subtle of men. But now I see, in guile and artifice, I must cede all such honors to my own High Wazir. By sending you to me he's saved his own daughter for yet another night."

"I don't understand," said Snow.

"Nor did I, until now. But finally the veil has been lifted and I understand why a foreign woman, who could have stood exempt from my decree, has inexplicably offered herself up to my executioner's ax."

"You're going to kill me?"

"At dawn, dear Snow, but only with the greatest of reluctance."

"But, why?"

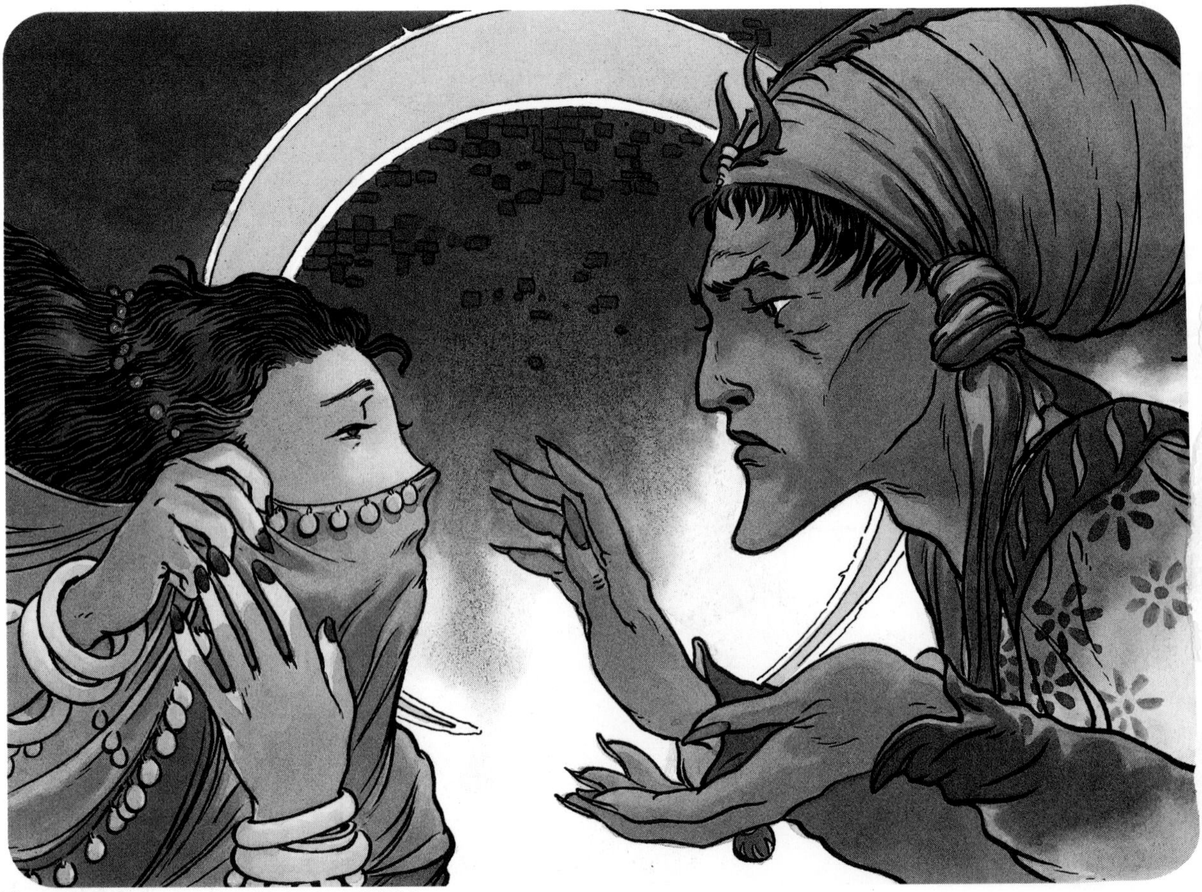

It's according to my own unbreakable edict. You're now doomed to suffer the same fate as the thousand virgins who've preceded you. Every night I take a new bride from among the daughters of my subjects, and every morning I give her over to my Wazir to be executed. In this wise I have continued for the space of three years."

"That's insane! Why would you do such a monstrous thing?"

"Mind your tongue, woman! Remember who it is you're talking to! It's hardly insanity to recognize the endless perfidy of womankind. Nor is it monstrous to revenge myself for it."

"I'm astonished," Snow said, unbullied by the Sultan's rebuke, for in truth she was once a princess in her own right and long accustomed to the presence of high royal personages. Her poise did not go unappreciated by the Sultan, who'd expected the foreign woman to beg and weep and plead for her life.

"What could possibly have occurred to make you act in such a way?" Snow continued.

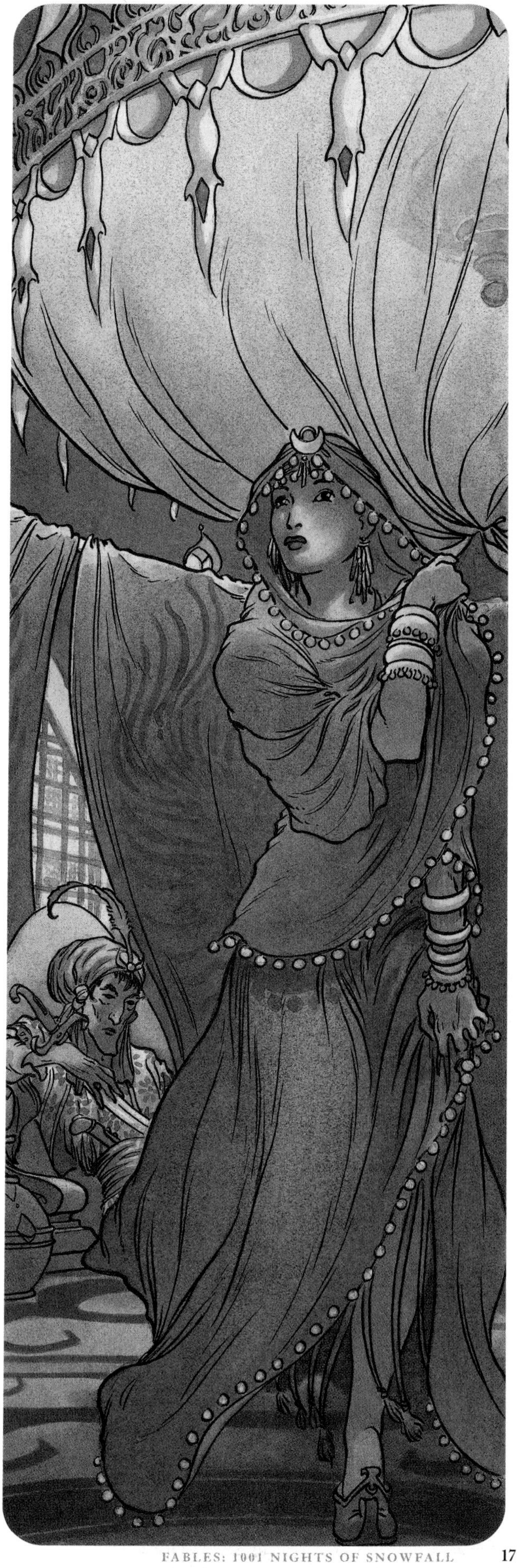

t's a tale already known to all within my lands, but come closer and I'll repeat it to you. Facing my unquenchable wrath in the morning, you deserve at least that much. Years past I was married to the finest flower in a hundred scattered kingdoms – a woman whose radiance outshone the sun and moon and the hurtling stars. One day I went forth to hunt and course and take my pleasure and pastime, as men will do. The hunting was inadequate that season, and so I returned days earlier than I had originally planned, only to discover the Queen, my wife, in my own carpet bed, writhing in carnal embrace with the filthiest of the palace slaves."

"And that's when you decided all women were evil?"

"Not yet, but I was truly stricken. For long months I sank into a black despair, believing the curse of Allah – praise be to he who set up the firmament without pillars in its stead – was on me, that such infamy could occur under my very nose. I neglected all but my own misery, until later when I discovered that my own brother, Shah Zaman, the King of far Samarcand, had suffered a similar fate. His bride had put horns on him as well, satisfying her lusts with Mameluke slaves and blackamoor cooks and goatherds and any dusty peasant from off the city streets. I saw then that Allah – praise be to the benificent King – had at least not singled me out for his harsh lessons."

"Did either woman mention why she would do such a thing?"

"Howsoever can one question a headless corpse? Immediately upon discovering their perfidies we sent them off to the headsman, as is only just and proper. By then we had no concerns with kingship, realizing that only in solitude can man be safe from the doings of this vile world. Know, then, that my brother and I forswore our thrones and riches and all finery, to overwander Allah's earth. With Him we sought refuge from women's malice and sleight."

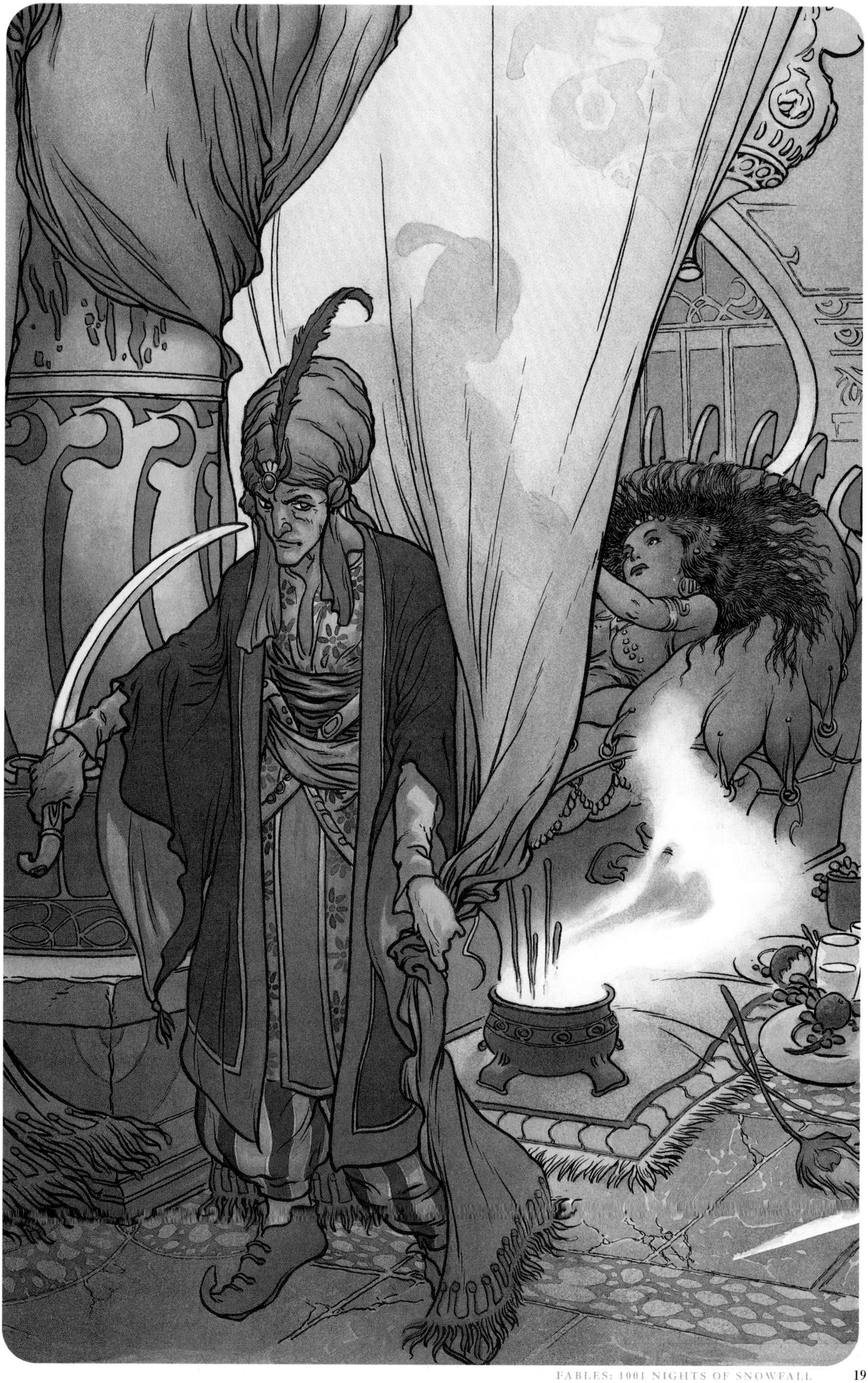

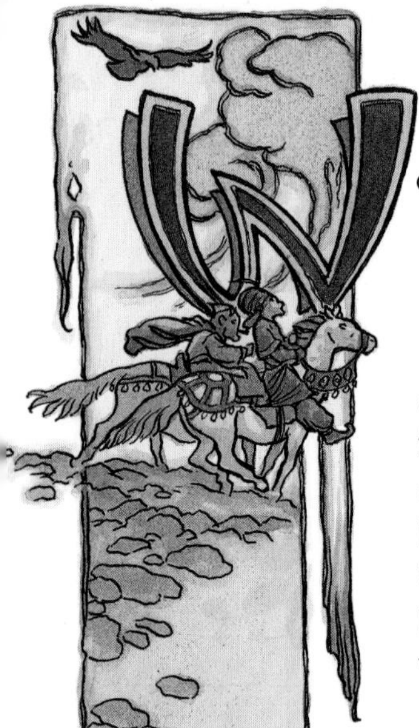
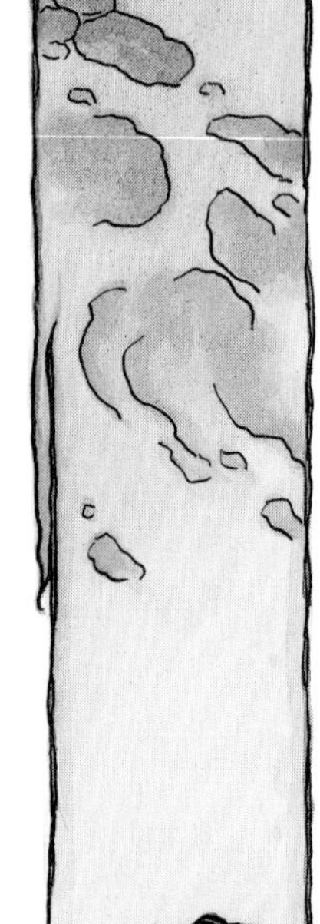

Worshipping the Almighty, we did not stint by day or night in our wayfaring, living as mean as the lowliest beggars, until one day when we happened upon a sleeping Jinni whose own wife cuckolded him a thousand times a thousand times. It is then that the melancholy and despondency fell away from me, as suddenly as the gazelle springs away from the lion. Turning to my only beloved brother, I exclaimed, 'Consider the ways of this magical lady with an ifrit who is so much more powerful than we are. Now since there has happened to him a greater mishap than that which befell us and which should bear us abundant consolation, so we should return to our countries and capitals.'

"Then did my brother return to far Samarcand in the barbarian lands, and I returned here to take up my imperial raiment once more. Upon arriving I took my great scimitar in hand and repaired to my seraglio, where I slew all the concubines and their Mamelukes. Then I sat upon my throne and mustered the Wazirs and Emirs, chamberlains and high officials, and my Chief Minister, and before them I swore a binding oath that whatever wife I married I would abate her maidenhead at night and slay her the next morning, to make sure of her honor. 'For,' said I, 'there never was nor is there one chaste woman upon the face of the earth.'"

"And since then you've married a woman each night and killed her each following day, for three years?" Snow asked.

"Even so," the Sultan answered.

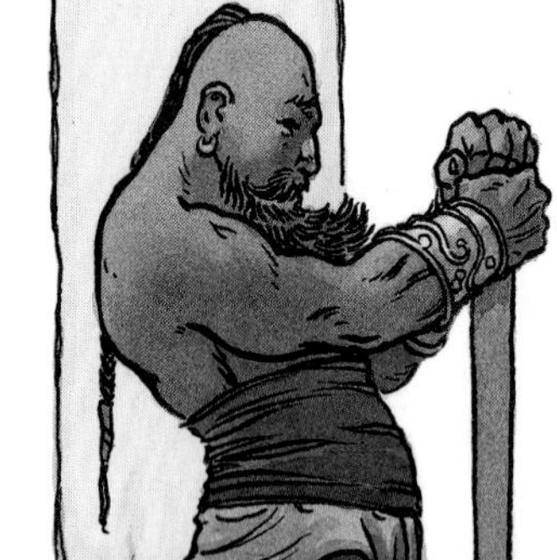

"And you intend to do the same to me tonight, even though I'm not one of your subjects, not a virgin, and have already been married?"

"Yet here you are, adrift in my lands, unaccompanied by any husband."

"We were divorced."

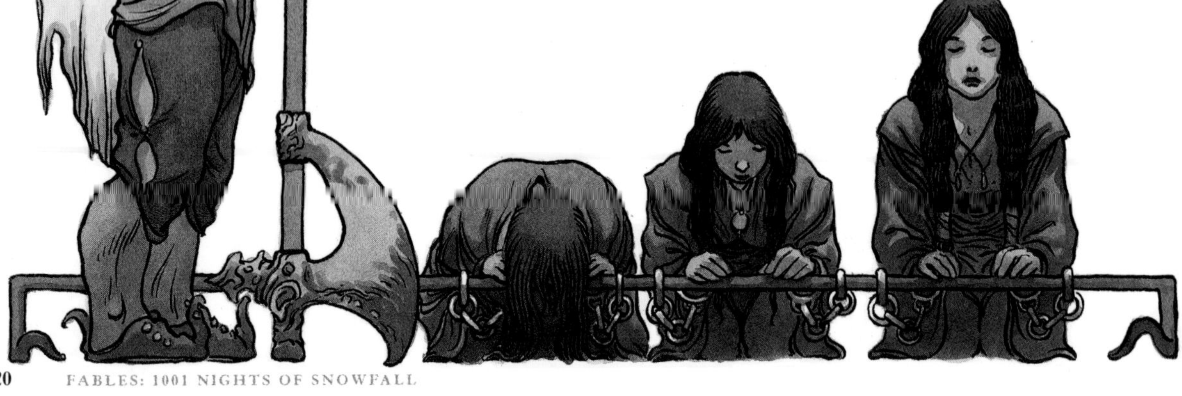

"Ah, I see," said the Sultan, and a haughty look came to his eyes, as if to suggest that some truth had been confirmed to him once again. "You should have mentioned that earlier. Now it is too late to find me another bride for the evening, so I'm afraid you'll just have to do. Speaking of which, the night wears on and the lamp oil runs low. I'll summon the minister, so that we may be about our business."

"Not just yet, O King of the Age," Snow said. And it's here that she summoned all of her wit and subtlety, artifice and subterfuge, for she had no intention to lie with the Sultan that night, or die with the coming dawn. "It's not fit that you've entertained me with a tale of your past, but received no such gift in return. It's not so late. The bright moon rises to take up the work of the flickering oil lamps, and I have my own small tale of revenge and its terrible lessons. Would you like to hear it?"

And here the Sultan was intrigued, for in all the years of his wanderings and the following years of his terrible daily ritual of marriage and murder, he'd forsaken other entertainments. He'd forgotten the joys of stories heard and told, and was surprised to rediscover how his heart still yearned for such simple pleasures.

"Yes," the Sultan said. "We can tarry a while longer. Tell me your tale, Snow White."

THE FENCING LESSONS

In which a wedding gift is given, bad doings are discovered, and two neighboring kingdoms begin to beat the drums of war.

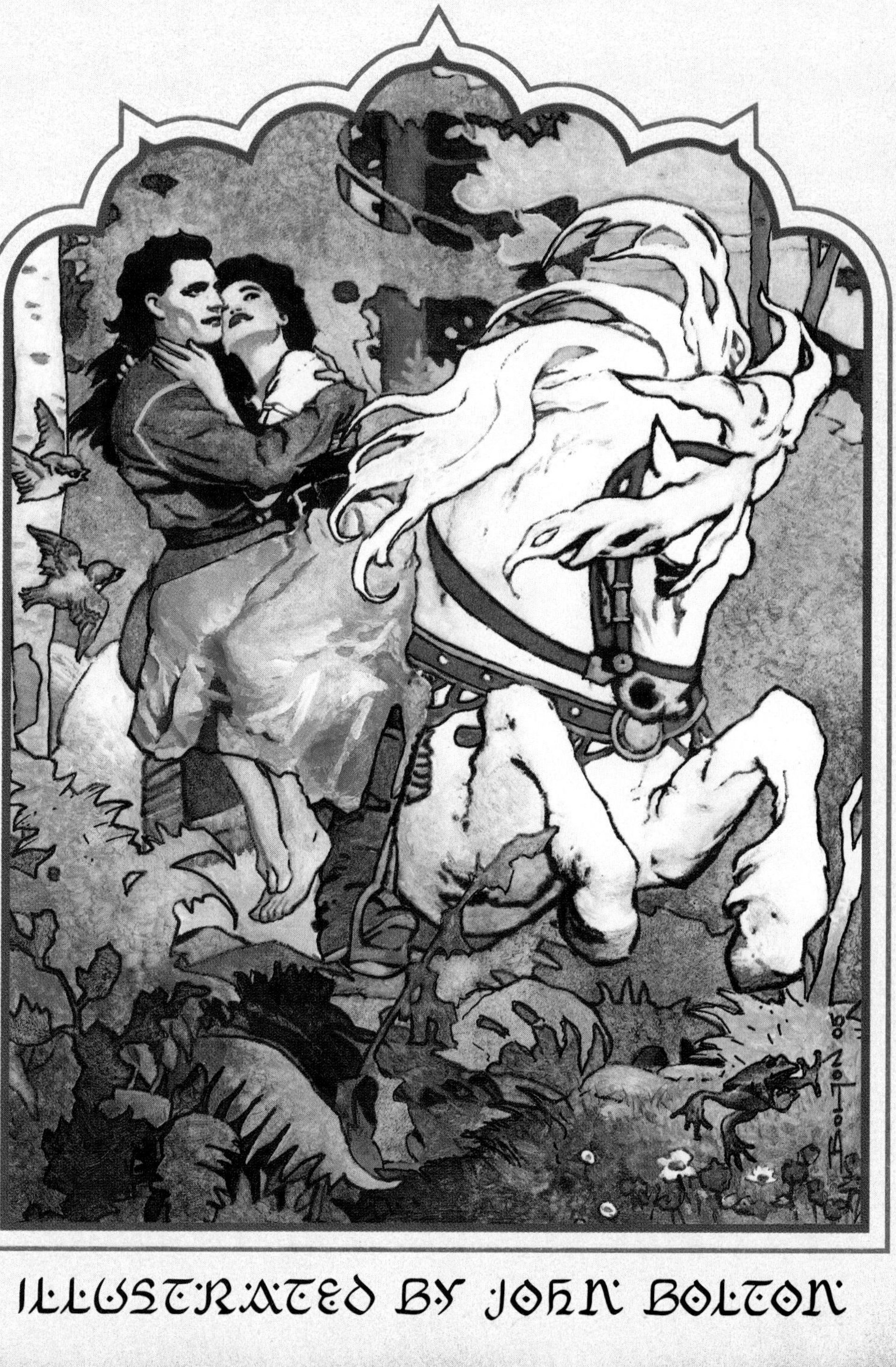

ILLUSTRATED BY JOHN BOLTON

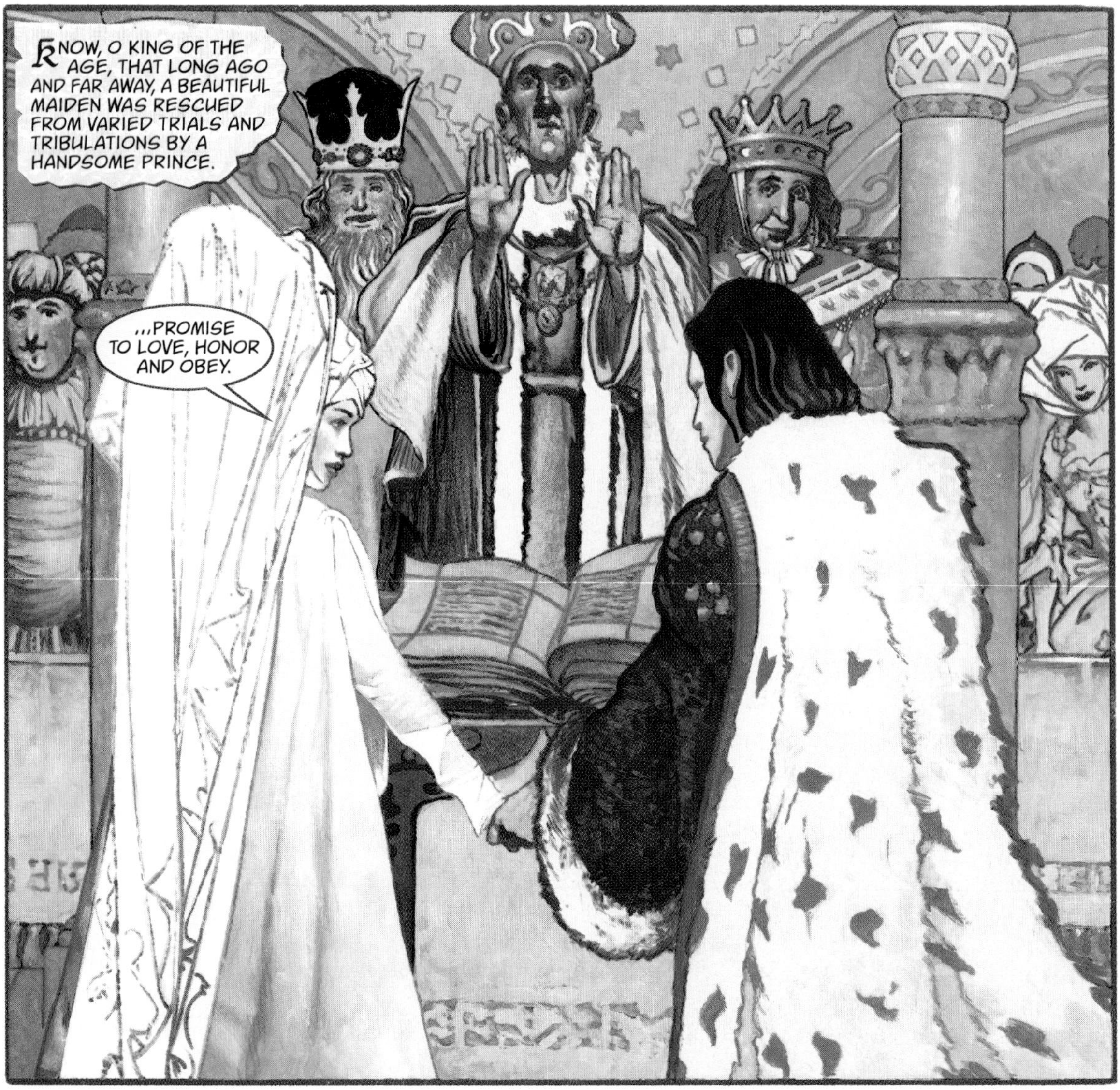
KNOW, O KING OF THE AGE, THAT LONG AGO AND FAR AWAY, A BEAUTIFUL MAIDEN WAS RESCUED FROM VARIED TRIALS AND TRIBULATIONS BY A HANDSOME PRINCE.
...PROMISE TO LOVE, HONOR AND OBEY.

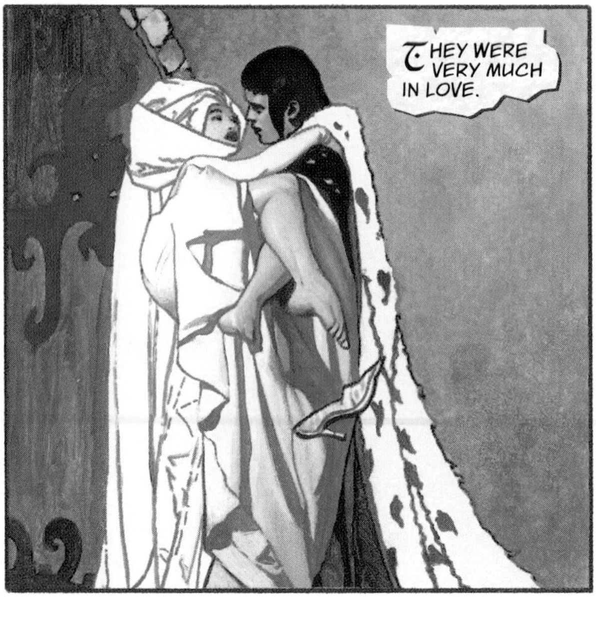
THEY WERE VERY MUCH IN LOVE.

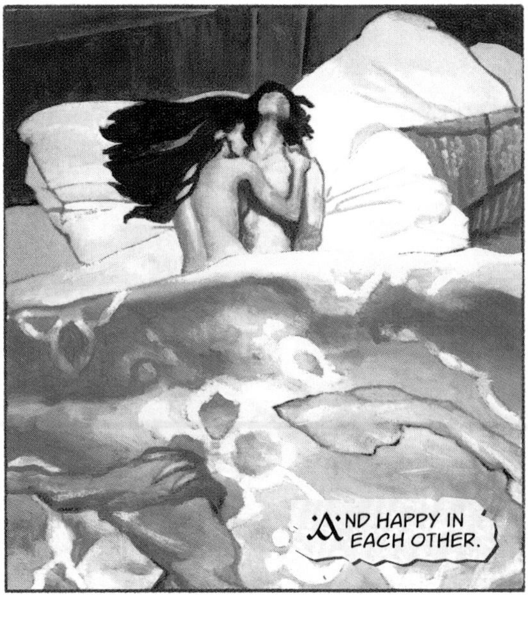
AND HAPPY IN EACH OTHER.

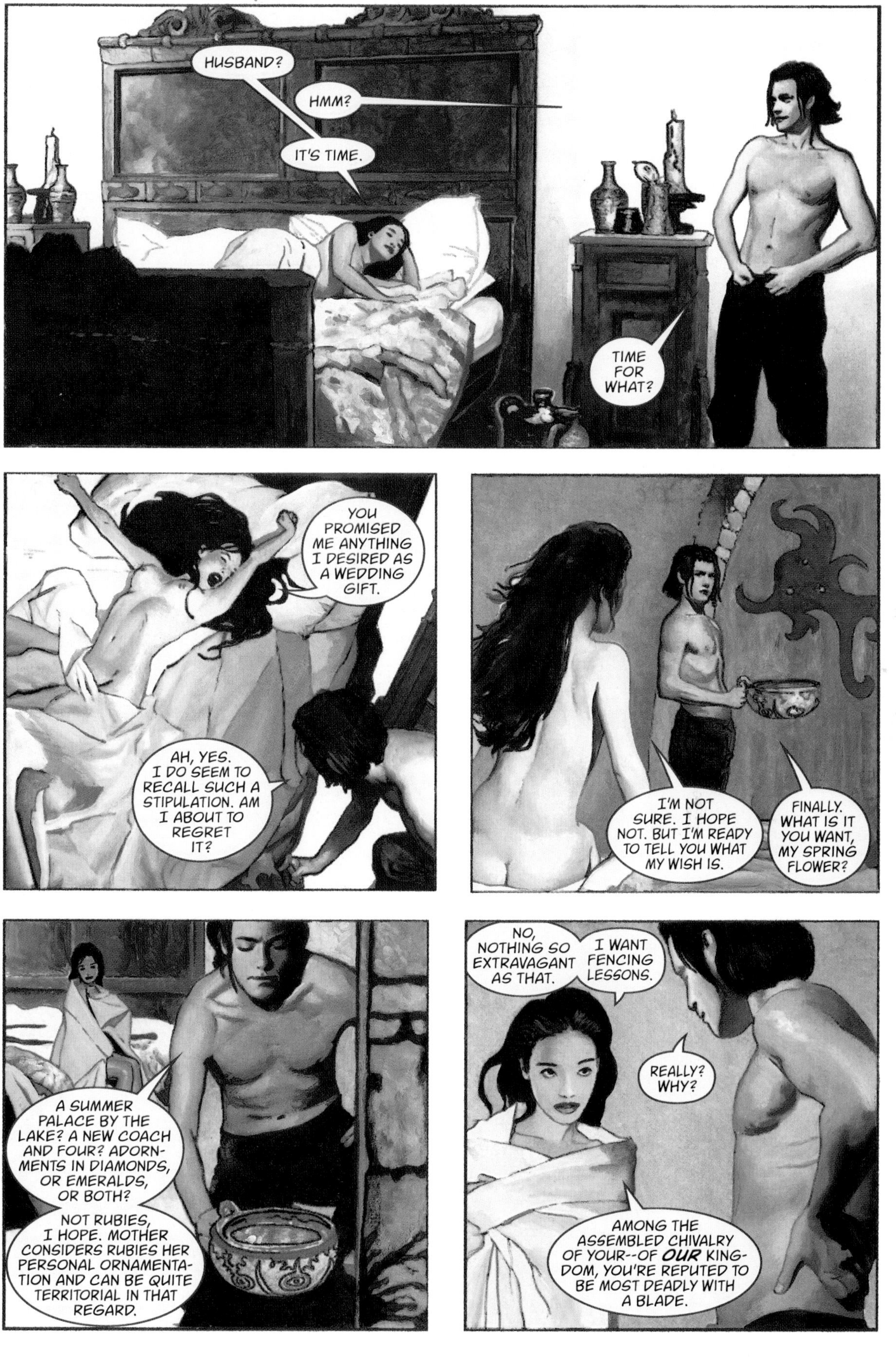
HUSBAND?
HMM?
IT'S TIME.
TIME FOR WHAT?
YOU PROMISED ME ANYTHING I DESIRED AS A WEDDING GIFT.
AH, YES. I DO SEEM TO RECALL SUCH A STIPULATION. AM I ABOUT TO REGRET IT?
I'M NOT SURE. I HOPE NOT. BUT I'M READY TO TELL YOU WHAT MY WISH IS.
FINALLY. WHAT IS IT YOU WANT, MY SPRING FLOWER?
A SUMMER PALACE BY THE LAKE? A NEW COACH AND FOUR? ADORN-MENTS IN DIAMONDS, OR EMERALDS, OR BOTH?
NOT RUBIES, I HOPE. MOTHER CONSIDERS RUBIES HER PERSONAL ORNAMENTA-TION AND CAN BE QUITE TERRITORIAL IN THAT REGARD.
NO, NOTHING SO EXTRAVAGANT AS THAT.
I WANT FENCING LESSONS.
REALLY? WHY?
AMONG THE ASSEMBLED CHIVALRY OF YOUR--OF OUR KING-DOM, YOU'RE REPUTED TO BE MOST DEADLY WITH A BLADE.

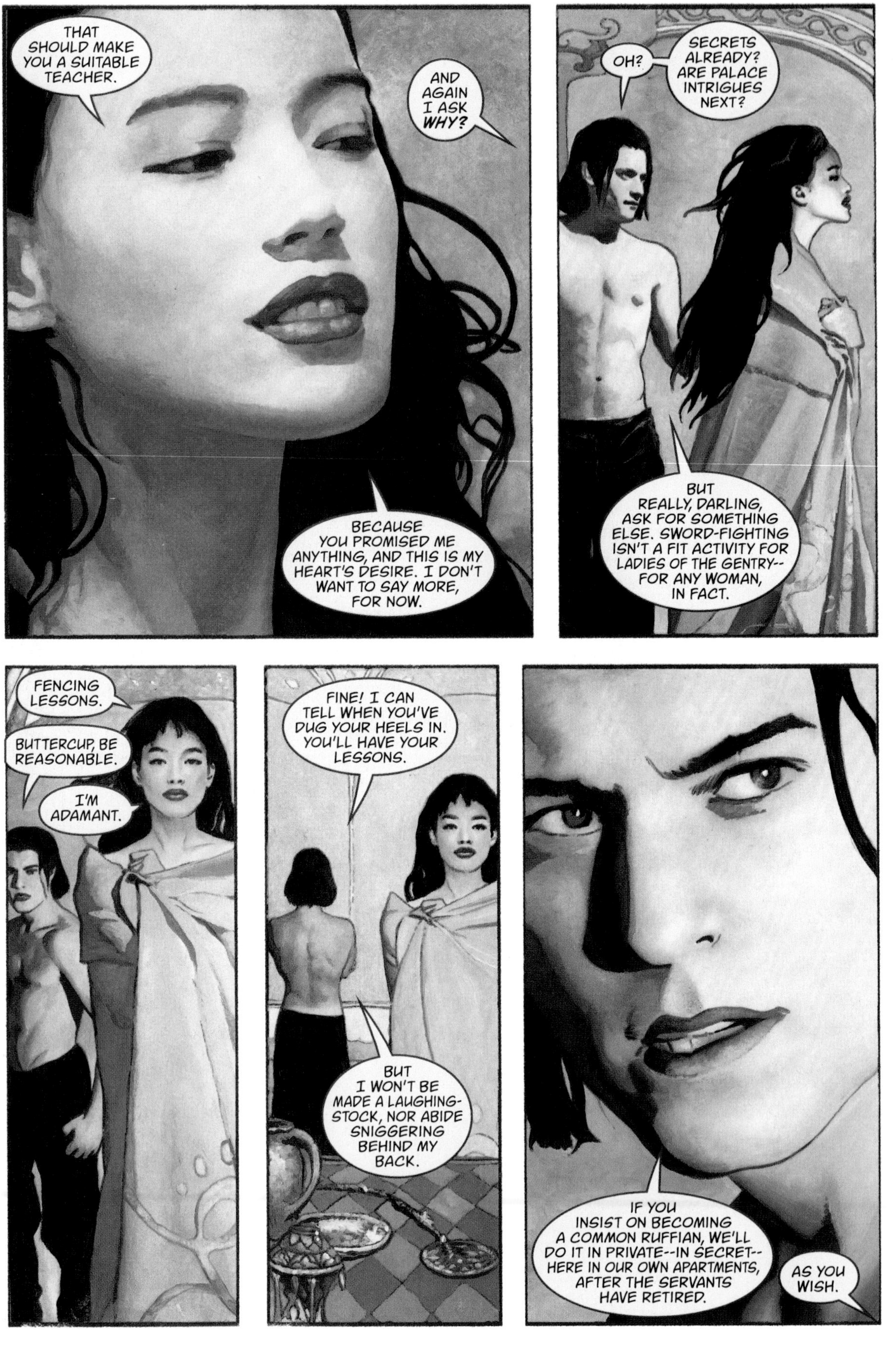
THAT SHOULD MAKE YOU A SUITABLE TEACHER.
AND AGAIN I ASK WHY?
BECAUSE YOU PROMISED ME ANYTHING, AND THIS IS MY HEART'S DESIRE. I DON'T WANT TO SAY MORE, FOR NOW.
OH?
SECRETS ALREADY? ARE PALACE INTRIGUES NEXT?
BUT REALLY, DARLING, ASK FOR SOMETHING ELSE. SWORD-FIGHTING ISN'T A FIT ACTIVITY FOR LADIES OF THE GENTRY-- FOR ANY WOMAN, IN FACT.
FENCING LESSONS.
BUTTERCUP, BE REASONABLE.
I'M ADAMANT.
FINE! I CAN TELL WHEN YOU'VE DUG YOUR HEELS IN. YOU'LL HAVE YOUR LESSONS.
BUT I WON'T BE MADE A LAUGHING-STOCK, NOR ABIDE SNIGGERING BEHIND MY BACK.
IF YOU INSIST ON BECOMING A COMMON RUFFIAN, WE'LL DO IT IN PRIVATE--IN SECRET-- HERE IN OUR OWN APARTMENTS, AFTER THE SERVANTS HAVE RETIRED.
AS YOU WISH.

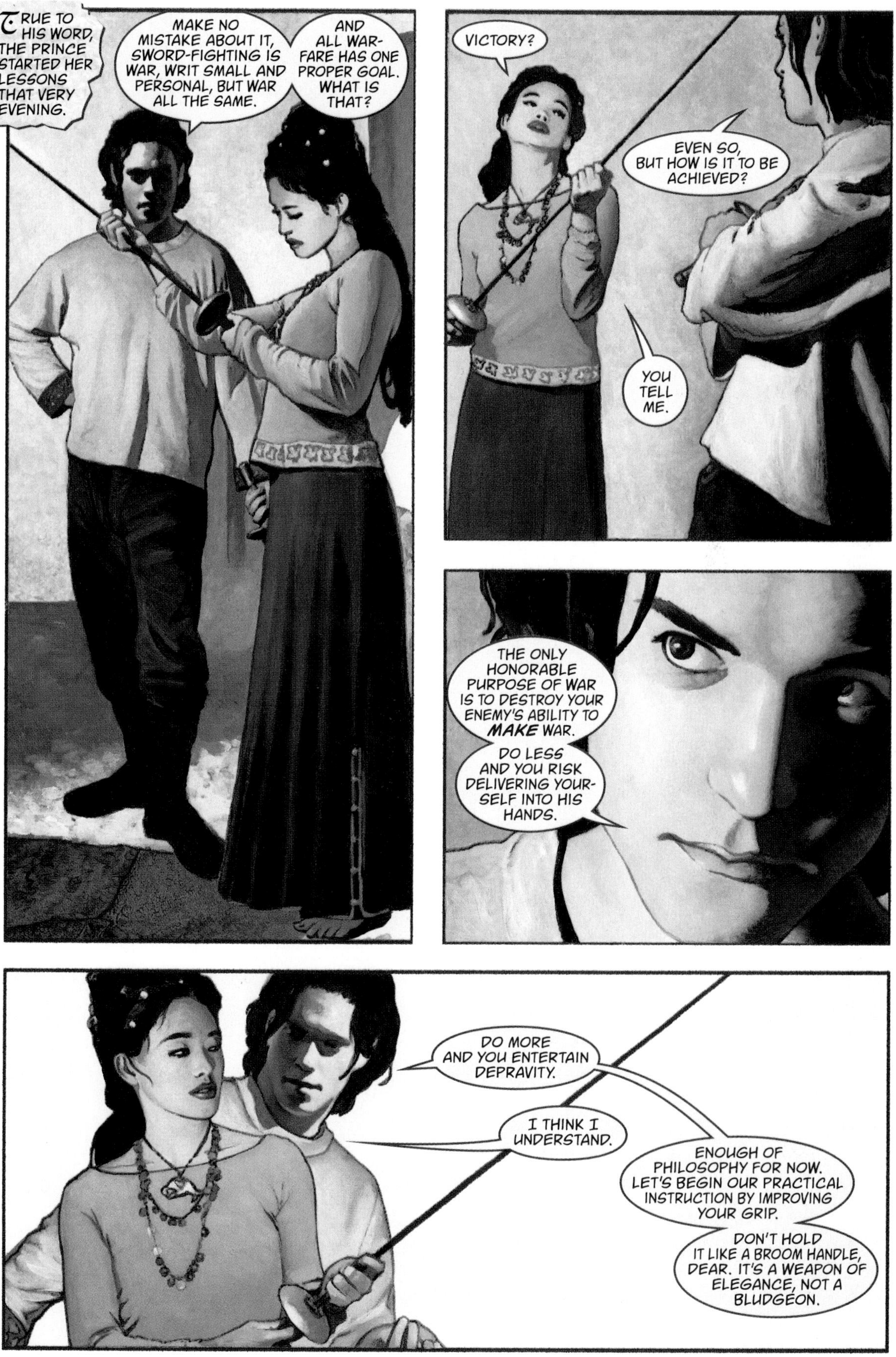
TRUE TO HIS WORD, THE PRINCE STARTED HER LESSONS THAT VERY EVENING.
MAKE NO MISTAKE ABOUT IT, SWORD-FIGHTING IS WAR, WRIT SMALL AND PERSONAL, BUT WAR ALL THE SAME.
AND ALL WARFARE HAS ONE PROPER GOAL. WHAT IS THAT?
VICTORY?
EVEN SO, BUT HOW IS IT TO BE ACHIEVED?
YOU TELL ME.
THE ONLY HONORABLE PURPOSE OF WAR IS TO DESTROY YOUR ENEMY'S ABILITY TO *MAKE* WAR.
DO LESS AND YOU RISK DELIVERING YOURSELF INTO HIS HANDS.
DO MORE AND YOU ENTERTAIN DEPRAVITY.
I THINK I UNDERSTAND.
ENOUGH OF PHILOSOPHY FOR NOW. LET'S BEGIN OUR PRACTICAL INSTRUCTION BY IMPROVING YOUR GRIP.
DON'T HOLD IT LIKE A BROOM HANDLE, DEAR. IT'S A WEAPON OF ELEGANCE, NOT A BLUDGEON.

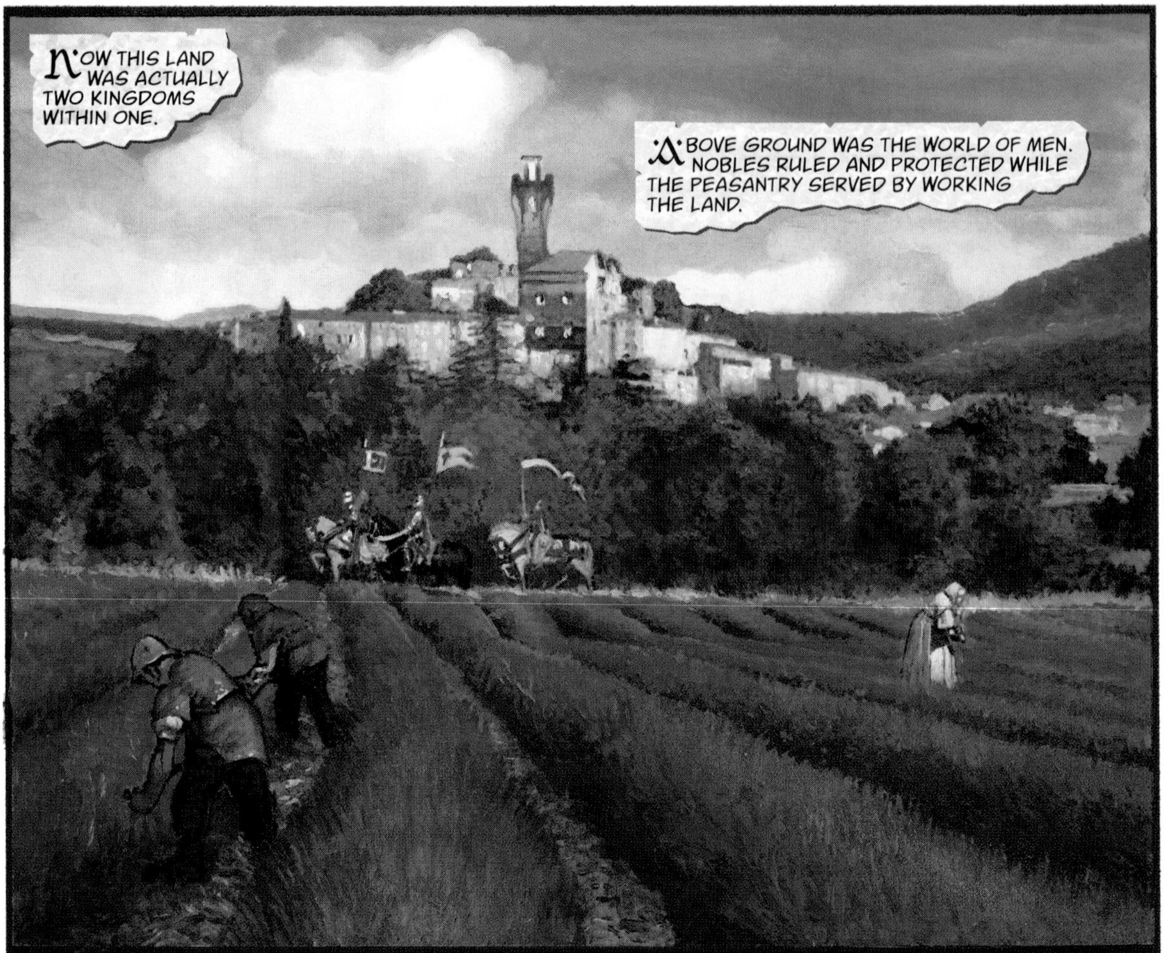
NOW THIS LAND WAS ACTUALLY TWO KINGDOMS WITHIN ONE.
ABOVE GROUND WAS THE WORLD OF MEN. NOBLES RULED AND PROTECTED WHILE THE PEASANTRY SERVED BY WORKING THE LAND.

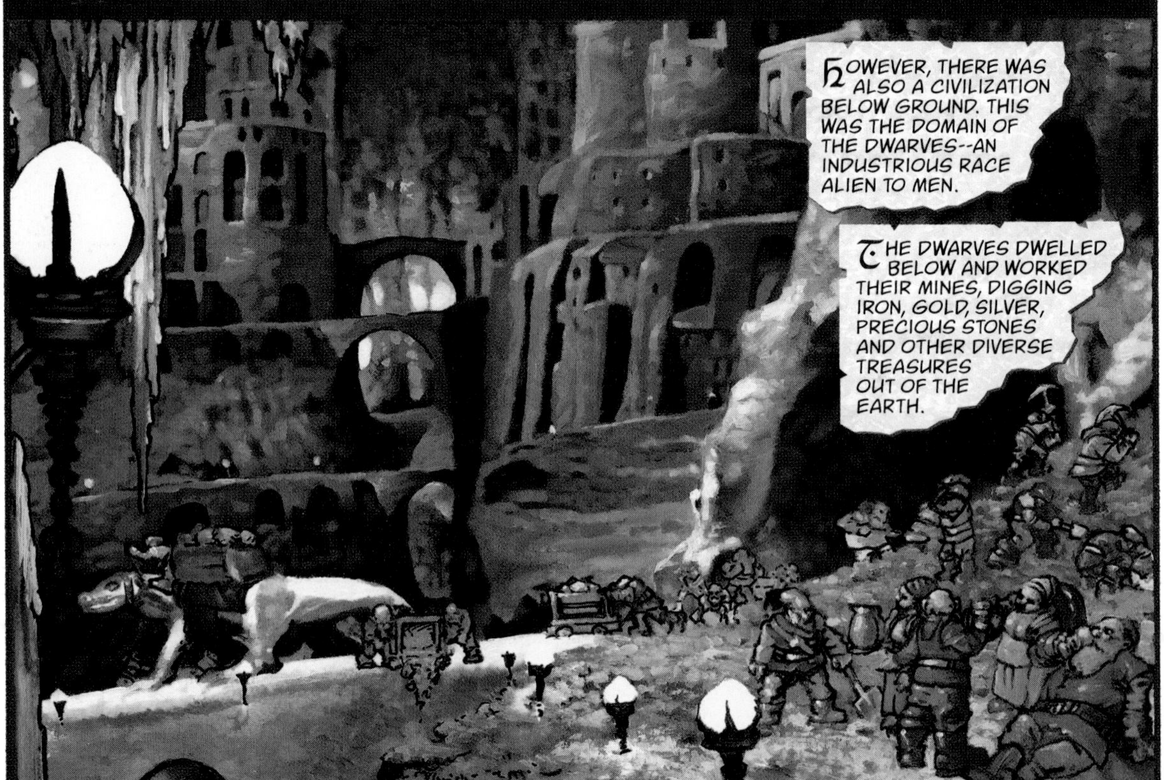
HOWEVER, THERE WAS ALSO A CIVILIZATION BELOW GROUND. THIS WAS THE DOMAIN OF THE DWARVES--AN INDUSTRIOUS RACE ALIEN TO MEN.
THE DWARVES DWELLED BELOW AND WORKED THEIR MINES, DIGGING IRON, GOLD, SILVER, PRECIOUS STONES AND OTHER DIVERSE TREASURES OUT OF THE EARTH.

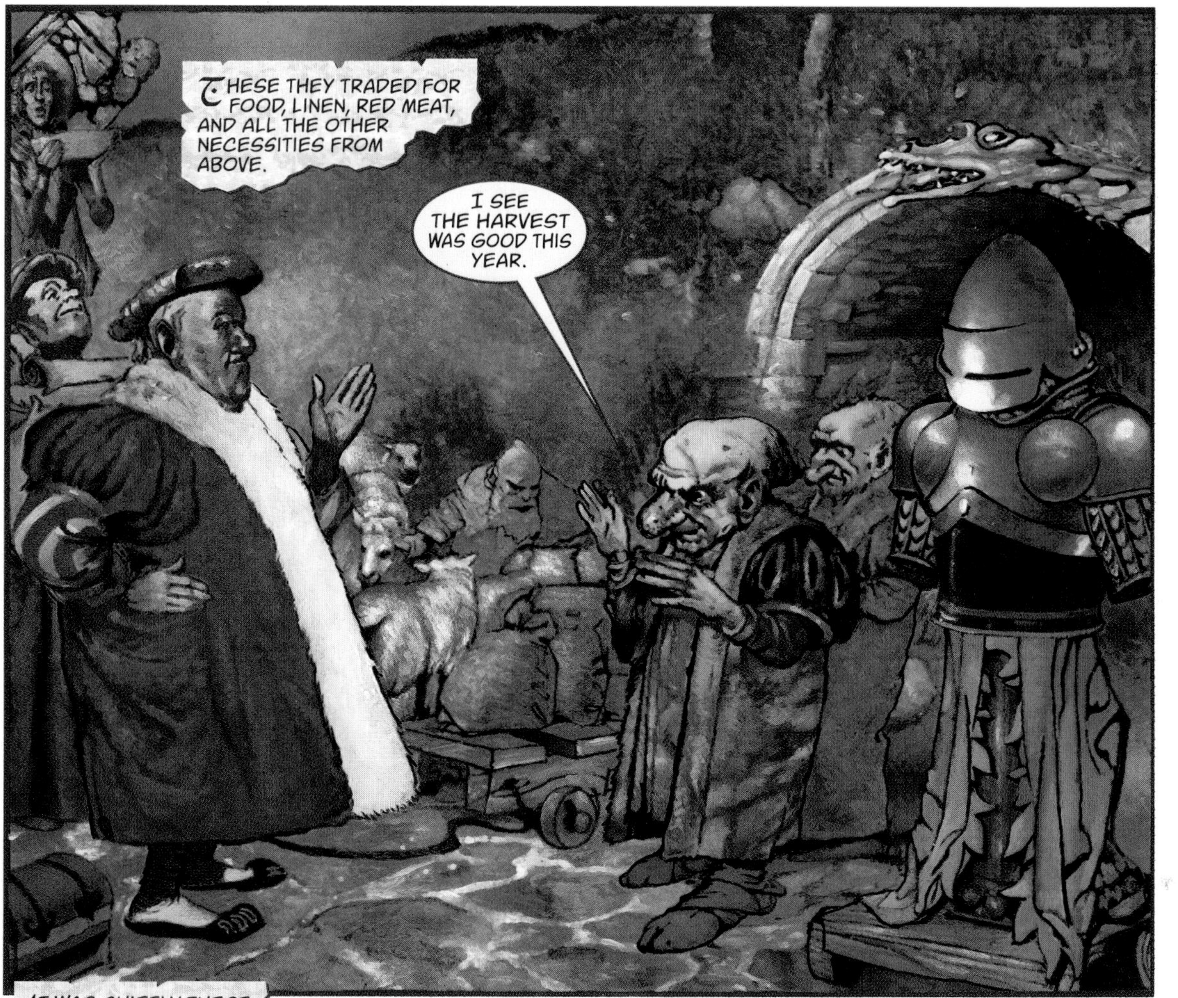
THESE THEY TRADED FOR FOOD, LINEN, RED MEAT, AND ALL THE OTHER NECESSITIES FROM ABOVE.
I SEE THE HARVEST WAS GOOD THIS YEAR.

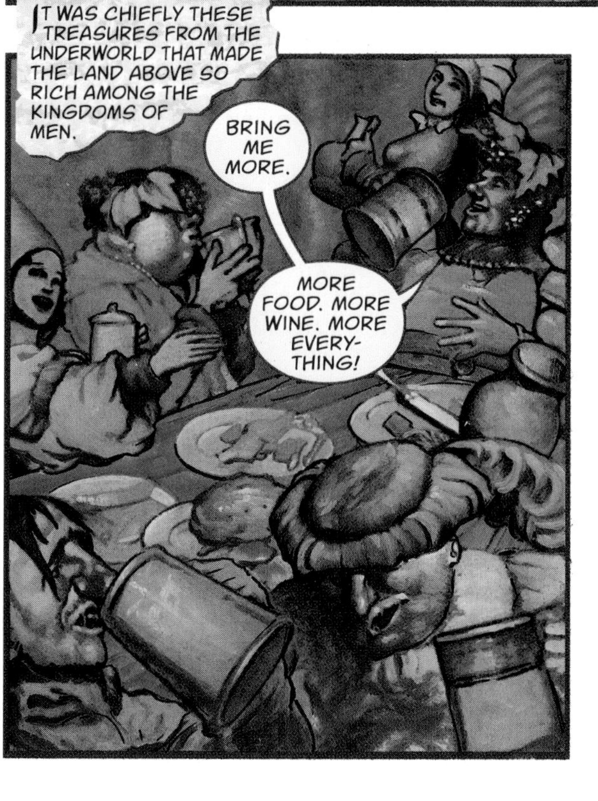
IT WAS CHIEFLY THESE TREASURES FROM THE UNDERWORLD THAT MADE THE LAND ABOVE SO RICH AMONG THE KINGDOMS OF MEN.
BRING ME MORE.
MORE FOOD. MORE WINE. MORE EVERY-THING!

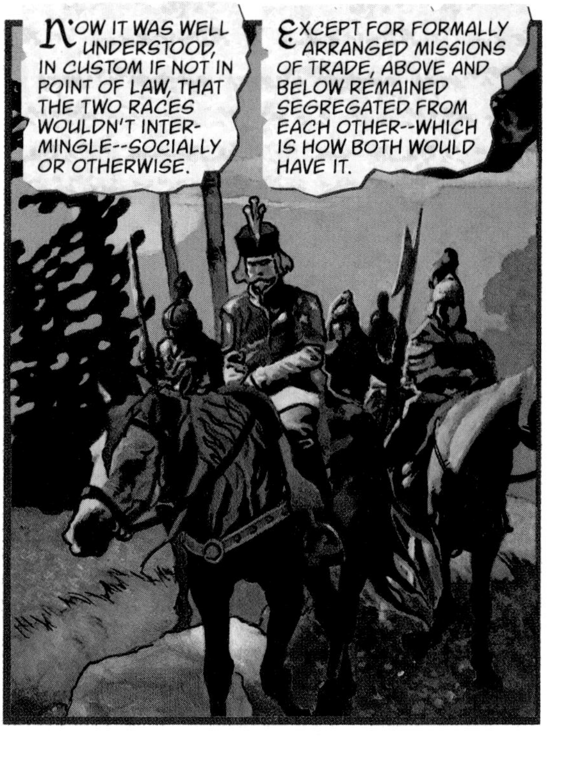
NOW IT WAS WELL UNDERSTOOD, IN CUSTOM IF NOT IN POINT OF LAW, THAT THE TWO RACES WOULDN'T INTER-MINGLE--SOCIALLY OR OTHERWISE.
EXCEPT FOR FORMALLY ARRANGED MISSIONS OF TRADE, ABOVE AND BELOW REMAINED SEGREGATED FROM EACH OTHER--WHICH IS HOW BOTH WOULD HAVE IT.

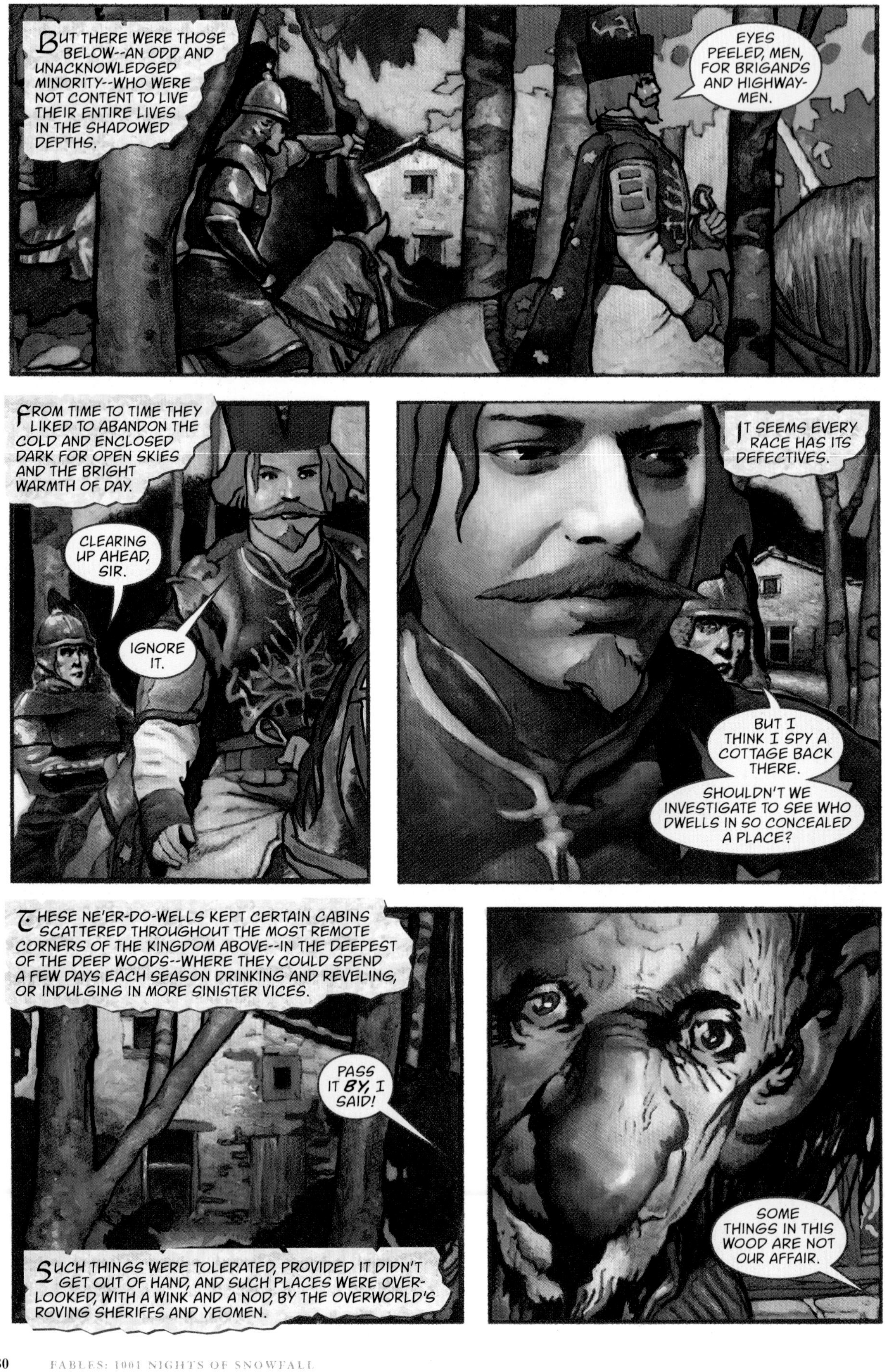
But there were those below--an odd and unacknowledged minority--who were not content to live their entire lives in the shadowed depths.
Eyes peeled, men, for brigands and highway-men.
From time to time they liked to abandon the cold and enclosed dark for open skies and the bright warmth of day.
Clearing up ahead, sir.
Ignore it.
It seems every race has its defectives.
But I think I spy a cottage back there.
Shouldn't we investigate to see who dwells in so concealed a place?
These ne'er-do-wells kept certain cabins scattered throughout the most remote corners of the kingdom above--in the deepest of the deep woods--where they could spend a few days each season drinking and reveling, or indulging in more sinister vices.
Pass it BY, I said!
Such things were tolerated, provided it didn't get out of hand, and such places were over-looked, with a wink and a nod, by the overworld's roving sheriffs and yeomen.
Some things in this wood are not our affair.

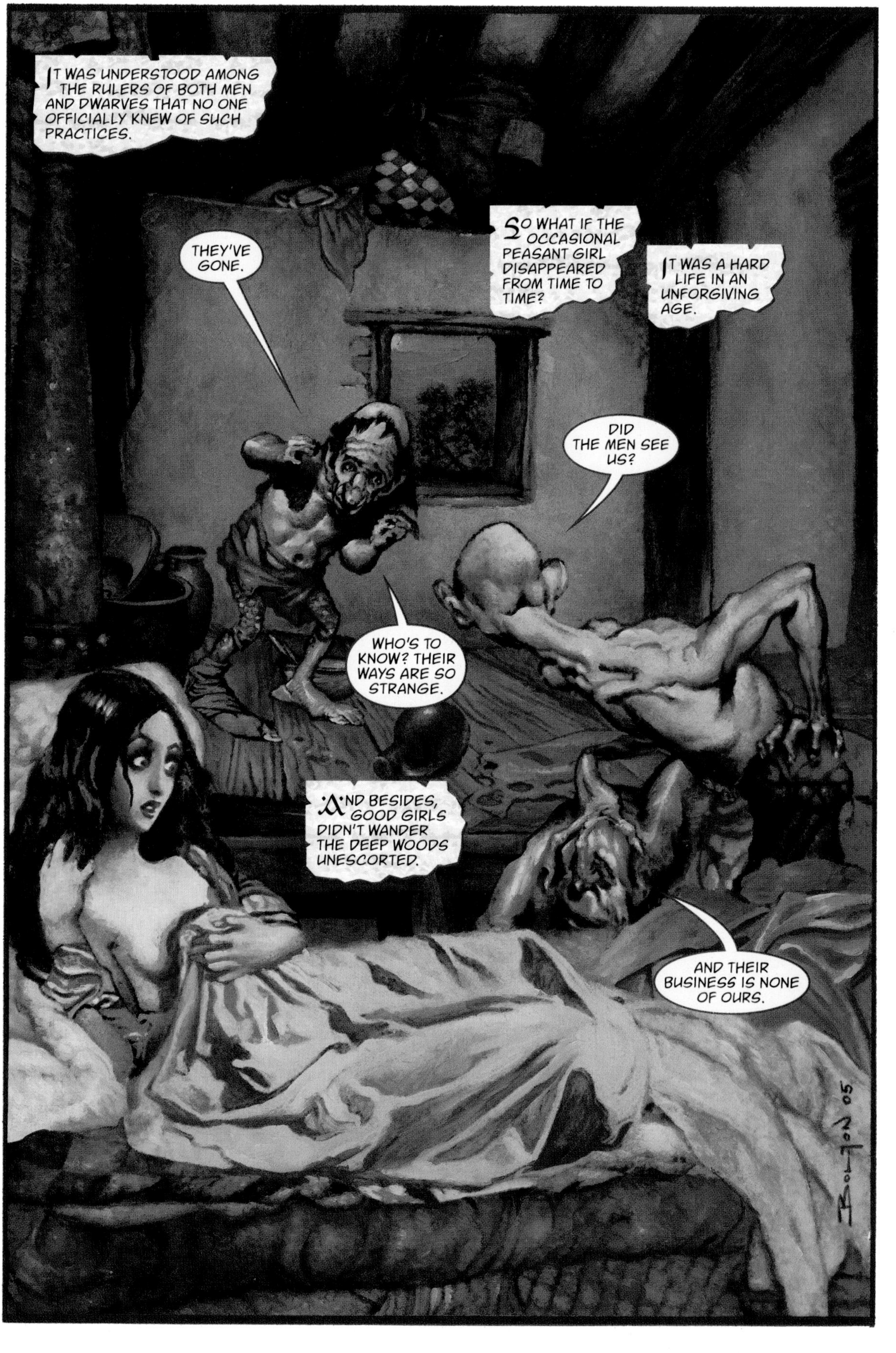
IT WAS UNDERSTOOD AMONG THE RULERS OF BOTH MEN AND DWARVES THAT NO ONE OFFICIALLY KNEW OF SUCH PRACTICES.
THEY'VE GONE.
SO WHAT IF THE OCCASIONAL PEASANT GIRL DISAPPEARED FROM TIME TO TIME?
IT WAS A HARD LIFE IN AN UNFORGIVING AGE.
DID THE MEN SEE US?
WHO'S TO KNOW? THEIR WAYS ARE SO STRANGE.
AND BESIDES, GOOD GIRLS DIDN'T WANDER THE DEEP WOODS UNESCORTED.
AND THEIR BUSINESS IS NONE OF OURS.
BOLTON 05

NO, NO *NO!*

YOU'RE NOT *DOING* IT RIGHT!

DON'T LEAP FORWARD AND START JABBING, WILLY NILLY!

STRAIGHTEN YOUR ARM *FIRST,* THEN LET YOUR LUNGE GUIDE YOUR BLADE TO ITS TARGET!

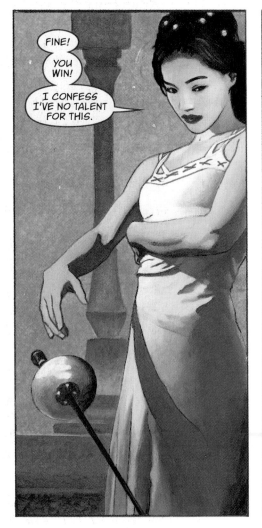

FINE! YOU WIN!

I CONFESS I'VE NO TALENT FOR THIS.

YOU'LL IMPROVE.

YOU'RE A *TOUCH* BETTER TODAY THAN YESTERDAY, AND YESTERDAY YOU WERE A *SMIDGEN* BETTER THAN THE DAY BEFORE.

NOW, RESUME YOUR STANCE.

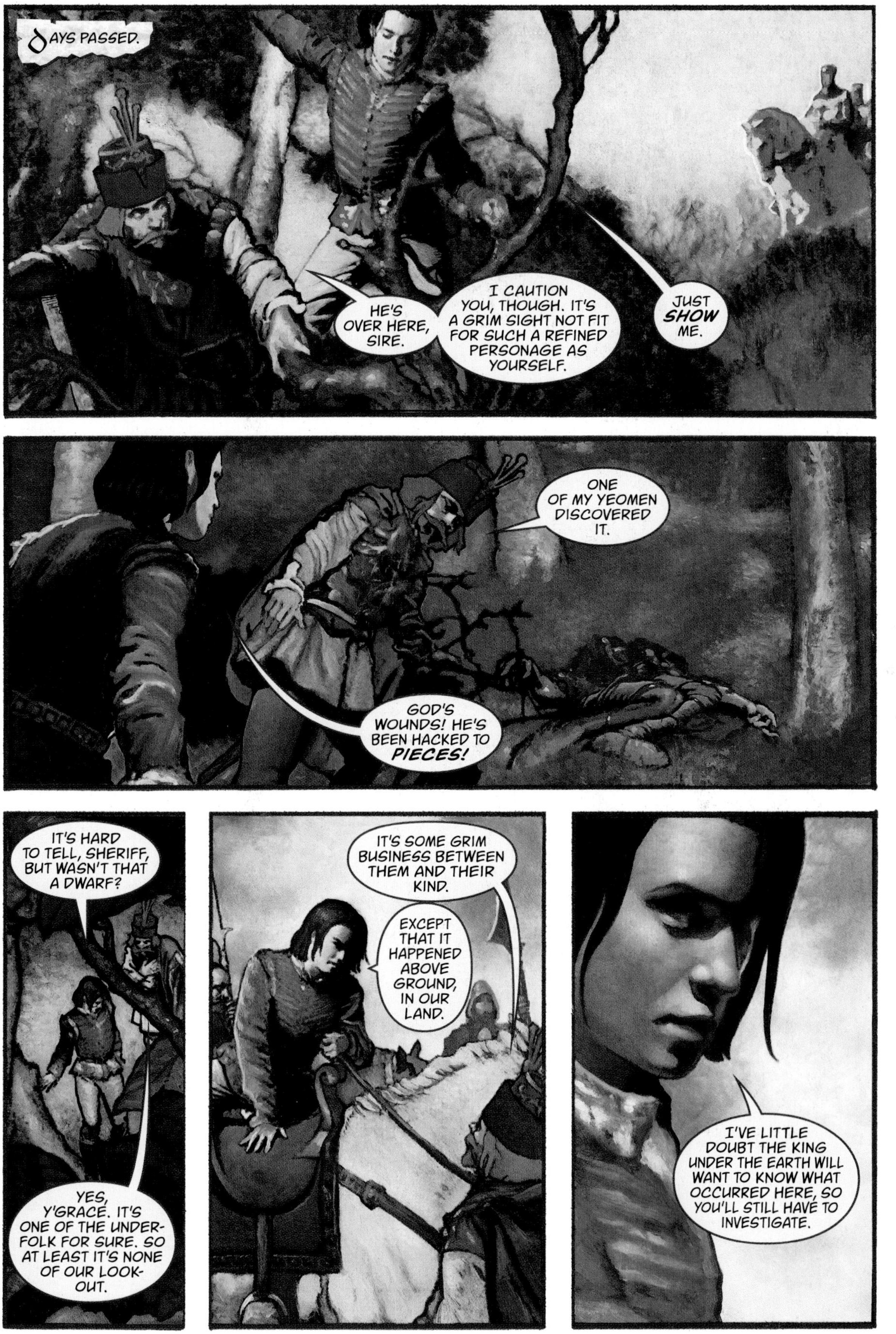
DAYS PASSED.
HE'S OVER HERE, SIRE.
I CAUTION YOU, THOUGH. IT'S A GRIM SIGHT NOT FIT FOR SUCH A REFINED PERSONAGE AS YOURSELF.
JUST SHOW ME.
ONE OF MY YEOMEN DISCOVERED IT.
GOD'S WOUNDS! HE'S BEEN HACKED TO PIECES!
IT'S HARD TO TELL, SHERIFF, BUT WASN'T THAT A DWARF?
YES, Y'GRACE. IT'S ONE OF THE UNDER-FOLK FOR SURE. SO AT LEAST IT'S NONE OF OUR LOOK-OUT.
IT'S SOME GRIM BUSINESS BETWEEN THEM AND THEIR KIND.
EXCEPT THAT IT HAPPENED ABOVE GROUND, IN OUR LAND.
I'VE LITTLE DOUBT THE KING UNDER THE EARTH WILL WANT TO KNOW WHAT OCCURRED HERE, SO YOU'LL STILL HAVE TO INVESTIGATE.

NEARLY A WEEK LATER THEY FOUND A SECOND BODY.

IT'S ANOTHER DWARF, PRINCE CHARMING, KILLED IN A DIFFERENT WAY, THOUGH.

THIS ONE'S LESS HACKED UP. MORE STAB WOUNDS.

LOTS OF THEM, THOUGH. THE KILLER SEEMS TO HAVE NEEDED SEVERAL TRIES TO FIND THIS POOR SOUL'S VITALS.

BEGGING YOUR PARDON, SIR, BUT FATHER VILLALON SAYS THESE THINGS DON'T HAVE THEM--*SOULS*, I MEAN.

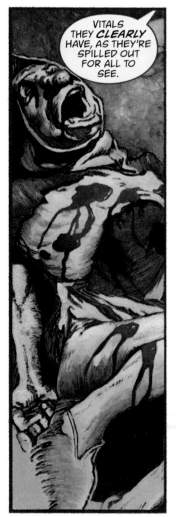

VITALS THEY *CLEARLY* HAVE, AS THEY'RE SPILLED OUT FOR ALL TO SEE.

FIND OUT WHO'S DOING THIS, SHERIFF. DO IT QUICKLY.

BY GOD, WE'LL HAVE AN *END* TO THIS MATTER!

YES, SIR, IMMEDIATELY, ONLY...I'M NOT SURE *HOW.*

AM I A COMMON SKULKER TO DO YOUR WORK *FOR* YOU? START BY ROUNDING UP EVERY ROGUE, CUT-PURSE AND VILLAIN YOU CAN LAY YOUR HANDS ON.

FILL THE DUNGEONS AND WE'LL LET OUR JACK KETCH START PUTTING THE QUESTION TO THEM.

A FEW DAYS OF HIS MERCIES AND *SOMEONE* WILL CONFESS. BET YOUR LAST PENNY ON THAT.

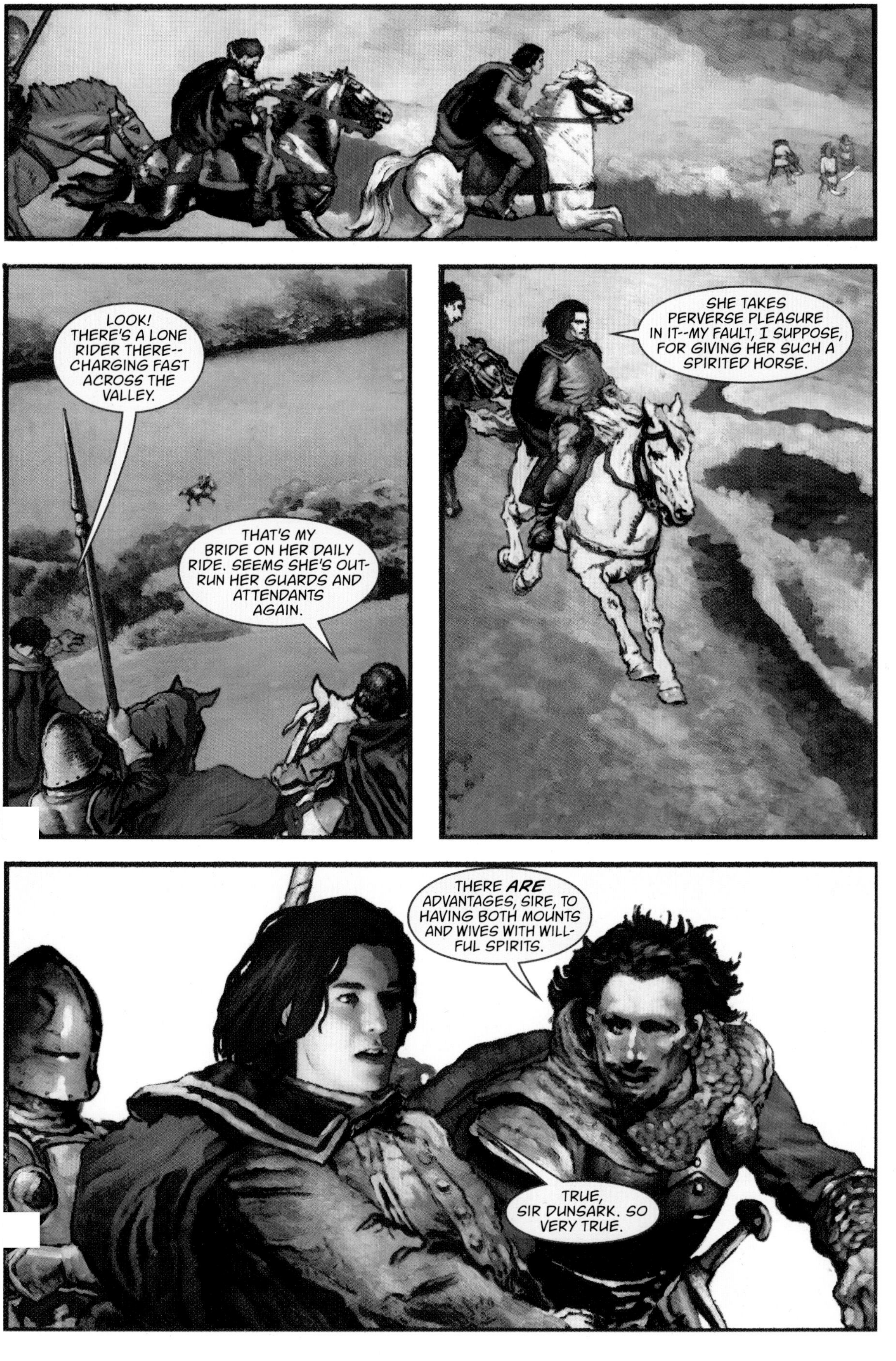
LOOK! THERE'S A LONE RIDER THERE--CHARGING FAST ACROSS THE VALLEY.
THAT'S MY BRIDE ON HER DAILY RIDE. SEEMS SHE'S OUT-RUN HER GUARDS AND ATTENDANTS AGAIN.
SHE TAKES PERVERSE PLEASURE IN IT--MY FAULT, I SUPPOSE, FOR GIVING HER SUCH A SPIRITED HORSE.
THERE *ARE* ADVANTAGES, SIRE, TO HAVING BOTH MOUNTS AND WIVES WITH WILL-FUL SPIRITS.
TRUE, SIR DUNSARK. SO VERY TRUE.

DAYS GO BY AND THE LESSONS CONTINUE.

YOU'VE GOTTEN MUCH BETTER.

BUT STILL TOO HESITANT IN YOUR ATTACKS.

I'M WORRIED ABOUT STICKING YOU.

WELL, DON'T. YOU WON'T TOUCH ME UNLESS I LET YOU.

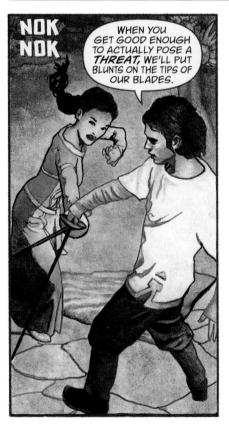

NOK NOK

WHEN YOU GET GOOD ENOUGH TO ACTUALLY POSE A *THREAT,* WE'LL PUT BLUNTS ON THE TIPS OF OUR BLADES.

DAMN, THERE'S THE DOOR.

HIDE YOURSELF, DEAR, SO OUR SECRET DOESN'T GET OUT.

BABCOCK! IS THAT YOU?

WHAT PROMPTS YOU TO BE LURKING OUTSIDE MY ROOMS AT THIS HOUR?

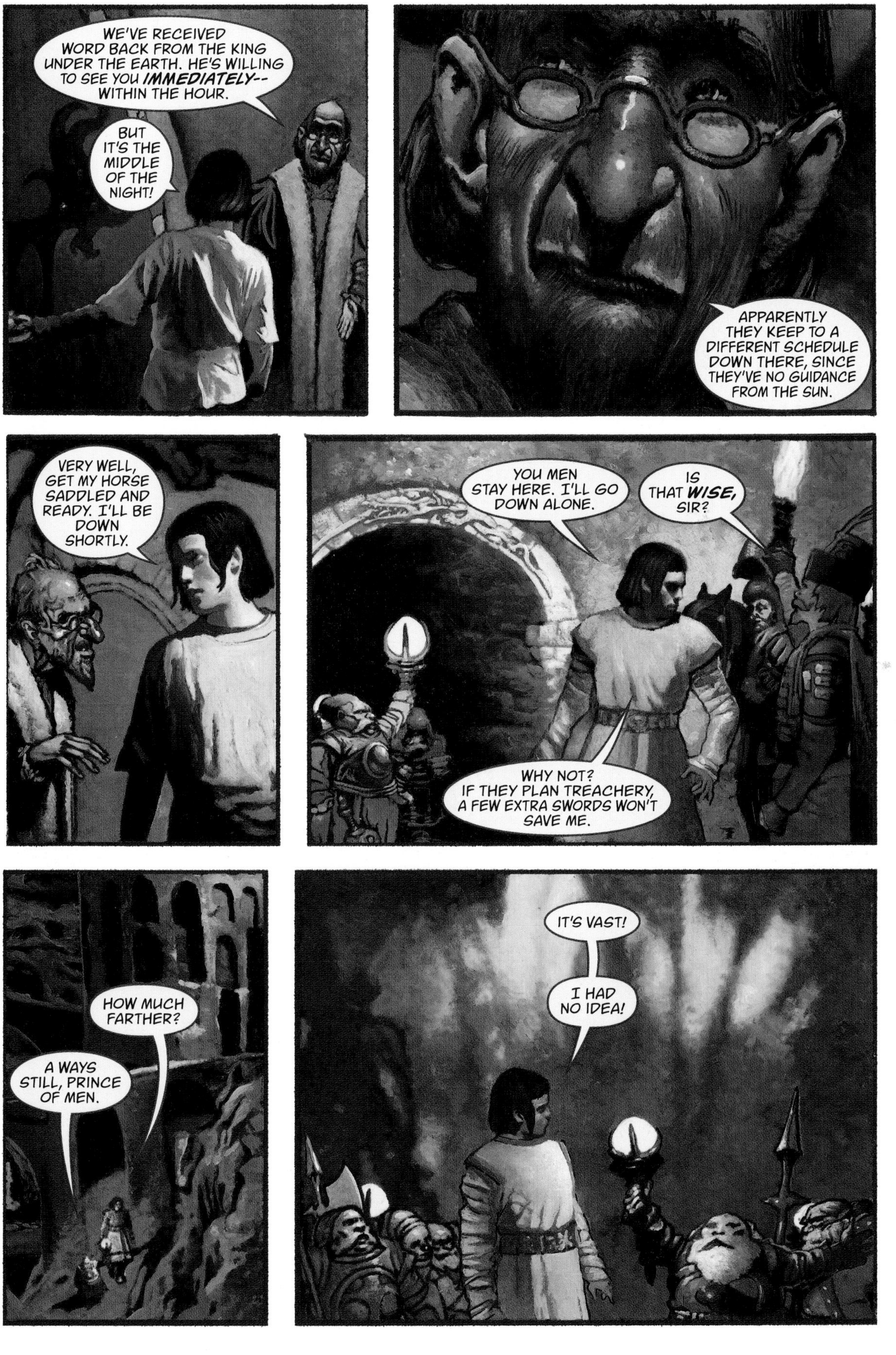
WE'VE RECEIVED WORD BACK FROM THE KING UNDER THE EARTH. HE'S WILLING TO SEE YOU *IMMEDIATELY*-- WITHIN THE HOUR.
BUT IT'S THE MIDDLE OF THE NIGHT!
APPARENTLY THEY KEEP TO A DIFFERENT SCHEDULE DOWN THERE, SINCE THEY'VE NO GUIDANCE FROM THE SUN.
VERY WELL, GET MY HORSE SADDLED AND READY. I'LL BE DOWN SHORTLY.
YOU MEN STAY HERE. I'LL GO DOWN ALONE.
IS THAT ***WISE,*** SIR?
WHY NOT? IF THEY PLAN TREACHERY, A FEW EXTRA SWORDS WON'T SAVE ME.
HOW MUCH FARTHER?
A WAYS STILL, PRINCE OF MEN.
IT'S VAST!
I HAD NO IDEA!

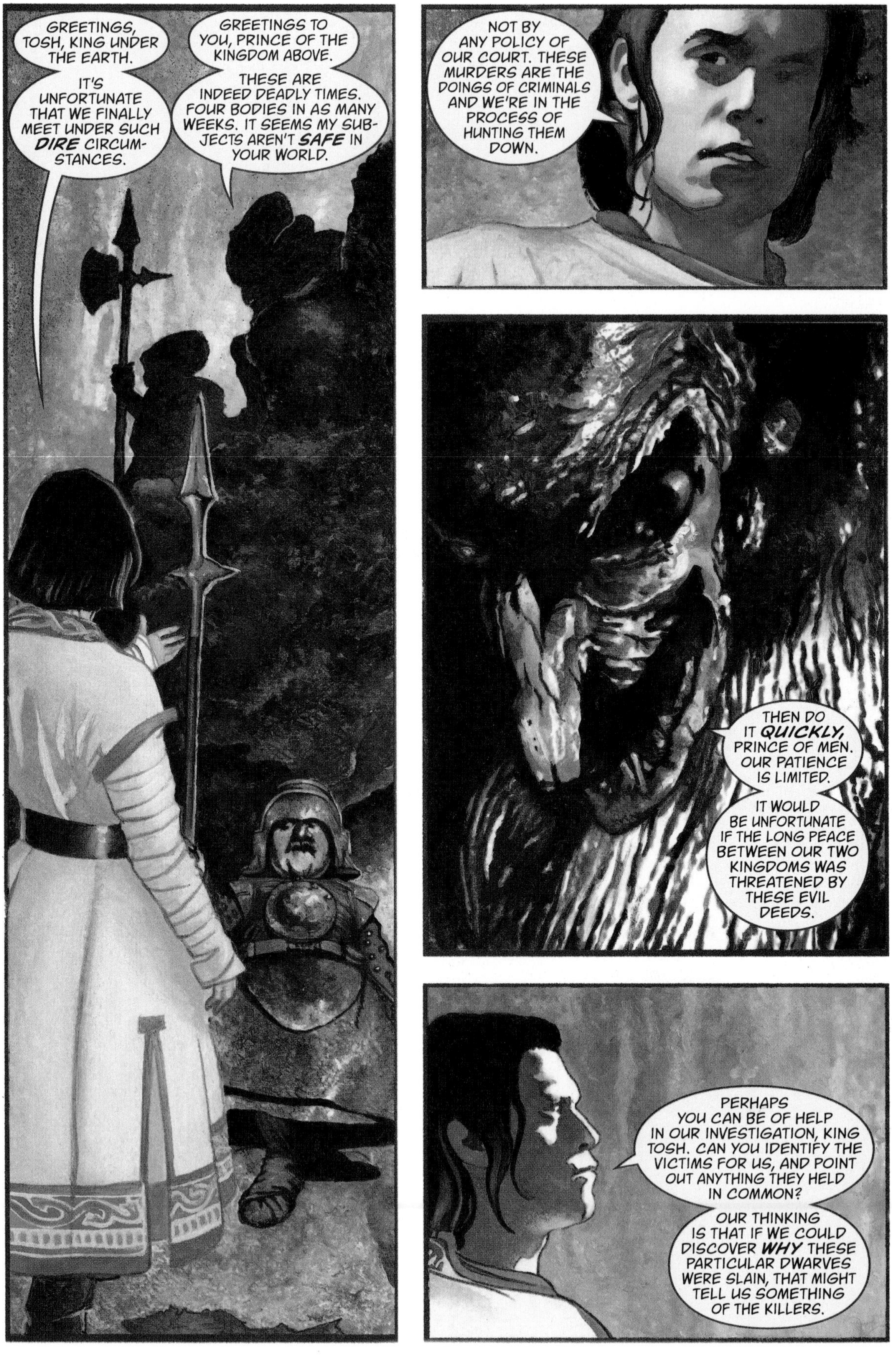
GREETINGS, TOSH, KING UNDER THE EARTH.
IT'S UNFORTUNATE THAT WE FINALLY MEET UNDER SUCH DIRE CIRCUMSTANCES.
GREETINGS TO YOU, PRINCE OF THE KINGDOM ABOVE.
THESE ARE INDEED DEADLY TIMES. FOUR BODIES IN AS MANY WEEKS. IT SEEMS MY SUBJECTS AREN'T SAFE IN YOUR WORLD.
NOT BY ANY POLICY OF OUR COURT. THESE MURDERS ARE THE DOINGS OF CRIMINALS AND WE'RE IN THE PROCESS OF HUNTING THEM DOWN.
THEN DO IT QUICKLY, PRINCE OF MEN. OUR PATIENCE IS LIMITED.
IT WOULD BE UNFORTUNATE IF THE LONG PEACE BETWEEN OUR TWO KINGDOMS WAS THREATENED BY THESE EVIL DEEDS.
PERHAPS YOU CAN BE OF HELP IN OUR INVESTIGATION, KING TOSH. CAN YOU IDENTIFY THE VICTIMS FOR US, AND POINT OUT ANYTHING THEY HELD IN COMMON?
OUR THINKING IS THAT IF WE COULD DISCOVER WHY THESE PARTICULAR DWARVES WERE SLAIN, THAT MIGHT TELL US SOMETHING OF THE KILLERS.

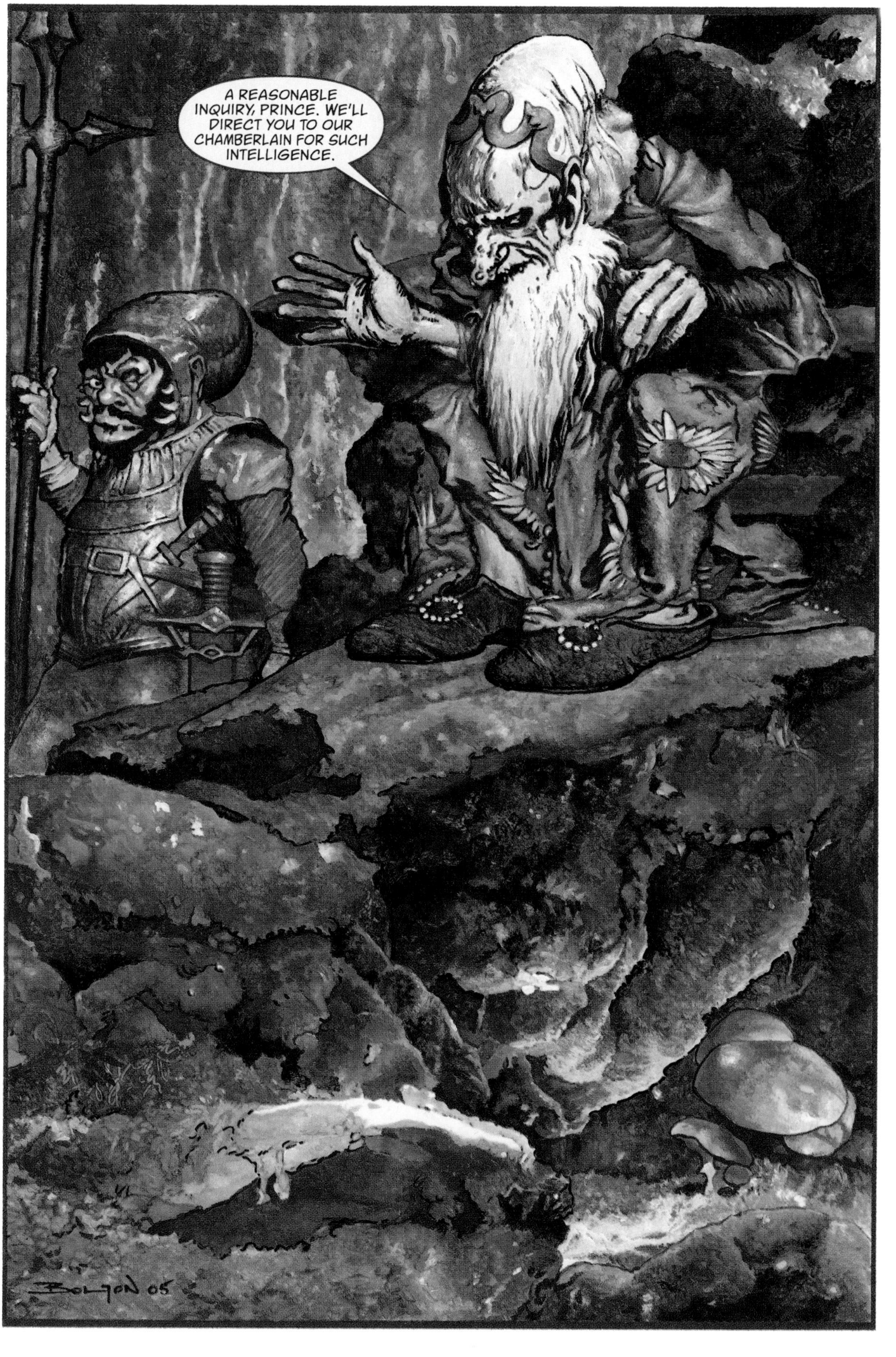
A REASONABLE INQUIRY, PRINCE. WE'LL DIRECT YOU TO OUR CHAMBERLAIN FOR SUCH INTELLIGENCE.
BOLTON 05

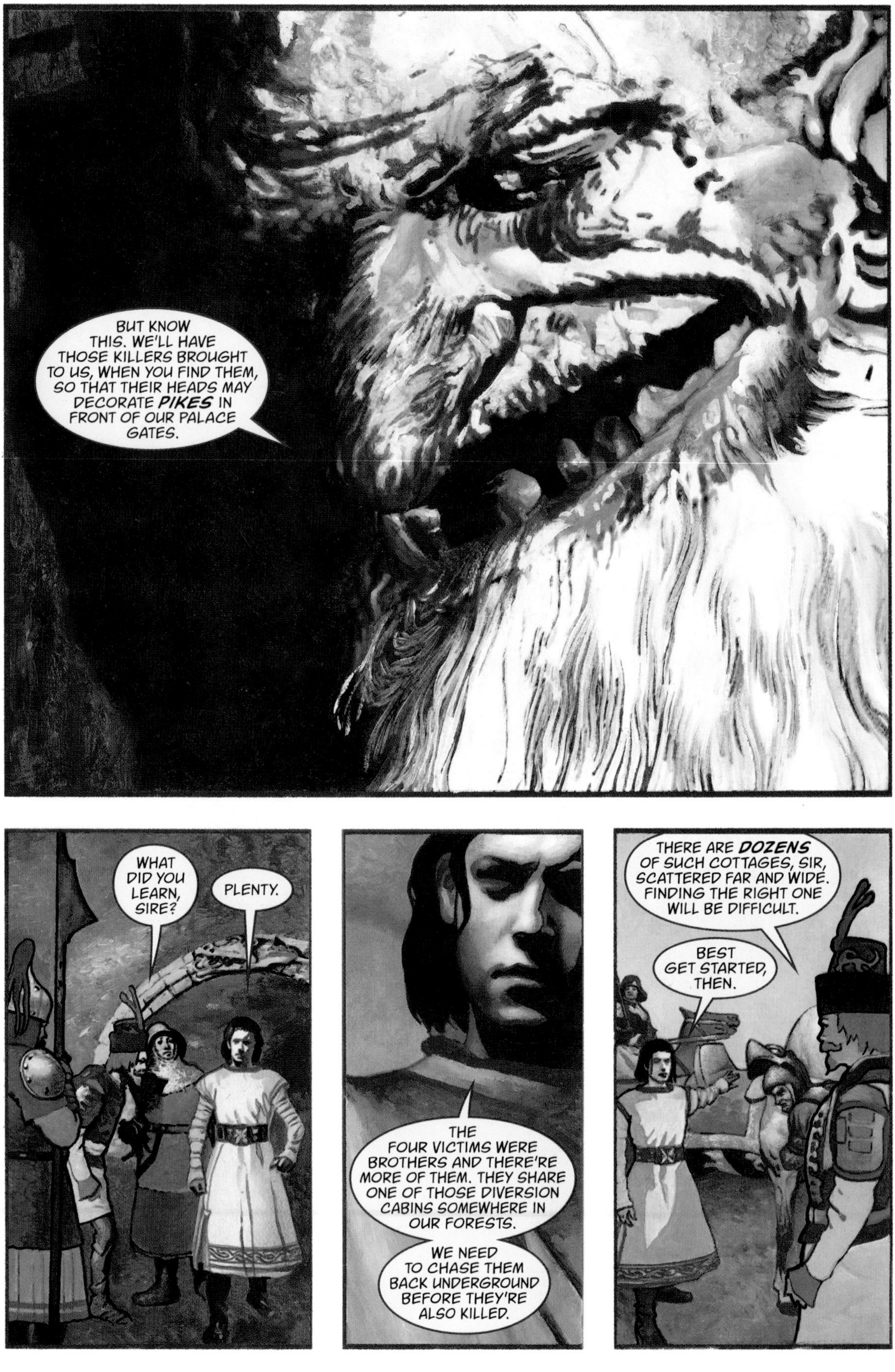
BUT KNOW THIS. WE'LL HAVE THOSE KILLERS BROUGHT TO US, WHEN YOU FIND THEM, SO THAT THEIR HEADS MAY DECORATE PIKES IN FRONT OF OUR PALACE GATES.
WHAT DID YOU LEARN, SIRE?
PLENTY.
THE FOUR VICTIMS WERE BROTHERS AND THERE'RE MORE OF THEM. THEY SHARE ONE OF THOSE DIVERSION CABINS SOMEWHERE IN OUR FORESTS.
WE NEED TO CHASE THEM BACK UNDERGROUND BEFORE THEY'RE ALSO KILLED.
THERE ARE DOZENS OF SUCH COTTAGES, SIR, SCATTERED FAR AND WIDE. FINDING THE RIGHT ONE WILL BE DIFFICULT.
BEST GET STARTED, THEN.

MORE BAD DREAMS?

YOU HAVEN'T BEEN SLEEPING WELL, HUSBAND, EVER SINCE YOU RETURNED FROM THE UNDERWORLD.

I'M JUST A LITTLE OVERWORKED THESE DAYS. NOTHING FOR YOU TO WORRY AT.

IT SEEMS PREVENTING A WAR DEPENDS ON SOLVING THESE MURDERS, BUT WE'VE HIT ONE DEAD END AFTER ANOTHER.

SUCH BLACK DEEDS CAN'T GO ON FOREVER. AND, FROM WHAT YOU TELL ME, THESE WERE NOT UPRIGHT CITIZENS OF ANY RACE--DWARF OR MAN.

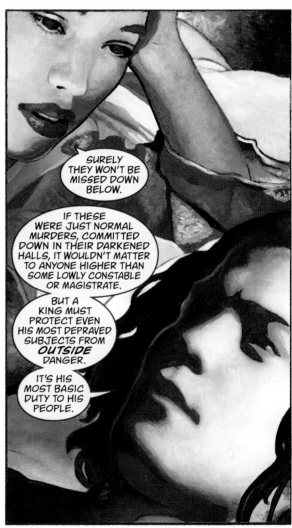

SURELY THEY WON'T BE MISSED DOWN BELOW.

IF THESE WERE JUST NORMAL MURDERS, COMMITTED DOWN IN THEIR DARKENED HALLS, IT WOULDN'T MATTER TO ANYONE HIGHER THAN SOME LOWLY CONSTABLE OR MAGISTRATE.

BUT A KING MUST PROTECT EVEN HIS MOST DEPRAVED SUBJECTS FROM *OUTSIDE* DANGER.

IT'S HIS MOST BASIC DUTY TO HIS PEOPLE.

THE MERE FACT THAT THE KILLER IS LIKELY SOMEONE OF *OUR* RACE IS ENOUGH TO WARRANT THEIR KING'S ATTENTION.

SUCH LOFTY MATTERS ARE BEYOND MY UNDERSTAND-ING.

BUT I WILL DO ONE THING TO HELP.

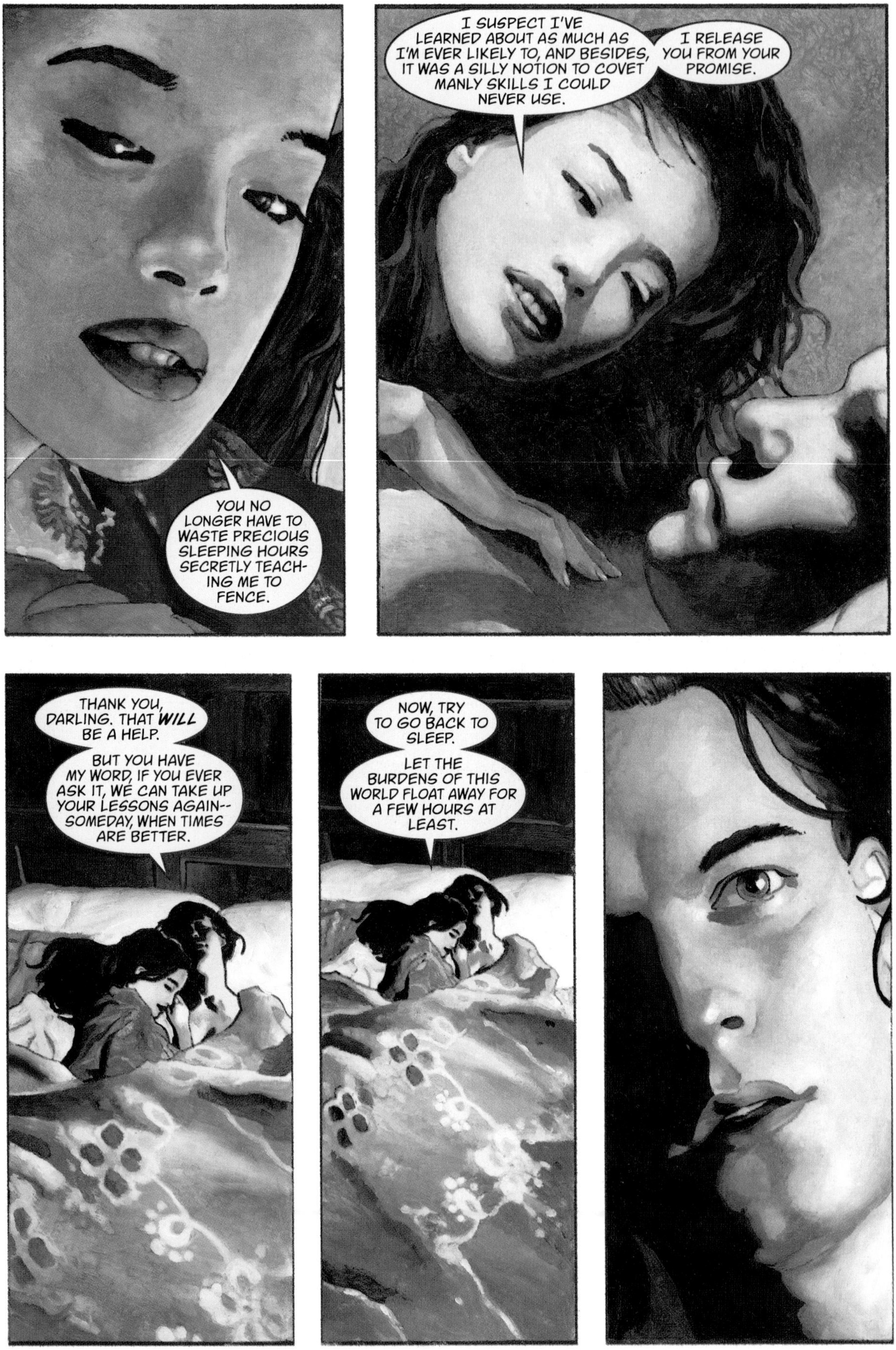
YOU NO LONGER HAVE TO WASTE PRECIOUS SLEEPING HOURS SECRETLY TEACHING ME TO FENCE.
I SUSPECT I'VE LEARNED ABOUT AS MUCH AS I'M EVER LIKELY TO, AND BESIDES, IT WAS A SILLY NOTION TO COVET MANLY SKILLS I COULD NEVER USE.
I RELEASE YOU FROM YOUR PROMISE.
THANK YOU, DARLING. THAT *WILL* BE A HELP.
BUT YOU HAVE MY WORD, IF YOU EVER ASK IT, WE CAN TAKE UP YOUR LESSONS AGAIN--SOMEDAY, WHEN TIMES ARE BETTER.
NOW, TRY TO GO BACK TO SLEEP.
LET THE BURDENS OF THIS WORLD FLOAT AWAY FOR A FEW HOURS AT LEAST.

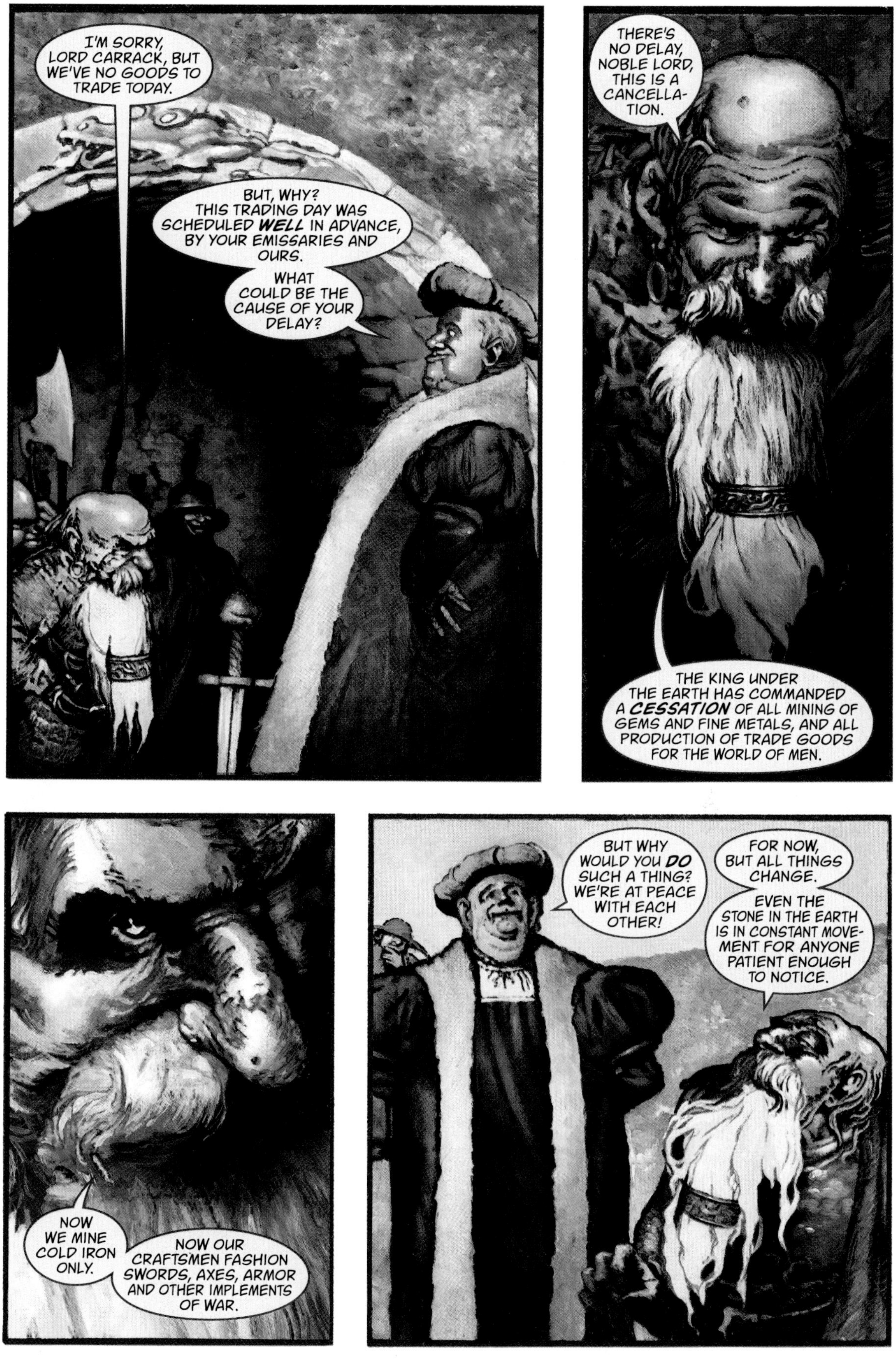
I'M SORRY, LORD CARRACK, BUT WE'VE NO GOODS TO TRADE TODAY.
BUT, WHY? THIS TRADING DAY WAS SCHEDULED **WELL** IN ADVANCE, BY YOUR EMISSARIES AND OURS.
WHAT COULD BE THE CAUSE OF YOUR DELAY?
THERE'S NO DELAY, NOBLE LORD, THIS IS A CANCELLATION.
THE KING UNDER THE EARTH HAS COMMANDED A **CESSATION** OF ALL MINING OF GEMS AND FINE METALS, AND ALL PRODUCTION OF TRADE GOODS FOR THE WORLD OF MEN.
NOW WE MINE COLD IRON ONLY.
NOW OUR CRAFTSMEN FASHION SWORDS, AXES, ARMOR AND OTHER IMPLEMENTS OF WAR.
BUT WHY WOULD YOU **DO** SUCH A THING? WE'RE AT PEACE WITH EACH OTHER!
FOR NOW, BUT ALL THINGS CHANGE.
EVEN THE STONE IN THE EARTH IS IN CONSTANT MOVEMENT FOR ANYONE PATIENT ENOUGH TO NOTICE.

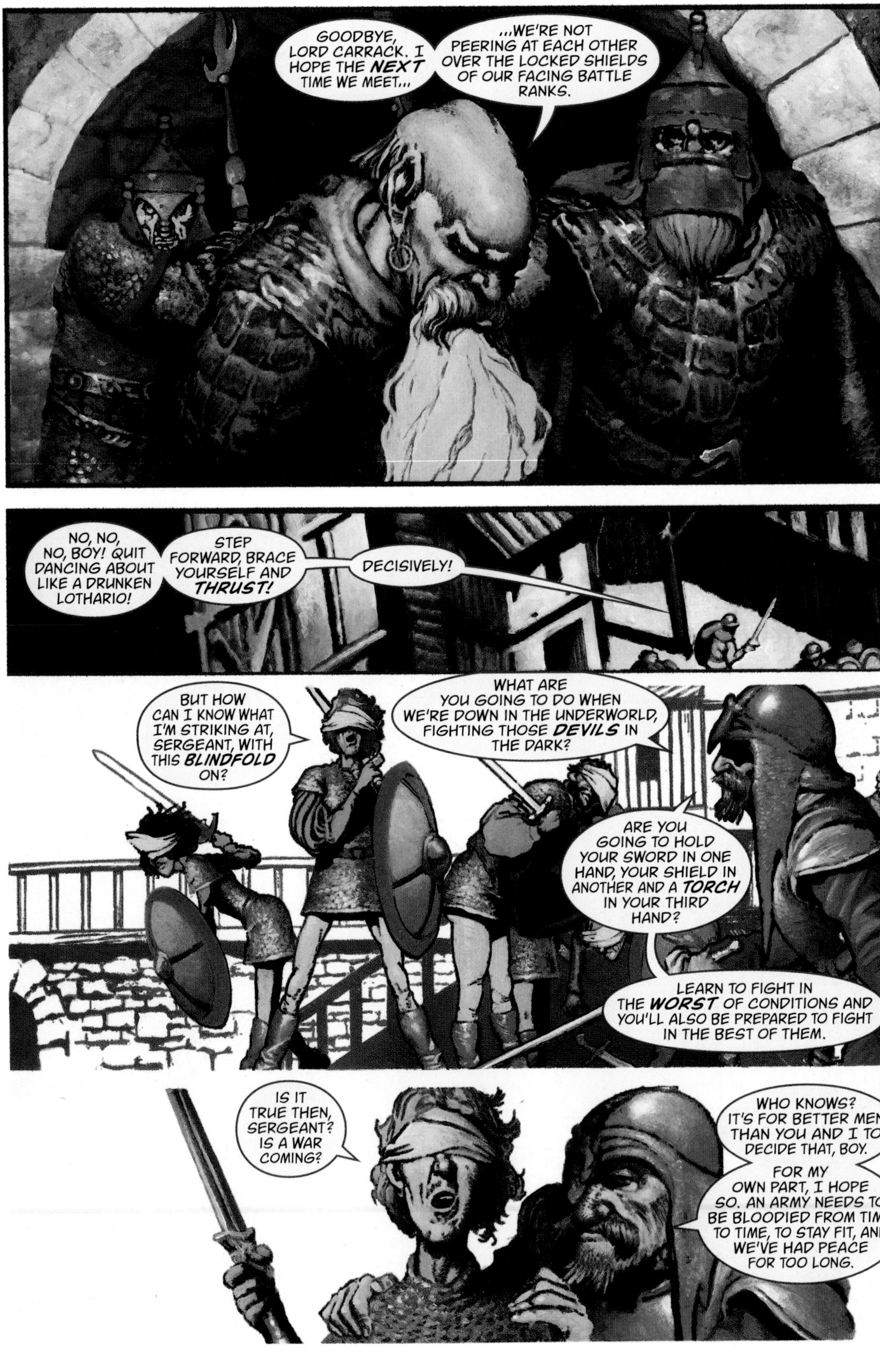
GOODBYE, LORD CARRACK. I HOPE THE NEXT TIME WE MEET...
...WE'RE NOT PEERING AT EACH OTHER OVER THE LOCKED SHIELDS OF OUR FACING BATTLE RANKS.
NO, NO, NO, BOY! QUIT DANCING ABOUT LIKE A DRUNKEN LOTHARIO!
STEP FORWARD, BRACE YOURSELF AND THRUST!
DECISIVELY!
BUT HOW CAN I KNOW WHAT I'M STRIKING AT, SERGEANT, WITH THIS BLINDFOLD ON?
WHAT ARE YOU GOING TO DO WHEN WE'RE DOWN IN THE UNDERWORLD, FIGHTING THOSE DEVILS IN THE DARK?
ARE YOU GOING TO HOLD YOUR SWORD IN ONE HAND, YOUR SHIELD IN ANOTHER AND A TORCH IN YOUR THIRD HAND?
LEARN TO FIGHT IN THE WORST OF CONDITIONS AND YOU'LL ALSO BE PREPARED TO FIGHT IN THE BEST OF THEM.
IS IT TRUE THEN, SERGEANT? IS A WAR COMING?
WHO KNOWS? IT'S FOR BETTER MEN THAN YOU AND I TO DECIDE THAT, BOY.
FOR MY OWN PART, I HOPE SO. AN ARMY NEEDS TO BE BLOODIED FROM TIME TO TIME, TO STAY FIT, AND WE'VE HAD PEACE FOR TOO LONG.

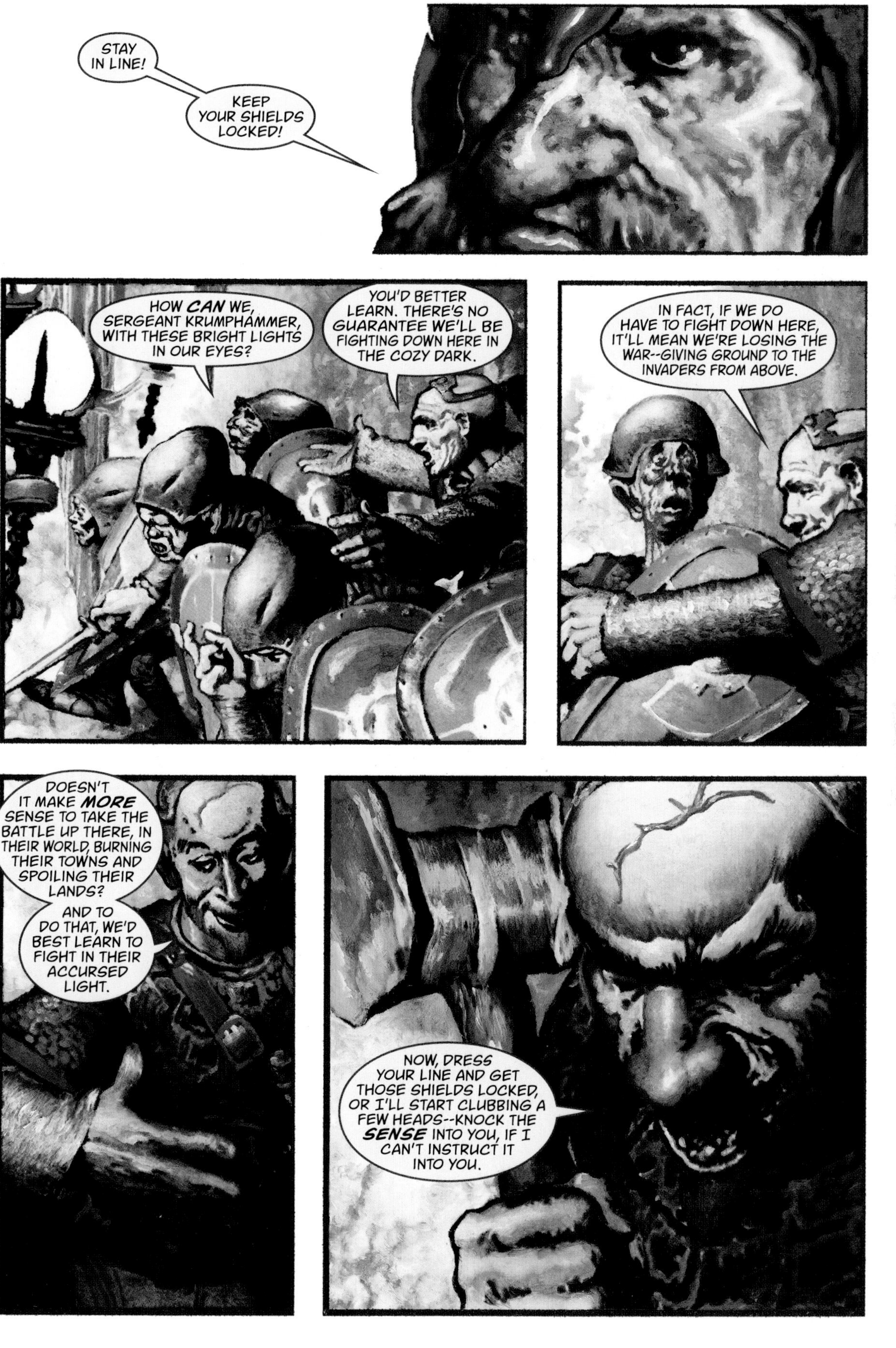
STAY IN LINE!
KEEP YOUR SHIELDS LOCKED!
HOW **CAN** WE, SERGEANT KRUMPHAMMER, WITH THESE BRIGHT LIGHTS IN OUR EYES?
YOU'D BETTER LEARN. THERE'S NO GUARANTEE **WE'LL** BE FIGHTING DOWN HERE IN THE COZY DARK.
IN FACT, IF WE DO HAVE TO FIGHT DOWN HERE, IT'LL MEAN WE'RE LOSING THE WAR--GIVING GROUND TO THE INVADERS FROM ABOVE.
DOESN'T IT MAKE **MORE** SENSE TO TAKE THE BATTLE UP THERE, IN THEIR WORLD, BURNING THEIR TOWNS AND SPOILING THEIR LANDS?
AND TO DO THAT, WE'D BEST LEARN TO FIGHT IN THEIR ACCURSED LIGHT.
NOW, DRESS YOUR LINE AND GET THOSE SHIELDS LOCKED, OR I'LL START CLUBBING A FEW HEADS--KNOCK THE **SENSE** INTO YOU, IF I CAN'T INSTRUCT IT INTO YOU.

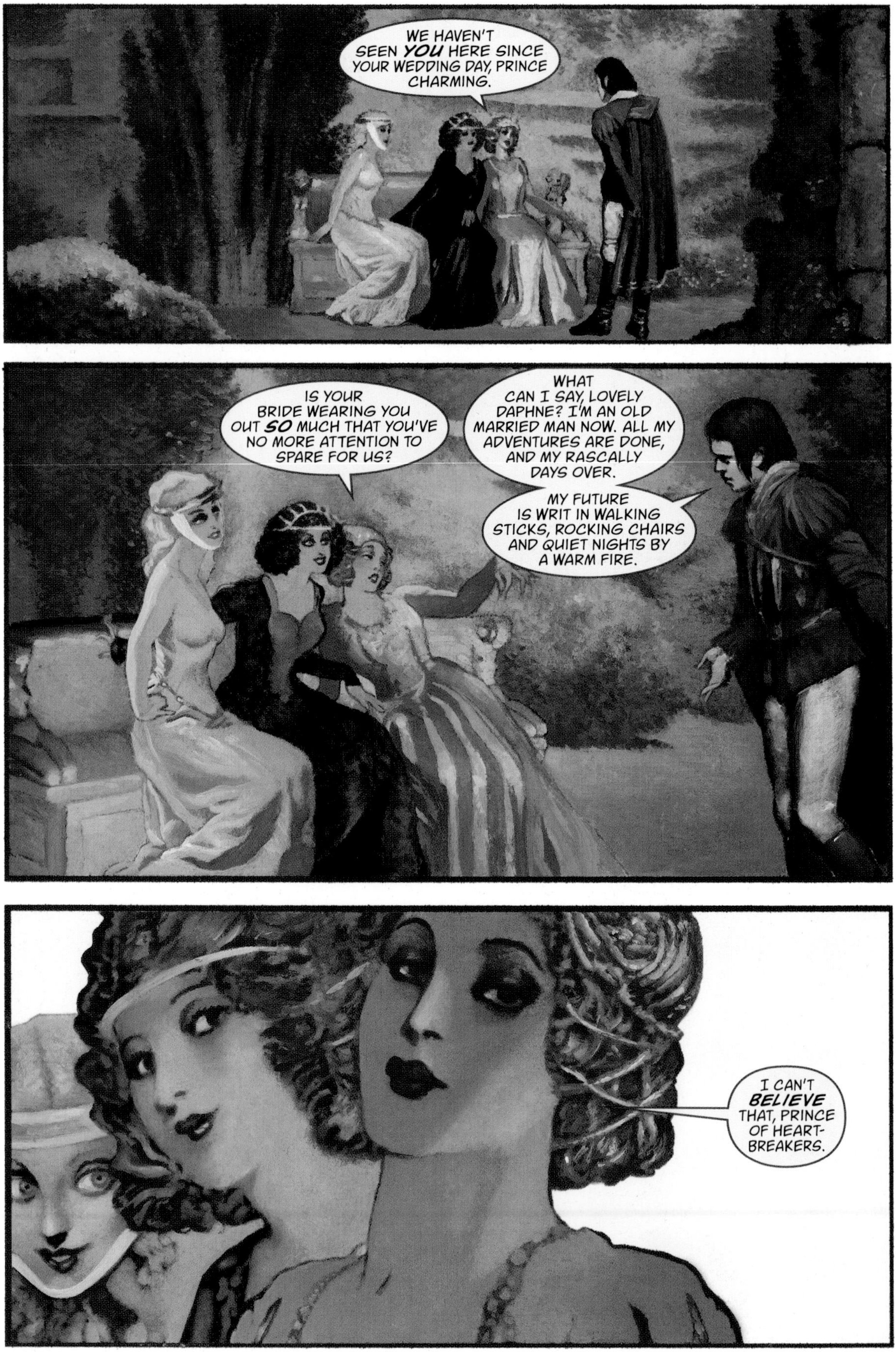
WE HAVEN'T SEEN YOU HERE SINCE YOUR WEDDING DAY, PRINCE CHARMING.
IS YOUR BRIDE WEARING YOU OUT SO MUCH THAT YOU'VE NO MORE ATTENTION TO SPARE FOR US?
WHAT CAN I SAY, LOVELY DAPHNE? I'M AN OLD MARRIED MAN NOW. ALL MY ADVENTURES ARE DONE, AND MY RASCALLY DAYS OVER.
MY FUTURE IS WRIT IN WALKING STICKS, ROCKING CHAIRS AND QUIET NIGHTS BY A WARM FIRE.
I CAN'T BELIEVE THAT, PRINCE OF HEART-BREAKERS.

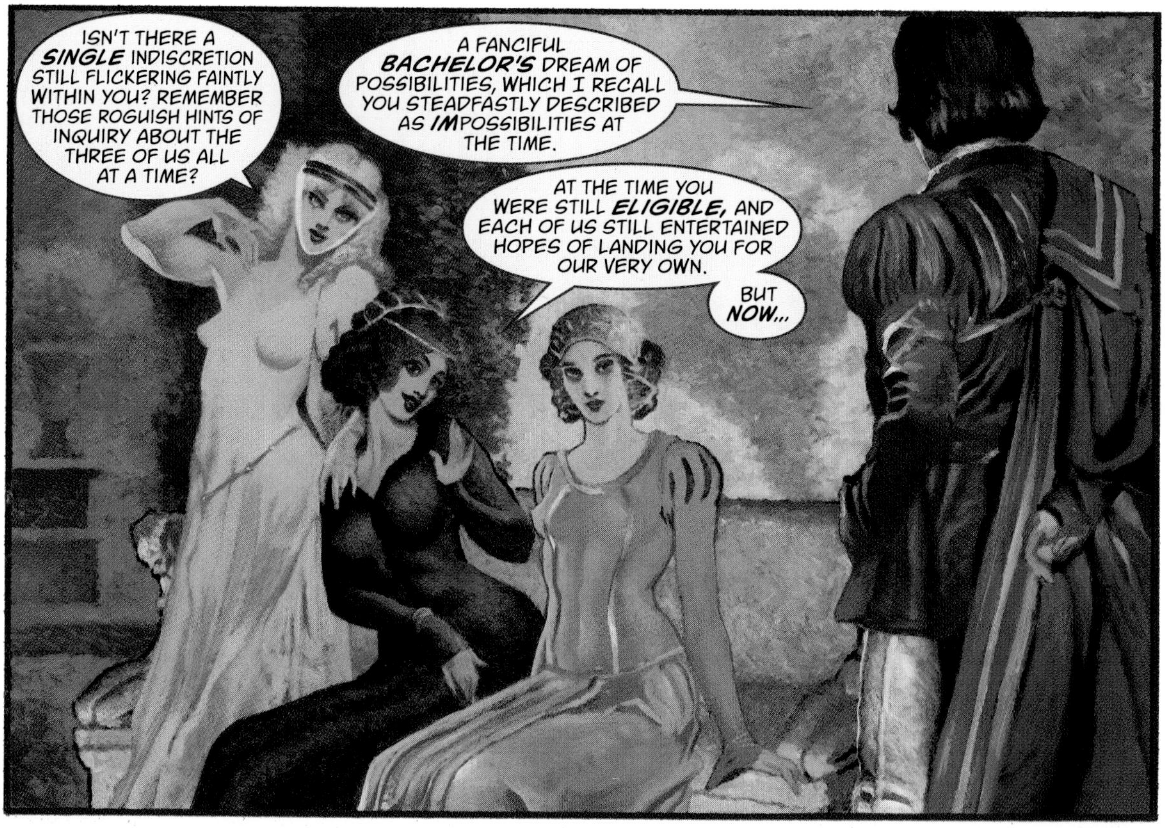
ISN'T THERE A SINGLE INDISCRETION STILL FLICKERING FAINTLY WITHIN YOU? REMEMBER THOSE ROGUISH HINTS OF INQUIRY ABOUT THE THREE OF US ALL AT A TIME?
A FANCIFUL BACHELOR'S DREAM OF POSSIBILITIES, WHICH I RECALL YOU STEADFASTLY DESCRIBED AS IMPOSSIBILITIES AT THE TIME.
AT THE TIME YOU WERE STILL ELIGIBLE, AND EACH OF US STILL ENTERTAINED HOPES OF LANDING YOU FOR OUR VERY OWN.
BUT NOW...

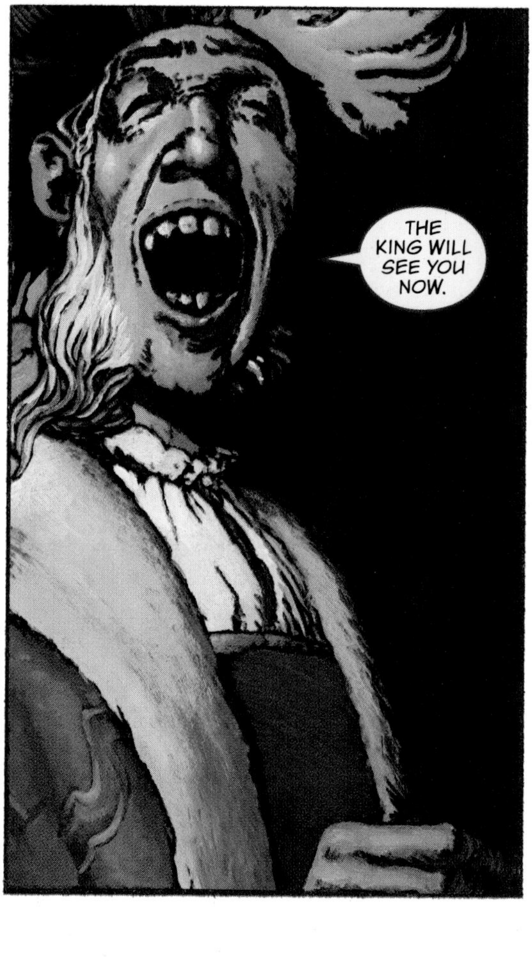
THE KING WILL SEE YOU NOW.

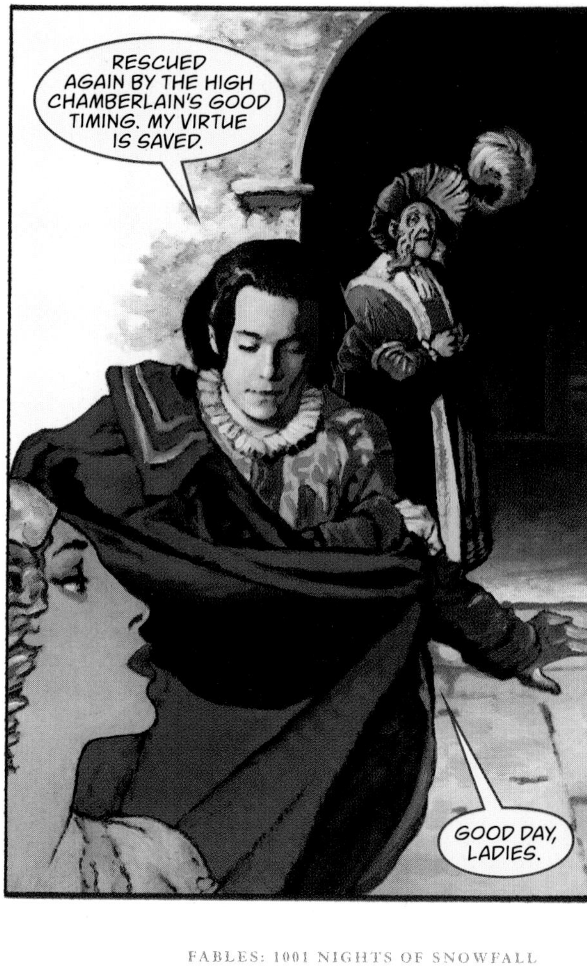
RESCUED AGAIN BY THE HIGH CHAMBERLAIN'S GOOD TIMING. MY VIRTUE IS SAVED.
GOOD DAY, LADIES.

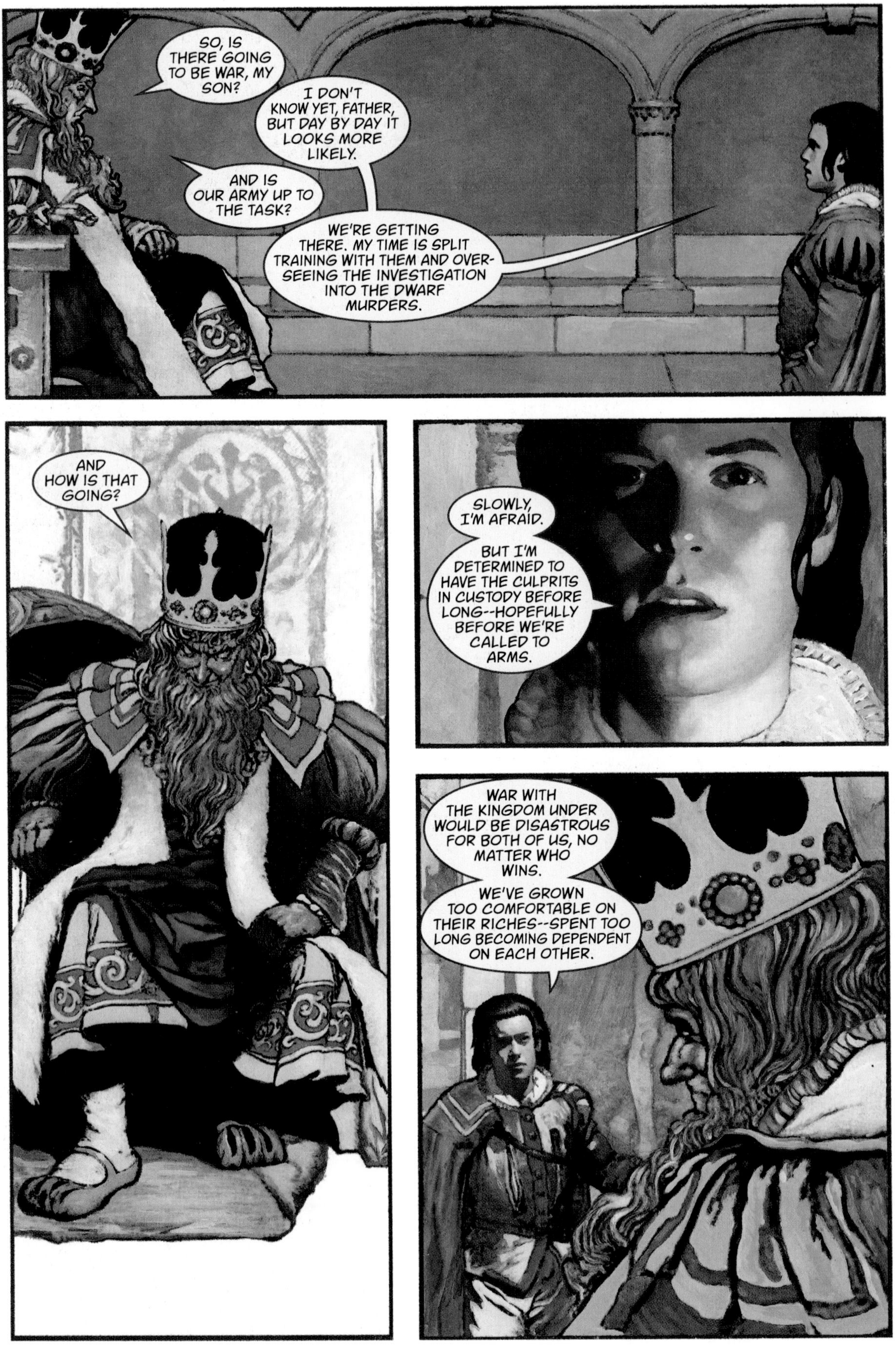
SO, IS THERE GOING TO BE WAR, MY SON?
I DON'T KNOW YET, FATHER, BUT DAY BY DAY IT LOOKS MORE LIKELY.
AND IS OUR ARMY UP TO THE TASK?
WE'RE GETTING THERE. MY TIME IS SPLIT TRAINING WITH THEM AND OVER-SEEING THE INVESTIGATION INTO THE DWARF MURDERS.
AND HOW IS THAT GOING?
SLOWLY, I'M AFRAID.
BUT I'M DETERMINED TO HAVE THE CULPRITS IN CUSTODY BEFORE LONG--HOPEFULLY BEFORE WE'RE CALLED TO ARMS.
WAR WITH THE KINGDOM UNDER WOULD BE DISASTROUS FOR BOTH OF US, NO MATTER WHO WINS.
WE'VE GROWN TOO COMFORTABLE ON THEIR RICHES--SPENT TOO LONG BECOMING DEPENDENT ON EACH OTHER.

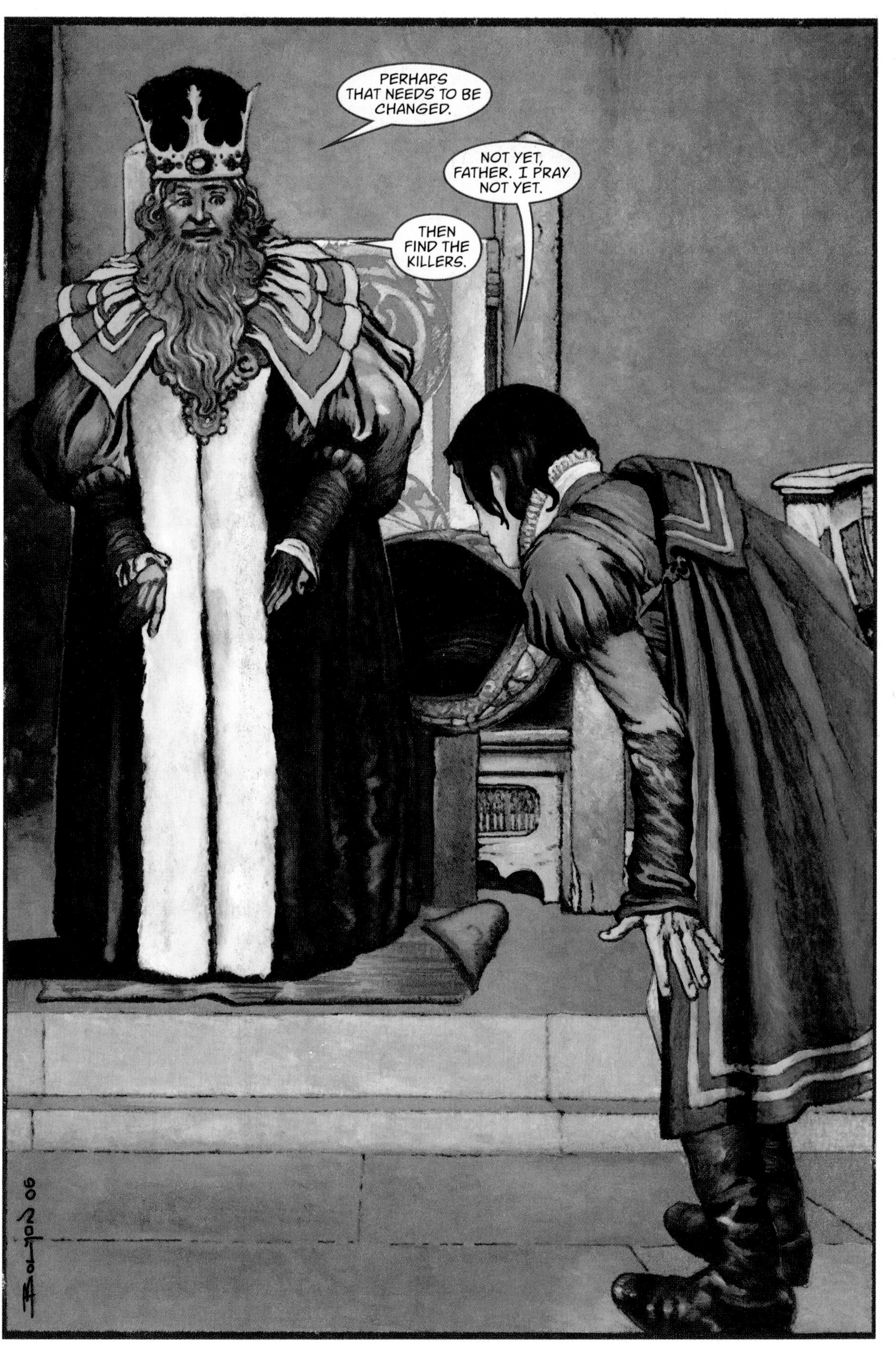
PERHAPS THAT NEEDS TO BE CHANGED.
NOT YET, FATHER. I PRAY NOT YET.
THEN FIND THE KILLERS.

I THINK THEY BURNED THE COTTAGE TO HIDE THE EVIDENCE OF MURDER.

BUT ALL THREE DWARF BODIES INSIDE WERE KILLED *BEFORE* THEY WERE COOKED--EACH BY A SINGLE SWORD THRUST THROUGH THE HEART.

I'LL BRING IN MORE MEN FROM THE OUTLYING COUNTIES TO EXPAND THE SIZE AND SCOPE OF THE SEARCH.

NO, DON'T BOTHER, SHERIFF. IT'S OVER. IT'S ALL SEVEN OF THEM NOW AND I BELIEVE THIS WILL BE THE LAST OF THE MURDERS.

YOUR INVESTIGATION IS DONE.

YOU'VE WORKED HARD THESE PAST MONTHS. GO HOME AND REST FOR A FEW WEEKS.

IT'S STRICTLY A POLITICAL MATTER FROM NOW ON.

TELL THE WARDEN OF THE DUNGEON THAT THE PRINCE WANTS TO SEE HIM, POST HASTE.

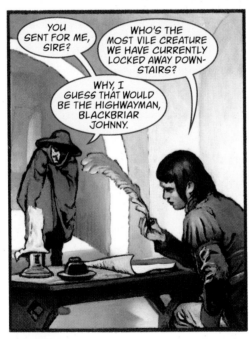

YOU SENT FOR ME, SIRE?

WHO'S THE MOST VILE CREATURE WE HAVE CURRENTLY LOCKED AWAY DOWN-STAIRS?

WHY, I GUESS THAT WOULD BE THE HIGHWAYMAN, BLACKBRIAR JOHNNY.

HE'D CUT DOWN A DOZEN TRAVELERS ALONG THE KING'S ROAD BEFORE WE CAUGHT HIM LAST YEAR.

SENTENCED TO BE HANGED ON THE PUBLIC GIBBET, BUT WE'VE PUT IT OFF. STILL HOPING TO COAX THE LOCATION OF SOME OF THE LOST PLUNDER FROM HIM.

WELL, CLEAN HIM UP. THEN HAVE HIS HEAD LOPPED OFF, IN SECRET, AND BRING IT HERE TO ME IN A BAG.

AND ALSO HAVE THESE PAPERS WITNESSED BY YOURSELF AND OUR JACK KETCH.

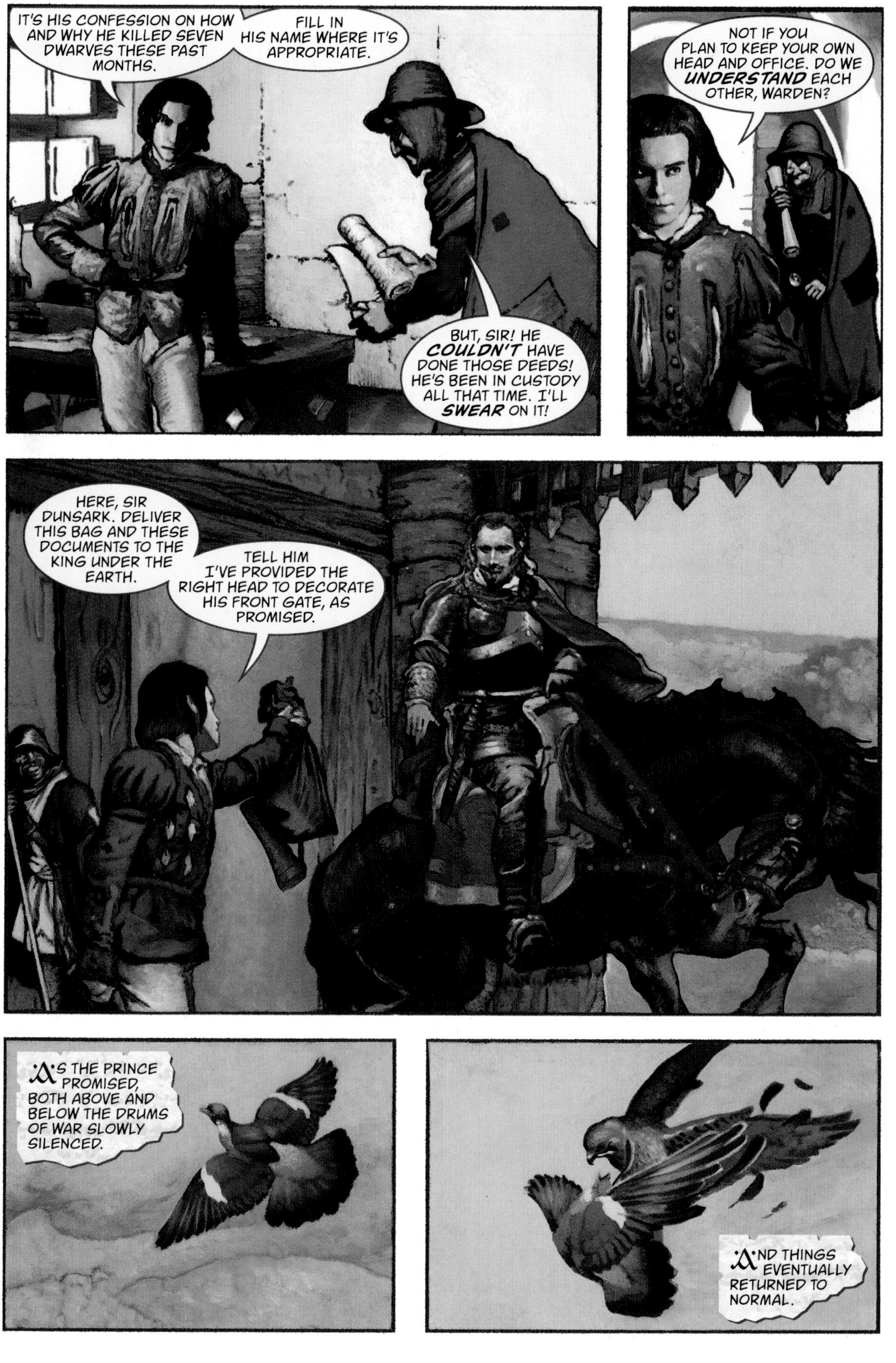
IT'S HIS CONFESSION ON HOW AND WHY HE KILLED SEVEN DWARVES THESE PAST MONTHS.
FILL IN HIS NAME WHERE IT'S APPROPRIATE.
BUT, SIR! HE COULDN'T HAVE DONE THOSE DEEDS! HE'S BEEN IN CUSTODY ALL THAT TIME. I'LL SWEAR ON IT!
NOT IF YOU PLAN TO KEEP YOUR OWN HEAD AND OFFICE. DO WE UNDERSTAND EACH OTHER, WARDEN?
HERE, SIR DUNSARK. DELIVER THIS BAG AND THESE DOCUMENTS TO THE KING UNDER THE EARTH.
TELL HIM I'VE PROVIDED THE RIGHT HEAD TO DECORATE HIS FRONT GATE, AS PROMISED.
AS THE PRINCE PROMISED, BOTH ABOVE AND BELOW THE DRUMS OF WAR SLOWLY SILENCED.
AND THINGS EVENTUALLY RETURNED TO NORMAL.

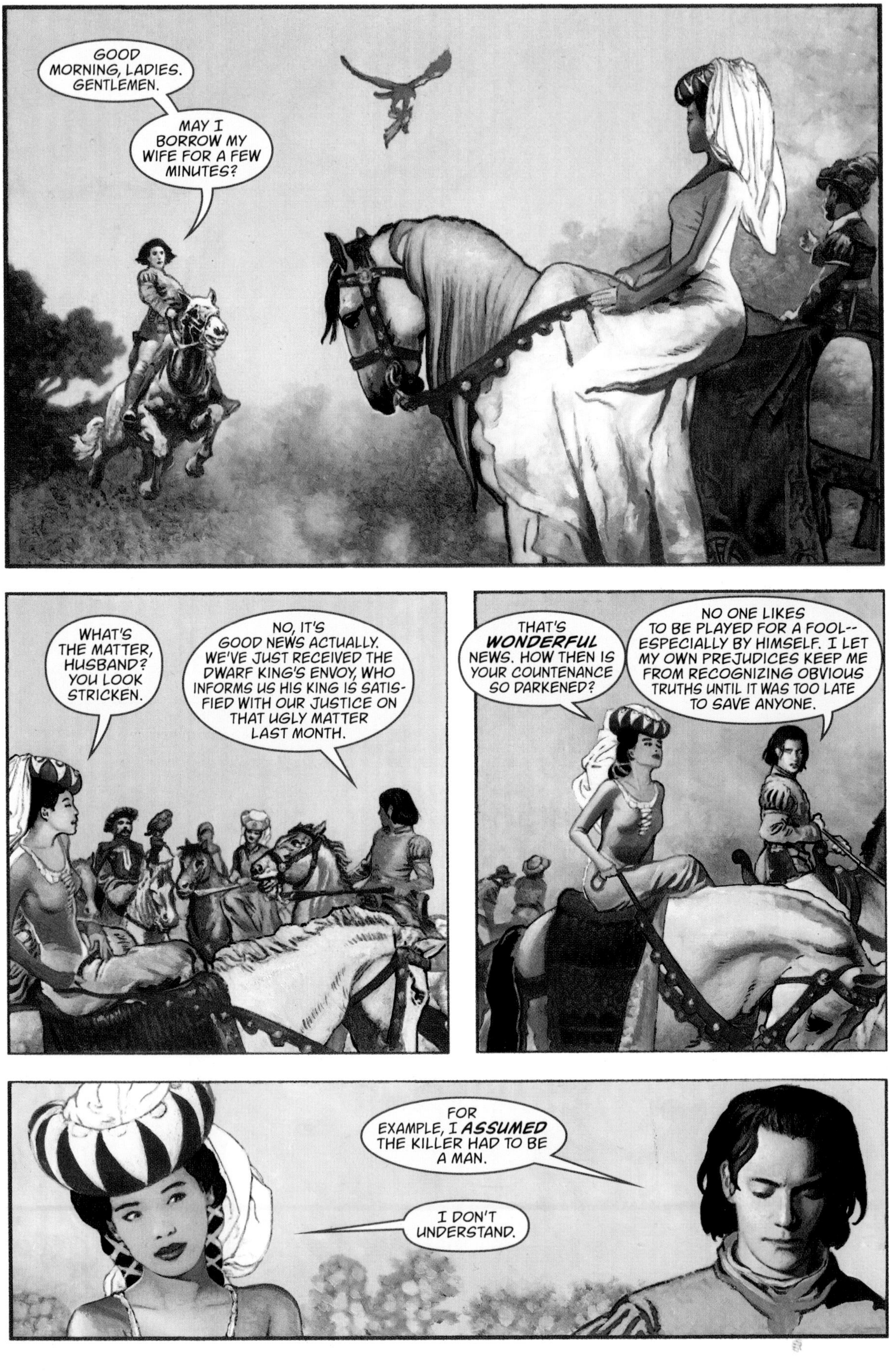
GOOD MORNING, LADIES. GENTLEMEN.
MAY I BORROW MY WIFE FOR A FEW MINUTES?
WHAT'S THE MATTER, HUSBAND? YOU LOOK STRICKEN.
NO, IT'S GOOD NEWS ACTUALLY. WE'VE JUST RECEIVED THE DWARF KING'S ENVOY, WHO INFORMS US HIS KING IS SATISFIED WITH OUR JUSTICE ON THAT UGLY MATTER LAST MONTH.
THAT'S **WONDERFUL** NEWS. HOW THEN IS YOUR COUNTENANCE SO DARKENED?
NO ONE LIKES TO BE PLAYED FOR A FOOL-- ESPECIALLY BY HIMSELF. I LET MY OWN PREJUDICES KEEP ME FROM RECOGNIZING OBVIOUS TRUTHS UNTIL IT WAS TOO LATE TO SAVE ANYONE.
FOR EXAMPLE, I **ASSUMED** THE KILLER HAD TO BE A MAN.
I DON'T UNDERSTAND.

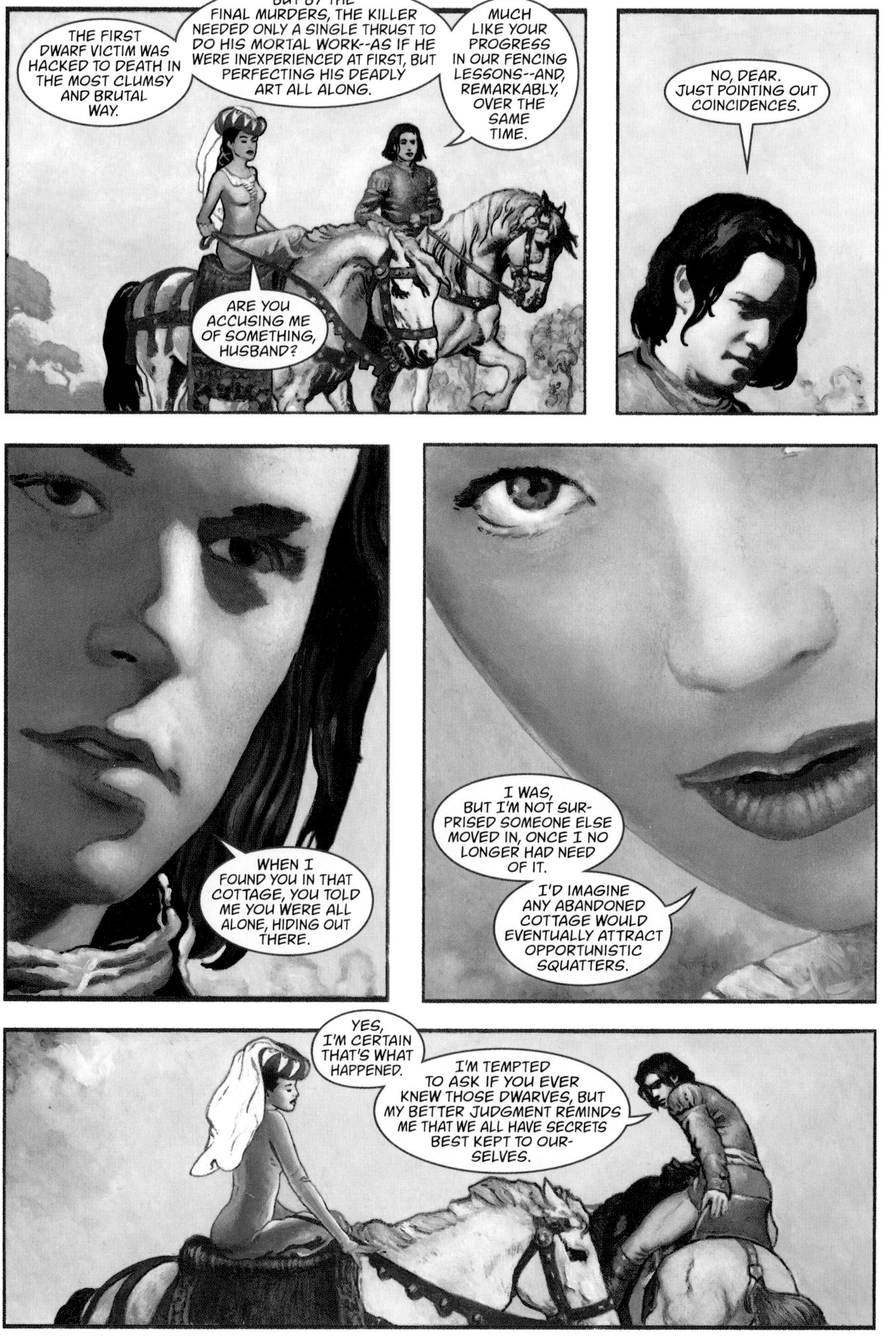
THE FIRST DWARF VICTIM WAS HACKED TO DEATH IN THE MOST CLUMSY AND BRUTAL WAY.
BUT BY THE FINAL MURDERS, THE KILLER NEEDED ONLY A SINGLE THRUST TO DO HIS MORTAL WORK--AS IF HE WERE INEXPERIENCED AT FIRST, BUT PERFECTING HIS DEADLY ART ALL ALONG.
MUCH LIKE YOUR PROGRESS IN OUR FENCING LESSONS--AND, REMARKABLY, OVER THE SAME TIME.
ARE YOU ACCUSING ME OF SOMETHING, HUSBAND?
NO, DEAR. JUST POINTING OUT COINCIDENCES.
WHEN I FOUND YOU IN THAT COTTAGE, YOU TOLD ME YOU WERE ALL ALONE, HIDING OUT THERE.
I WAS, BUT I'M NOT SUR-PRISED SOMEONE ELSE MOVED IN, ONCE I NO LONGER HAD NEED OF IT.
I'D IMAGINE ANY ABANDONED COTTAGE WOULD EVENTUALLY ATTRACT OPPORTUNISTIC SQUATTERS.
YES, I'M CERTAIN THAT'S WHAT HAPPENED.
I'M TEMPTED TO ASK IF YOU EVER KNEW THOSE DWARVES, BUT MY BETTER JUDGMENT REMINDS ME THAT WE ALL HAVE SECRETS BEST KEPT TO OUR-SELVES.

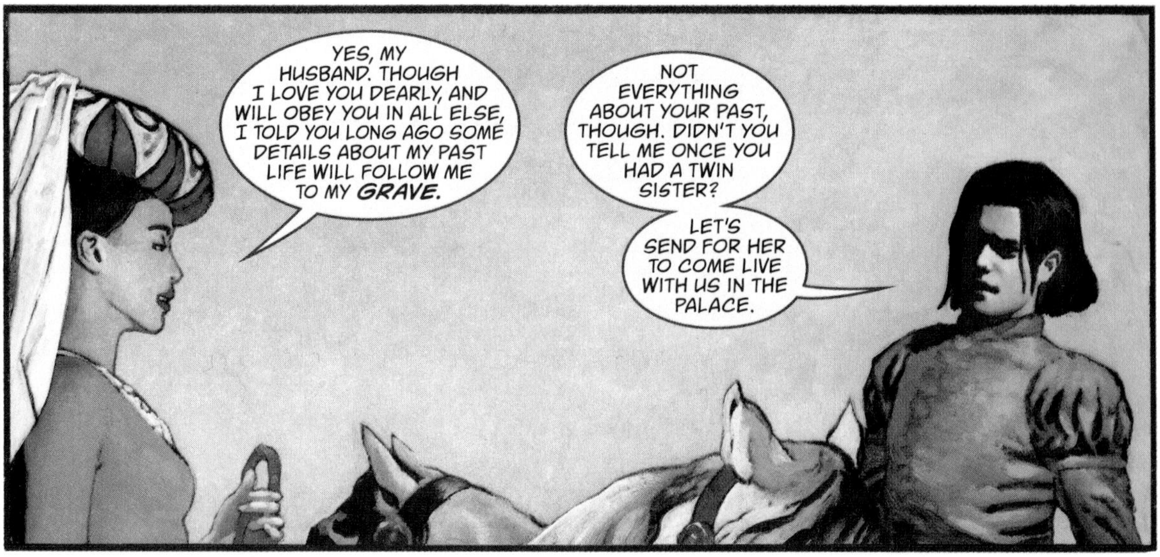
YES, MY HUSBAND. THOUGH I LOVE YOU DEARLY, AND WILL OBEY YOU IN ALL ELSE, I TOLD YOU LONG AGO SOME DETAILS ABOUT MY PAST LIFE WILL FOLLOW ME TO MY GRAVE.
NOT EVERYTHING ABOUT YOUR PAST, THOUGH. DIDN'T YOU TELL ME ONCE YOU HAD A TWIN SISTER?
LET'S SEND FOR HER TO COME LIVE WITH US IN THE PALACE.

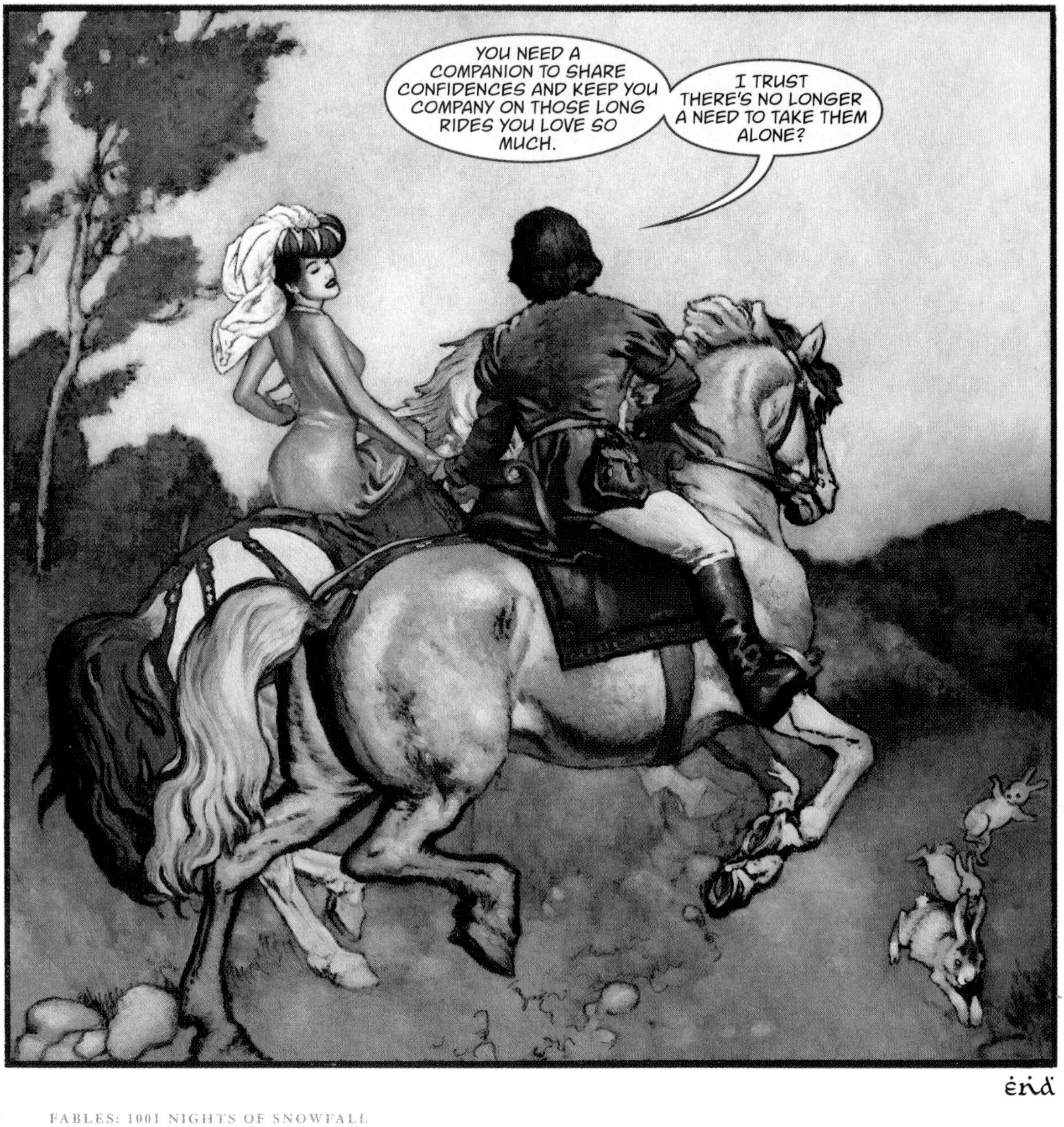
YOU NEED A COMPANION TO SHARE CONFIDENCES AND KEEP YOU COMPANY ON THOSE LONG RIDES YOU LOVE SO MUCH.
I TRUST THERE'S NO LONGER A NEED TO TAKE THEM ALONE?

end

At the conclusion of Snow White's tale the yawning Sultan noticed that the first rays of the new morning had begun to peek over the eastern ramparts.

"That was an intriguing story," King Shahryar said. "Though I suspect it wasn't chosen strictly as an entertainment. Is there some message in it for me?"

"Perhaps only that revenge is ultimately unsatisfying," Snow said. "It can't make up for the evil done to you, but can destroy the remaining good in your life."

"And what things did it ruin in the life of the young princess of your tale? War was averted, seven wicked rascals were executed, and she seems to have paid no price to accomplish it."

"Except that her husband never quite trusted her again. One version of the story has it that their marriage ended when he slept with the princess's sister, newly arrived to be a companion to her. But wiser listeners might conclude that the marriage really ended on the day she set out to become a destroyer."

"Every good story has a hundred different versions, Snow. That's what makes them endlessly wondrous and delightful." And here the King paused to yawn again and glance out of the window where a bright red finch sat on the sill singing his morning song. "But look, the day has come and I am tired. I should summon the headsman to do his terrible duty, so that I can get to my carpet bed."

"As you command, great King of the Age," Snow said. "I had another story I could have told you this evening, but since we've run out of time…"

"Another story?" King Shahryar said, his eyes widening with renewed interest. "Well, perhaps we can pause our mortal judgment for the space of a day, in the interest of hearing just one more tale that might otherwise never be known in this land."

And so, for the first time in three years the Sultan's headsman had no morning's work to do. Snow was escorted under guard, back to her rooms. With the fall of evening, having bathed and rested throughout the day, she was ushered back into the great Sultan's private rooms to begin her second night's story.

THE CHRISTMAS PIES

In which the bakeries of a dozen villages throughout a remote wooded valley are put to good use.

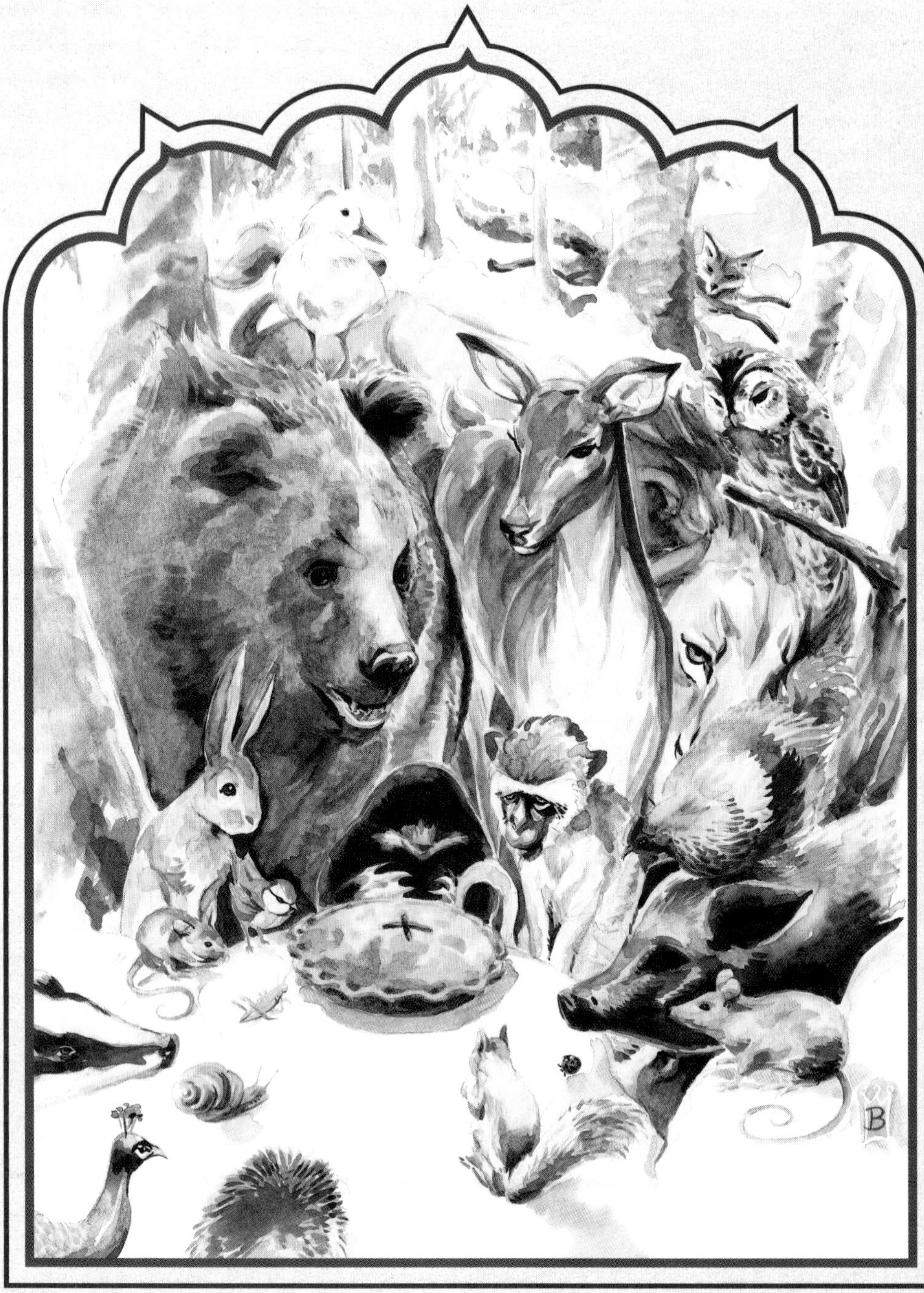

ILLUSTRATED BY MARK BUCKINGHAM

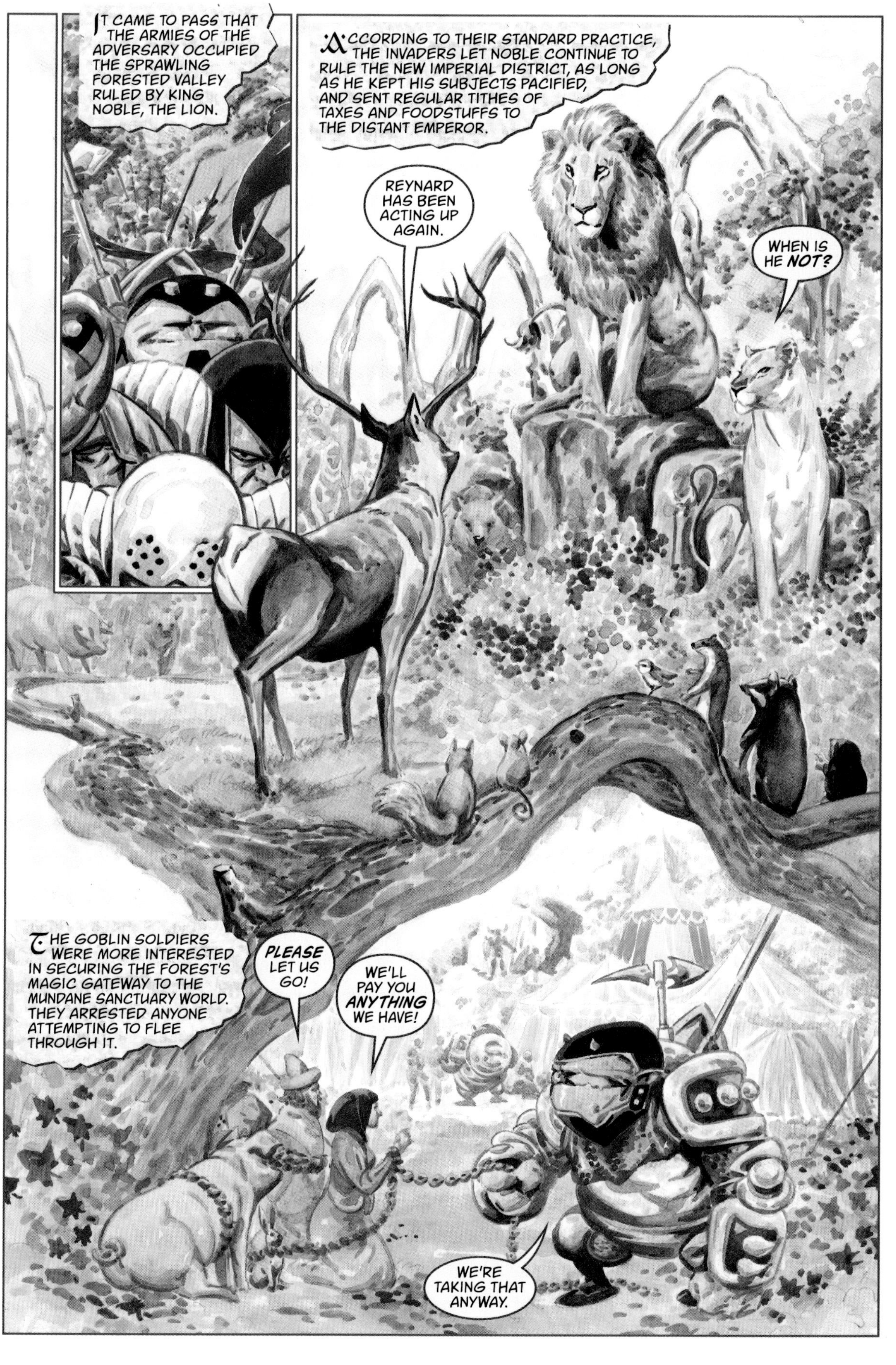
IT CAME TO PASS THAT THE ARMIES OF THE ADVERSARY OCCUPIED THE SPRAWLING FORESTED VALLEY RULED BY KING NOBLE, THE LION.
ACCORDING TO THEIR STANDARD PRACTICE, THE INVADERS LET NOBLE CONTINUE TO RULE THE NEW IMPERIAL DISTRICT, AS LONG AS HE KEPT HIS SUBJECTS PACIFIED, AND SENT REGULAR TITHES OF TAXES AND FOODSTUFFS TO THE DISTANT EMPEROR.
REYNARD HAS BEEN ACTING UP AGAIN.
WHEN IS HE *NOT?*
THE GOBLIN SOLDIERS WERE MORE INTERESTED IN SECURING THE FOREST'S MAGIC GATEWAY TO THE MUNDANE SANCTUARY WORLD. THEY ARRESTED ANYONE ATTEMPTING TO FLEE THROUGH IT.
PLEASE LET US GO!
WE'LL PAY YOU *ANYTHING* WE HAVE!
WE'RE TAKING THAT ANYWAY.

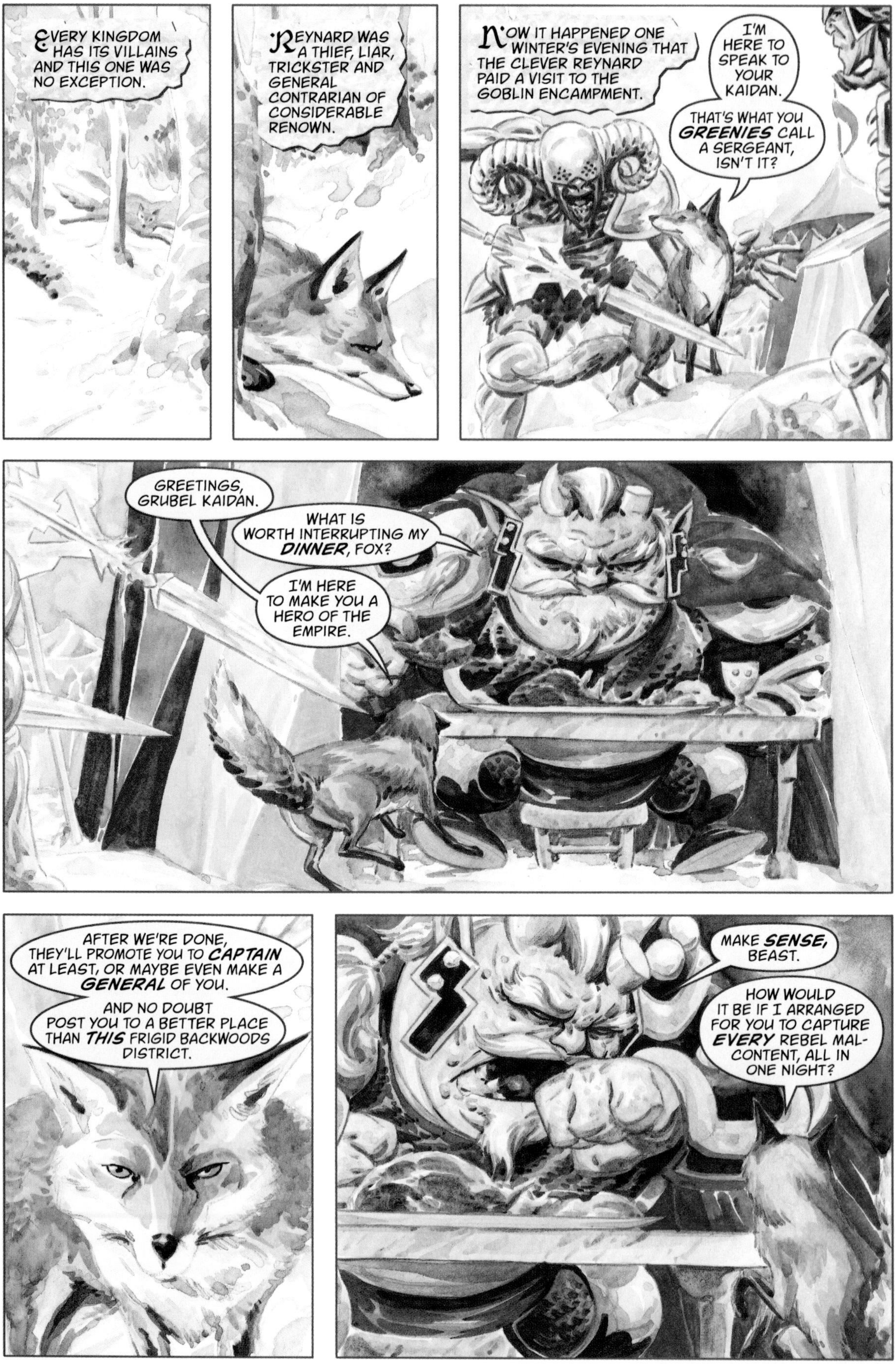
EVERY KINGDOM HAS ITS VILLAINS AND THIS ONE WAS NO EXCEPTION.
REYNARD WAS A THIEF, LIAR, TRICKSTER AND GENERAL CONTRARIAN OF CONSIDERABLE RENOWN.
NOW IT HAPPENED ONE WINTER'S EVENING THAT THE CLEVER REYNARD PAID A VISIT TO THE GOBLIN ENCAMPMENT.
I'M HERE TO SPEAK TO YOUR KAIDAN.
THAT'S WHAT YOU GREENIES CALL A SERGEANT, ISN'T IT?
GREETINGS, GRUBEL KAIDAN.
WHAT IS WORTH INTERRUPTING MY DINNER, FOX?
I'M HERE TO MAKE YOU A HERO OF THE EMPIRE.
AFTER WE'RE DONE, THEY'LL PROMOTE YOU TO CAPTAIN AT LEAST, OR MAYBE EVEN MAKE A GENERAL OF YOU.
AND NO DOUBT POST YOU TO A BETTER PLACE THAN THIS FRIGID BACKWOODS DISTRICT.
MAKE SENSE, BEAST.
HOW WOULD IT BE IF I ARRANGED FOR YOU TO CAPTURE EVERY REBEL MAL-CONTENT, ALL IN ONE NIGHT?

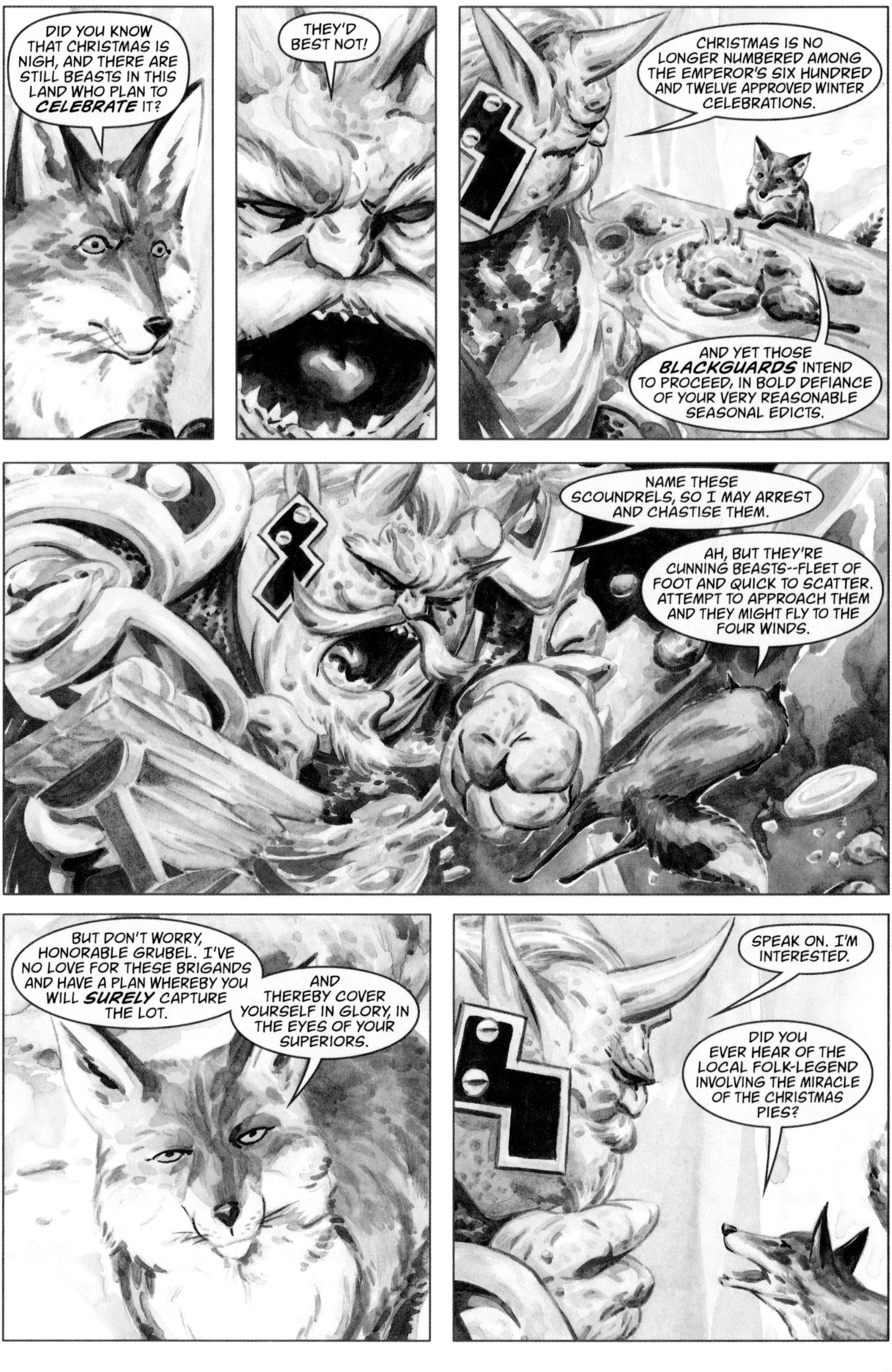
DID YOU KNOW THAT CHRISTMAS IS NIGH, AND THERE ARE STILL BEASTS IN THIS LAND WHO PLAN TO CELEBRATE IT?
THEY'D BEST NOT!
CHRISTMAS IS NO LONGER NUMBERED AMONG THE EMPEROR'S SIX HUNDRED AND TWELVE APPROVED WINTER CELEBRATIONS.
AND YET THOSE BLACKGUARDS INTEND TO PROCEED, IN BOLD DEFIANCE OF YOUR VERY REASONABLE SEASONAL EDICTS.
NAME THESE SCOUNDRELS, SO I MAY ARREST AND CHASTISE THEM.
AH, BUT THEY'RE CUNNING BEASTS--FLEET OF FOOT AND QUICK TO SCATTER. ATTEMPT TO APPROACH THEM AND THEY MIGHT FLY TO THE FOUR WINDS.
BUT DON'T WORRY, HONORABLE GRUBEL. I'VE NO LOVE FOR THESE BRIGANDS AND HAVE A PLAN WHEREBY YOU WILL SURELY CAPTURE THE LOT.
AND THEREBY COVER YOURSELF IN GLORY, IN THE EYES OF YOUR SUPERIORS.
SPEAK ON. I'M INTERESTED.
DID YOU EVER HEAR OF THE LOCAL FOLK-LEGEND INVOLVING THE MIRACLE OF THE CHRISTMAS PIES?

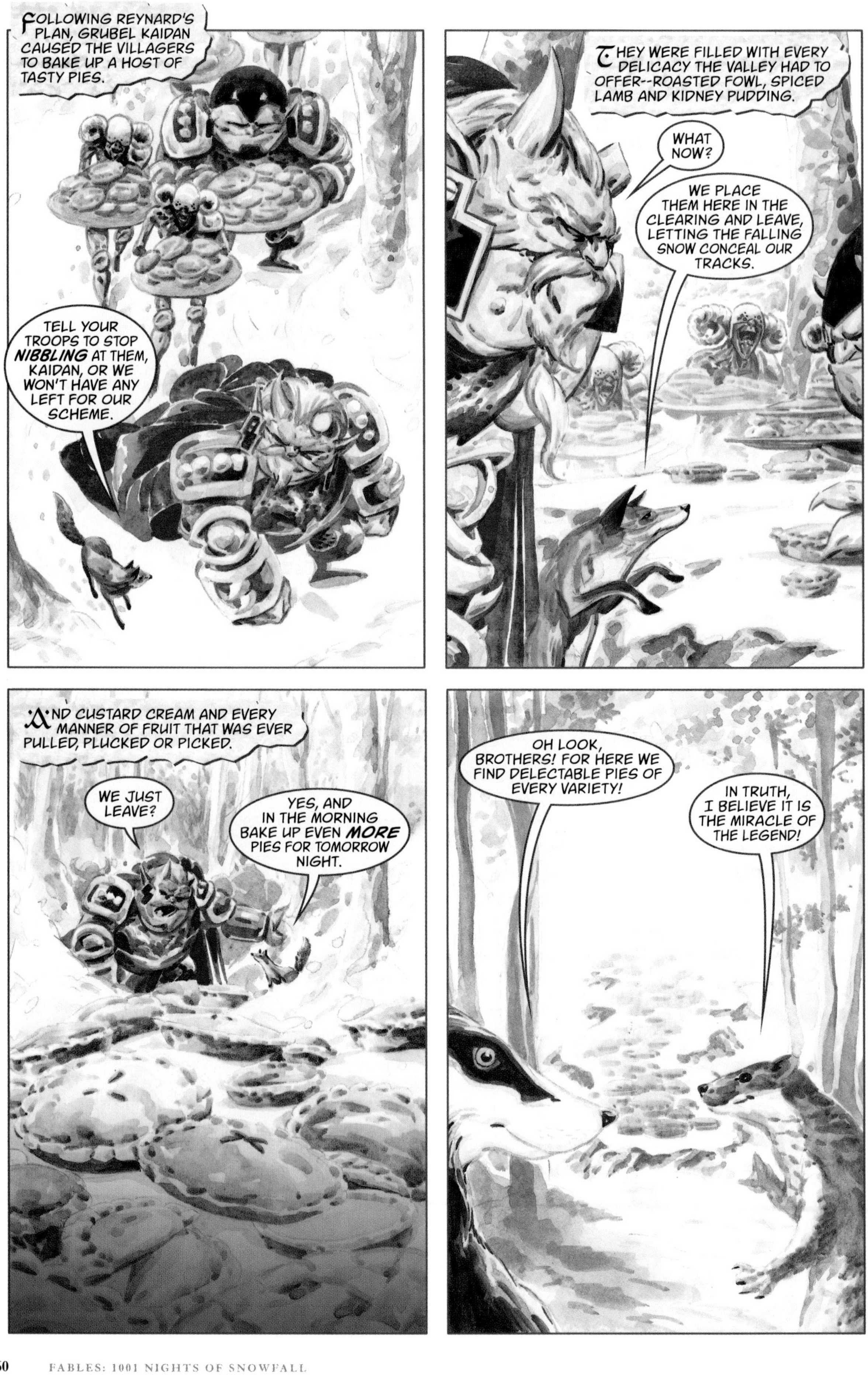
FOLLOWING REYNARD'S PLAN, GRUBEL KAIDAN CAUSED THE VILLAGERS TO BAKE UP A HOST OF TASTY PIES.
TELL YOUR TROOPS TO STOP NIBBLING AT THEM, KAIDAN, OR WE WON'T HAVE ANY LEFT FOR OUR SCHEME.
THEY WERE FILLED WITH EVERY DELICACY THE VALLEY HAD TO OFFER--ROASTED FOWL, SPICED LAMB AND KIDNEY PUDDING.
WHAT NOW?
WE PLACE THEM HERE IN THE CLEARING AND LEAVE, LETTING THE FALLING SNOW CONCEAL OUR TRACKS.
AND CUSTARD CREAM AND EVERY MANNER OF FRUIT THAT WAS EVER PULLED, PLUCKED OR PICKED.
WE JUST LEAVE?
YES, AND IN THE MORNING BAKE UP EVEN MORE PIES FOR TOMORROW NIGHT.
OH LOOK, BROTHERS! FOR HERE WE FIND DELECTABLE PIES OF EVERY VARIETY!
IN TRUTH, I BELIEVE IT IS THE MIRACLE OF THE LEGEND!

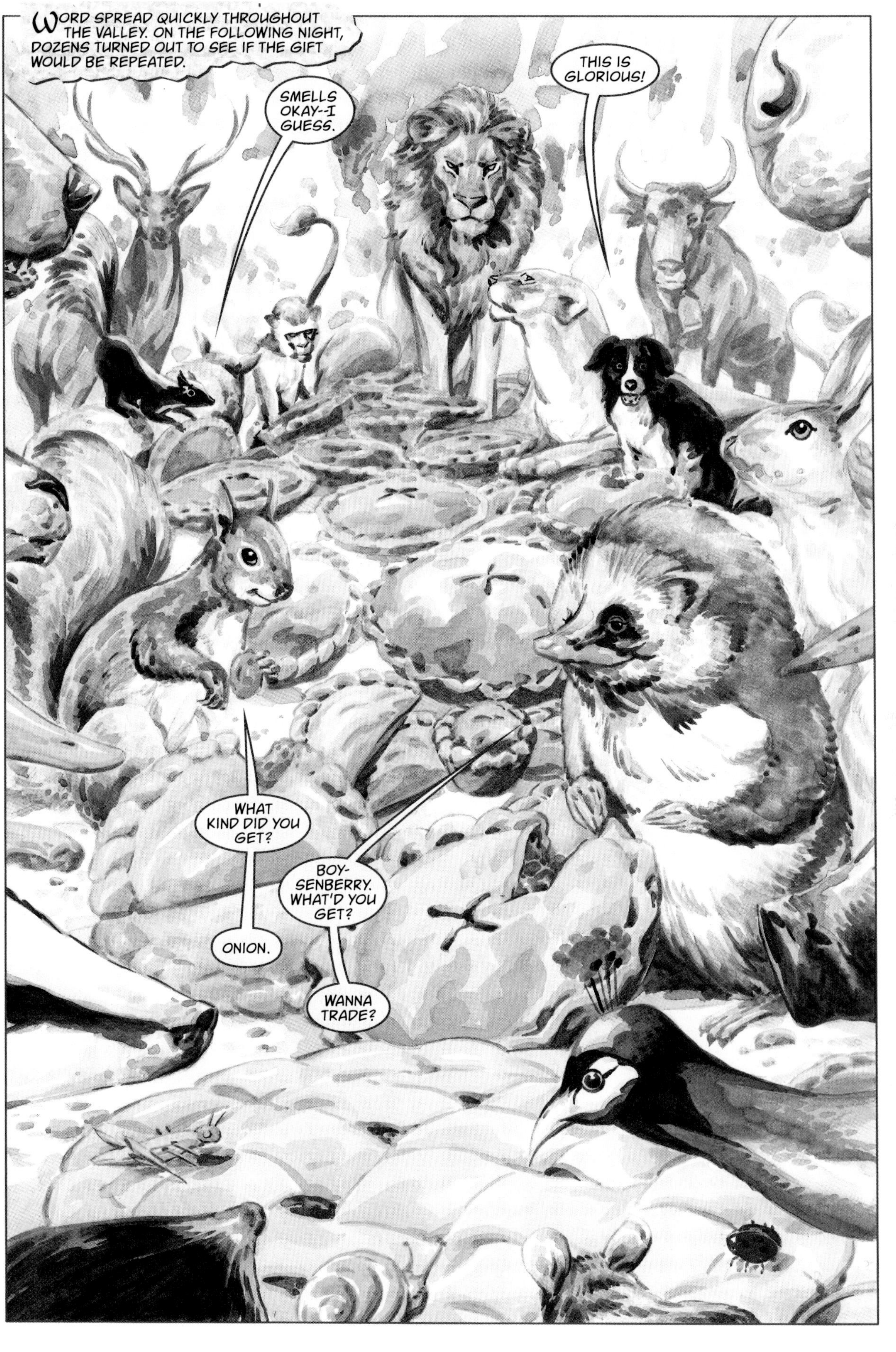
WORD SPREAD QUICKLY THROUGHOUT THE VALLEY. ON THE FOLLOWING NIGHT, DOZENS TURNED OUT TO SEE IF THE GIFT WOULD BE REPEATED.
SMELLS OKAY--I GUESS.
THIS IS GLORIOUS!
WHAT KIND DID YOU GET?
BOY-SENBERRY. WHAT'D YOU GET?
ONION.
WANNA TRADE?

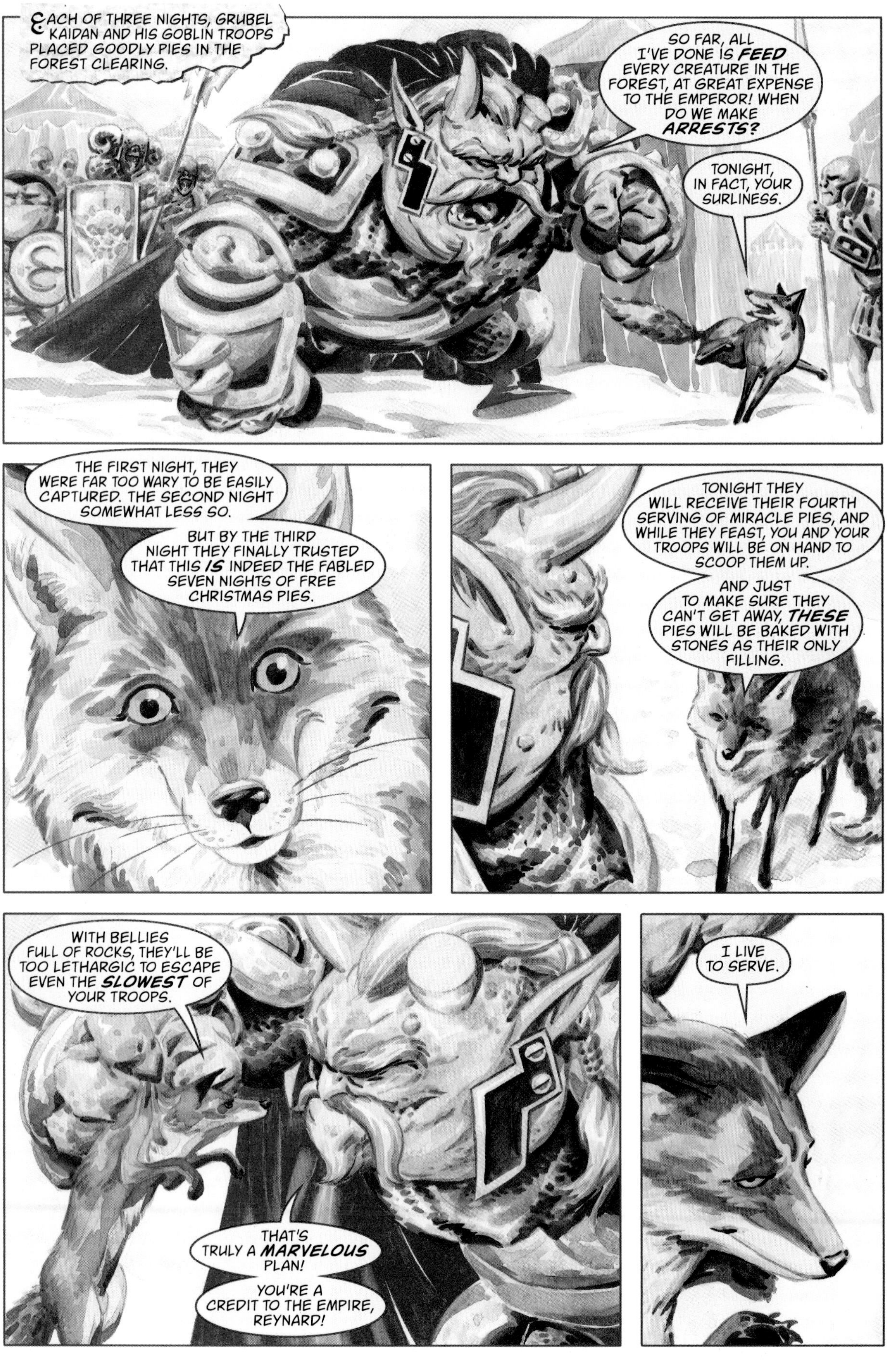
EACH OF THREE NIGHTS, GRUBEL KAIDAN AND HIS GOBLIN TROOPS PLACED GOODLY PIES IN THE FOREST CLEARING.
SO FAR, ALL I'VE DONE IS FEED EVERY CREATURE IN THE FOREST, AT GREAT EXPENSE TO THE EMPEROR! WHEN DO WE MAKE ARRESTS?
TONIGHT, IN FACT, YOUR SURLINESS.
THE FIRST NIGHT, THEY WERE FAR TOO WARY TO BE EASILY CAPTURED. THE SECOND NIGHT SOMEWHAT LESS SO.
BUT BY THE THIRD NIGHT THEY FINALLY TRUSTED THAT THIS IS INDEED THE FABLED SEVEN NIGHTS OF FREE CHRISTMAS PIES.
TONIGHT THEY WILL RECEIVE THEIR FOURTH SERVING OF MIRACLE PIES, AND WHILE THEY FEAST, YOU AND YOUR TROOPS WILL BE ON HAND TO SCOOP THEM UP.
AND JUST TO MAKE SURE THEY CAN'T GET AWAY, THESE PIES WILL BE BAKED WITH STONES AS THEIR ONLY FILLING.
WITH BELLIES FULL OF ROCKS, THEY'LL BE TOO LETHARGIC TO ESCAPE EVEN THE SLOWEST OF YOUR TROOPS.
THAT'S TRULY A MARVELOUS PLAN!
YOU'RE A CREDIT TO THE EMPIRE, REYNARD!
I LIVE TO SERVE.

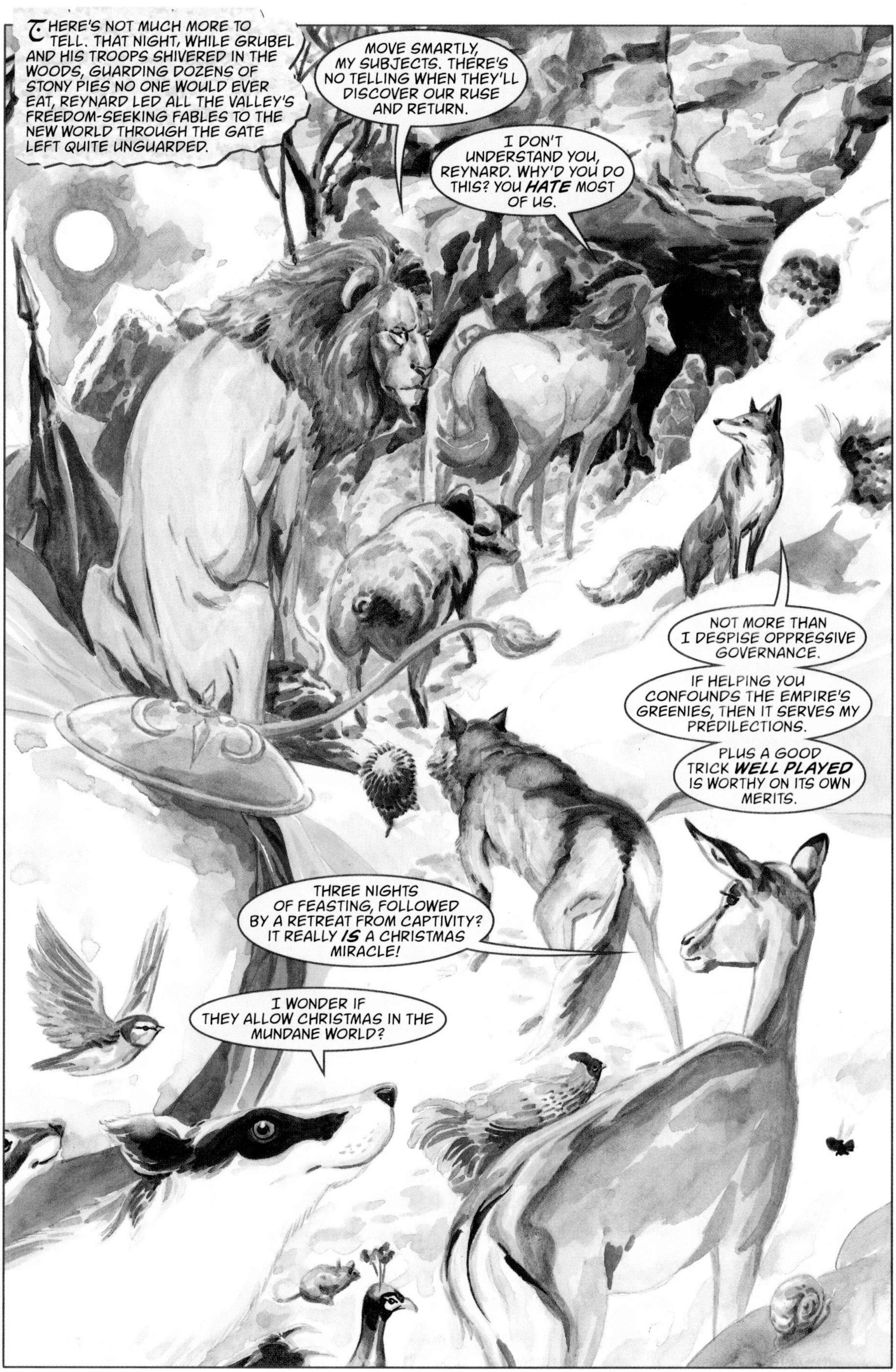
THERE'S NOT MUCH MORE TO TELL. THAT NIGHT, WHILE GRUBEL AND HIS TROOPS SHIVERED IN THE WOODS, GUARDING DOZENS OF STONY PIES NO ONE WOULD EVER EAT, REYNARD LED ALL THE VALLEY'S FREEDOM-SEEKING FABLES TO THE NEW WORLD THROUGH THE GATE LEFT QUITE UNGUARDED.
MOVE SMARTLY, MY SUBJECTS. THERE'S NO TELLING WHEN THEY'LL DISCOVER OUR RUSE AND RETURN.
I DON'T UNDERSTAND YOU, REYNARD. WHY'D YOU DO THIS? YOU HATE MOST OF US.
NOT MORE THAN I DESPISE OPPRESSIVE GOVERNANCE.
IF HELPING YOU CONFOUNDS THE EMPIRE'S GREENIES, THEN IT SERVES MY PREDILECTIONS.
PLUS A GOOD TRICK WELL PLAYED IS WORTHY ON ITS OWN MERITS.
THREE NIGHTS OF FEASTING, FOLLOWED BY A RETREAT FROM CAPTIVITY? IT REALLY IS A CHRISTMAS MIRACLE!
I WONDER IF THEY ALLOW CHRISTMAS IN THE MUNDANE WORLD?

end

A Frog's-Eye View

◆In which a frog gets a bride,
has a wonderful life with many children,
and lives happily ever after —
for a time.

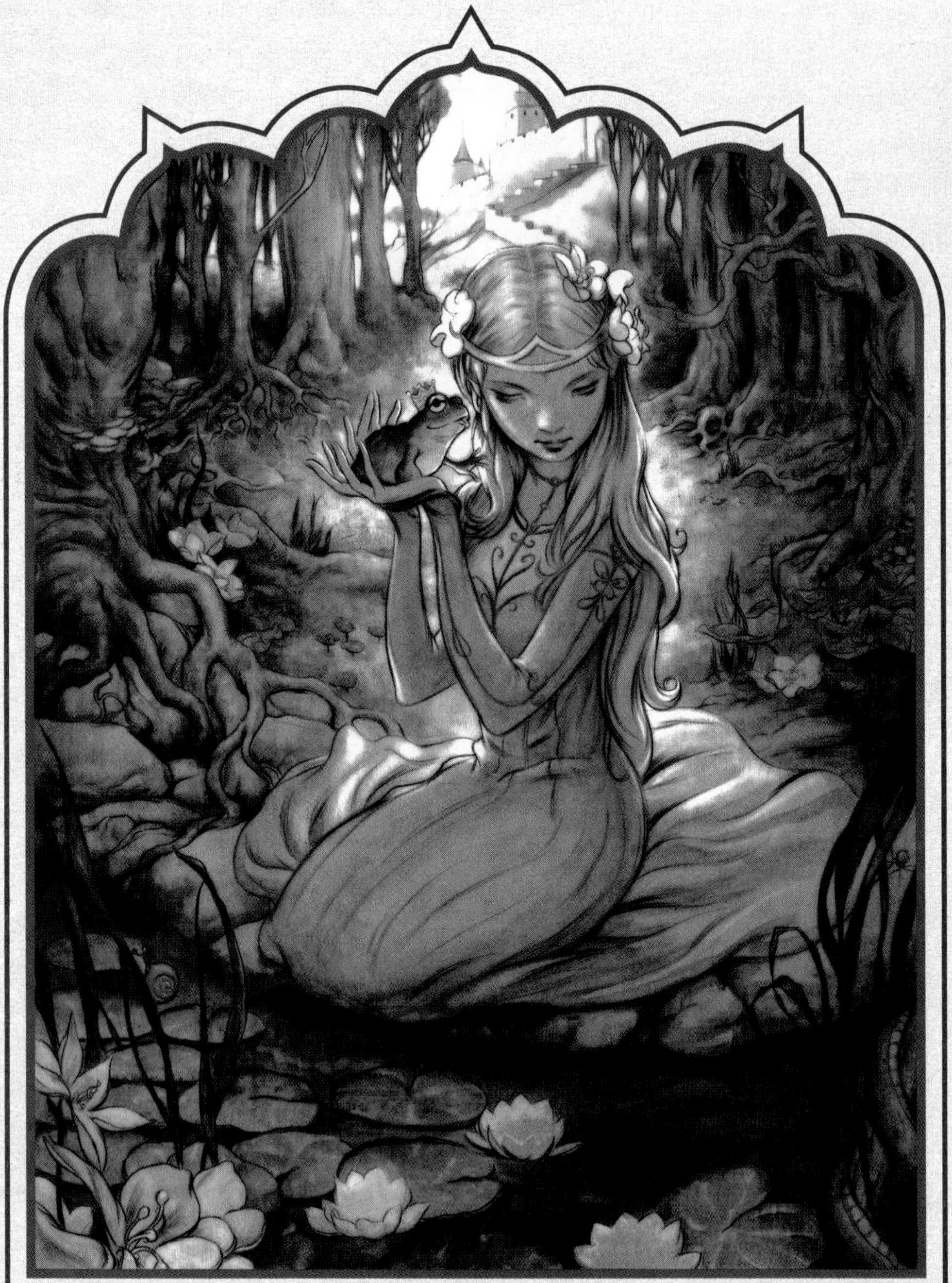

Illustrated by James Jean

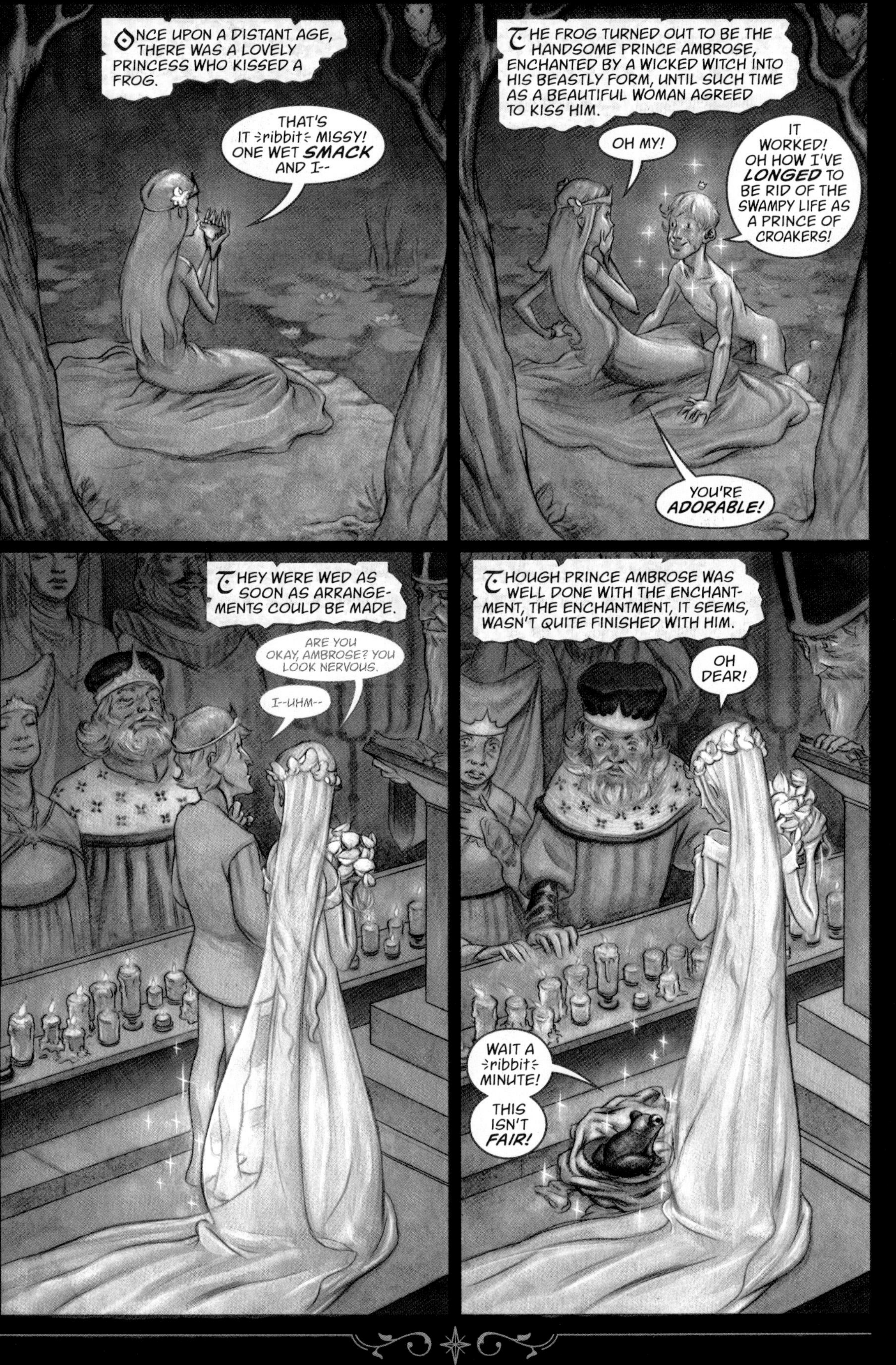
ONCE UPON A DISTANT AGE, THERE WAS A LOVELY PRINCESS WHO KISSED A FROG.
THAT'S IT ≶ribbit≶ MISSY! ONE WET SMACK AND I--
THE FROG TURNED OUT TO BE THE HANDSOME PRINCE AMBROSE, ENCHANTED BY A WICKED WITCH INTO HIS BEASTLY FORM, UNTIL SUCH TIME AS A BEAUTIFUL WOMAN AGREED TO KISS HIM.
OH MY!
IT WORKED! OH HOW I'VE LONGED TO BE RID OF THE SWAMPY LIFE AS A PRINCE OF CROAKERS!
YOU'RE ADORABLE!
THEY WERE WED AS SOON AS ARRANGEMENTS COULD BE MADE.
ARE YOU OKAY, AMBROSE? YOU LOOK NERVOUS.
I--UHM--
THOUGH PRINCE AMBROSE WAS WELL DONE WITH THE ENCHANTMENT, THE ENCHANTMENT, IT SEEMS, WASN'T QUITE FINISHED WITH HIM.
OH DEAR!
WAIT A ≶ribbit≶ MINUTE!
THIS ISN'T FAIR!

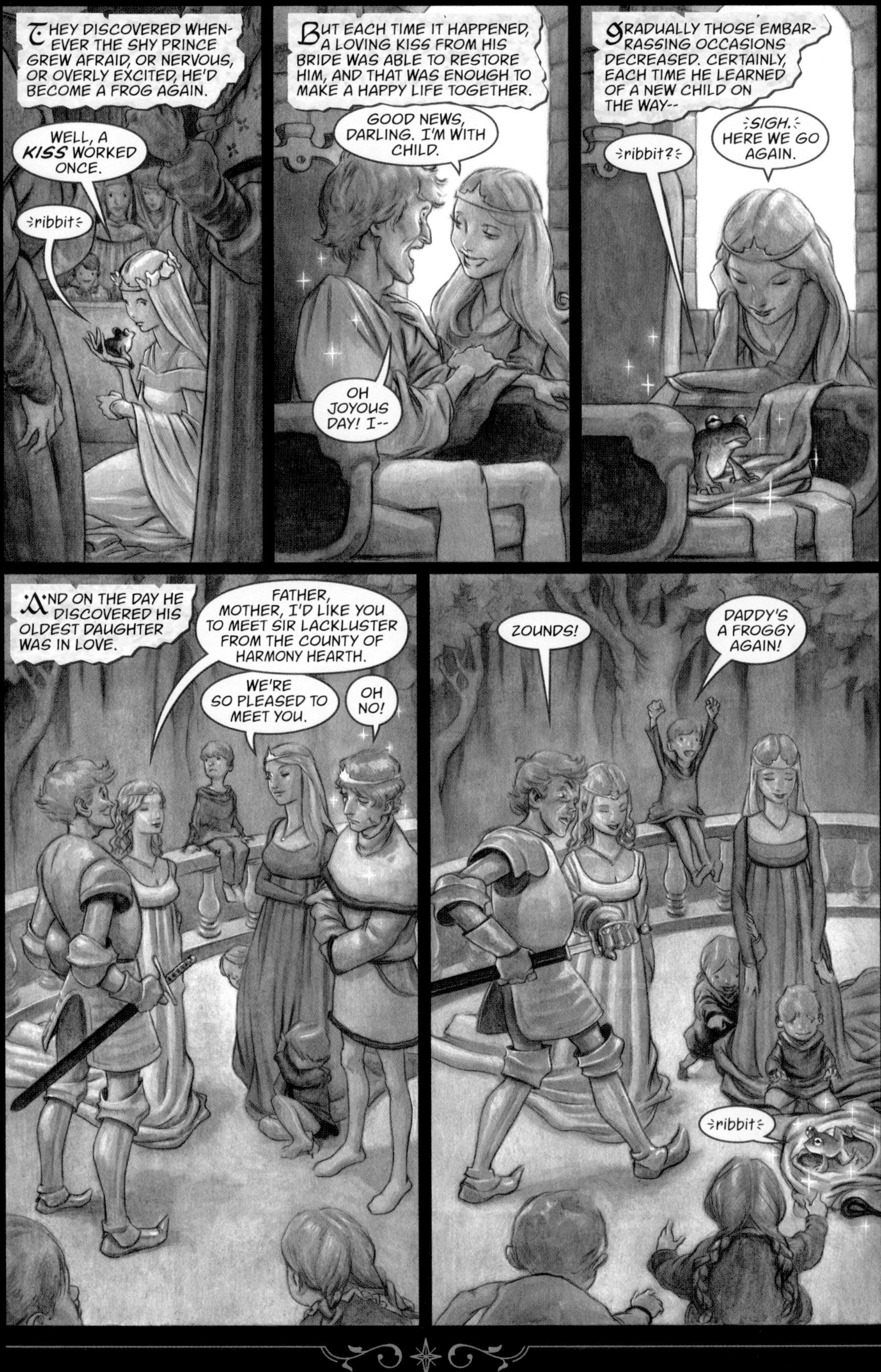
THEY DISCOVERED WHENEVER THE SHY PRINCE GREW AFRAID, OR NERVOUS, OR OVERLY EXCITED, HE'D BECOME A FROG AGAIN.
WELL, A KISS WORKED ONCE.
ribbit
BUT EACH TIME IT HAPPENED, A LOVING KISS FROM HIS BRIDE WAS ABLE TO RESTORE HIM, AND THAT WAS ENOUGH TO MAKE A HAPPY LIFE TOGETHER.
GOOD NEWS, DARLING. I'M WITH CHILD.
OH JOYOUS DAY! I--
GRADUALLY THOSE EMBARRASSING OCCASIONS DECREASED. CERTAINLY, EACH TIME HE LEARNED OF A NEW CHILD ON THE WAY--
ribbit?
SIGH. HERE WE GO AGAIN.
AND ON THE DAY HE DISCOVERED HIS OLDEST DAUGHTER WAS IN LOVE.
FATHER, MOTHER, I'D LIKE YOU TO MEET SIR LACKLUSTER FROM THE COUNTY OF HARMONY HEARTH.
WE'RE SO PLEASED TO MEET YOU.
OH NO!
ZOUNDS!
DADDY'S A FROGGY AGAIN!
ribbit

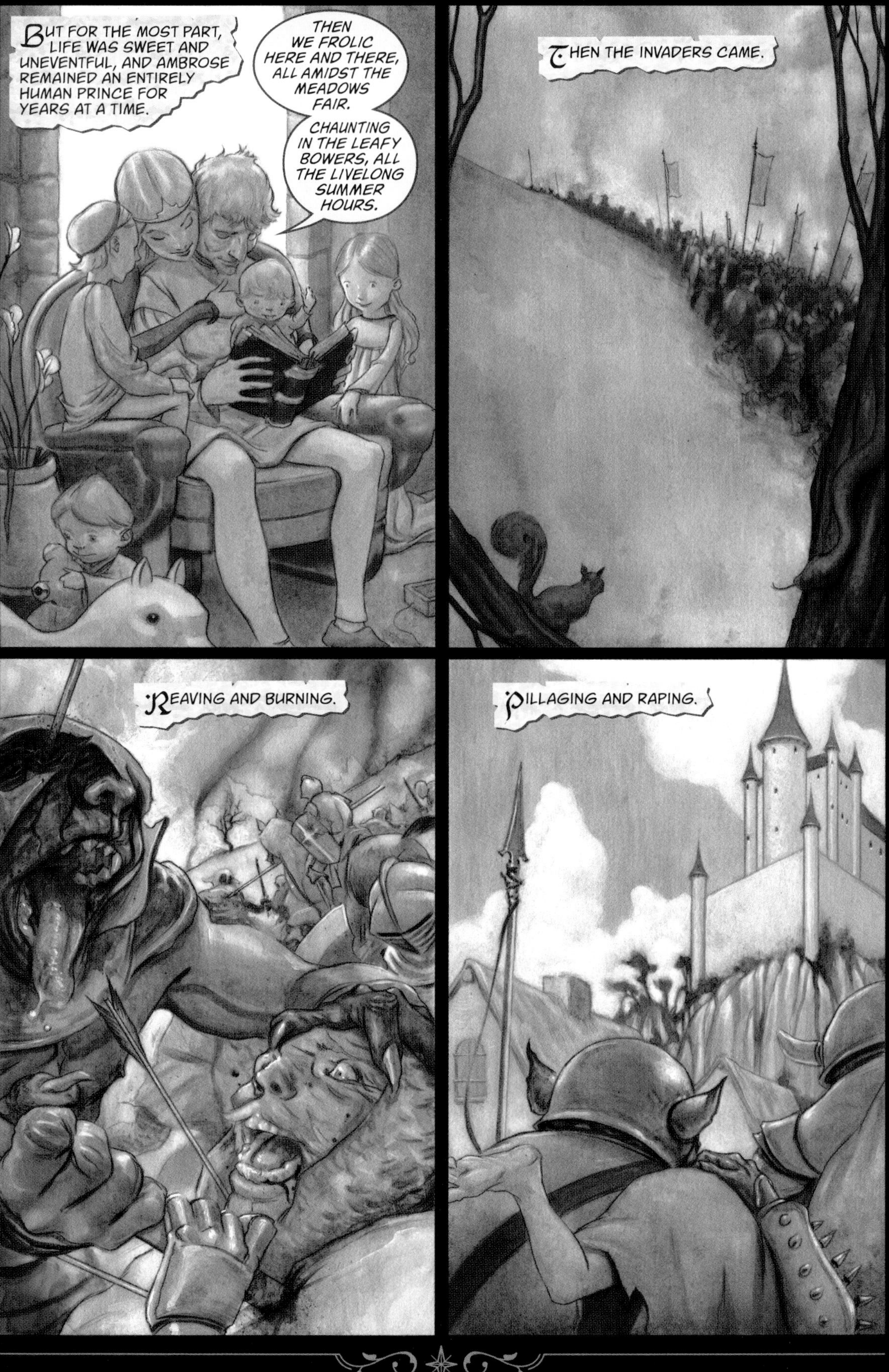

BUT FOR THE MOST PART, LIFE WAS SWEET AND UNEVENTFUL, AND AMBROSE REMAINED AN ENTIRELY HUMAN PRINCE FOR YEARS AT A TIME.
THEN WE FROLIC HERE AND THERE, ALL AMIDST THE MEADOWS FAIR.
CHAUNTING IN THE LEAFY BOWERS, ALL THE LIVELONG SUMMER HOURS.
THEN THE INVADERS CAME.
REAVING AND BURNING.
PILLAGING AND RAPING.

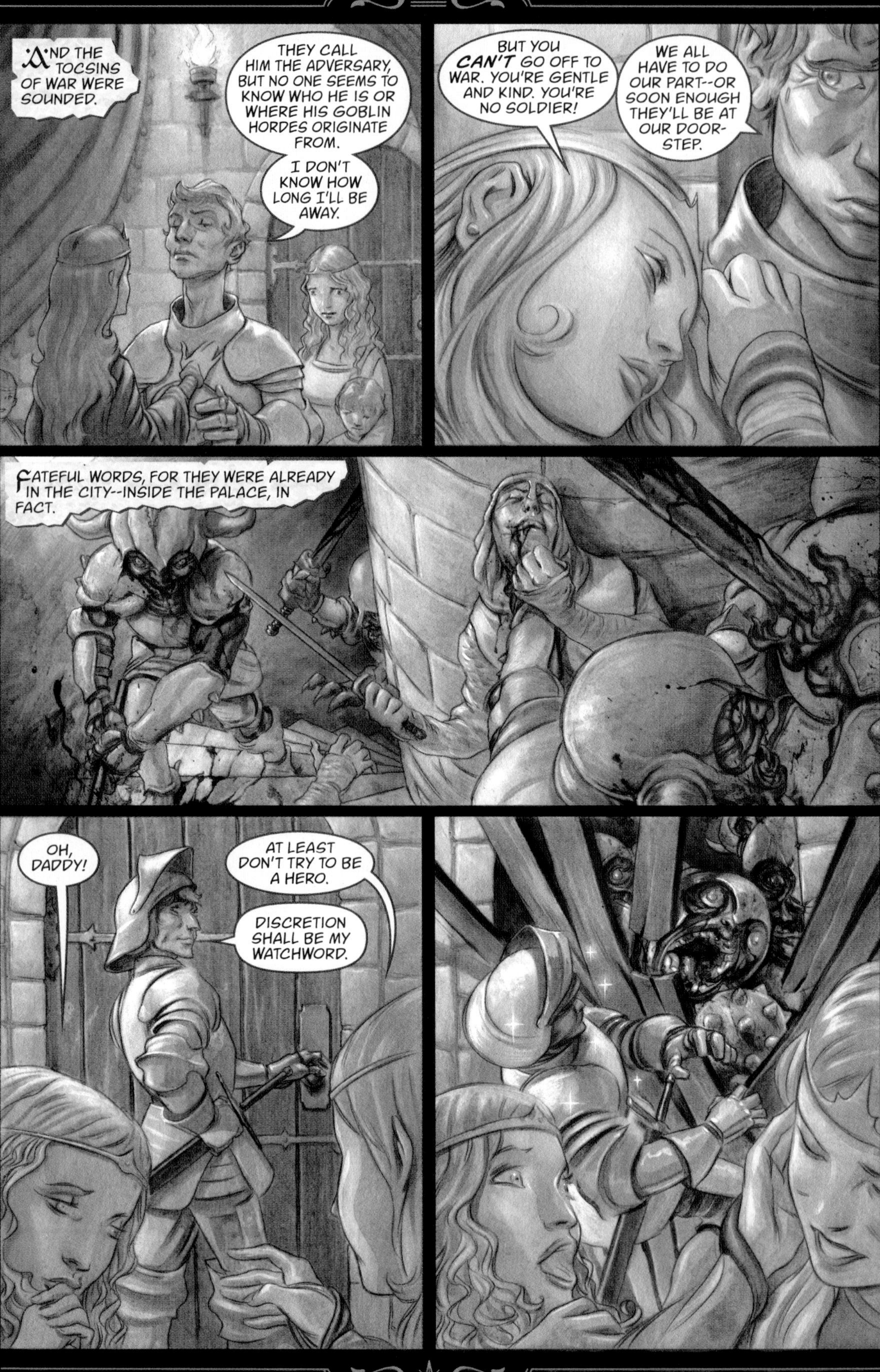
AND THE TOCSINS OF WAR WERE SOUNDED.
THEY CALL HIM THE ADVERSARY, BUT NO ONE SEEMS TO KNOW WHO HE IS OR WHERE HIS GOBLIN HORDES ORIGINATE FROM.
I DON'T KNOW HOW LONG I'LL BE AWAY.
BUT YOU CAN'T GO OFF TO WAR. YOU'RE GENTLE AND KIND. YOU'RE NO SOLDIER!
WE ALL HAVE TO DO OUR PART--OR SOON ENOUGH THEY'LL BE AT OUR DOOR-STEP.
FATEFUL WORDS, FOR THEY WERE ALREADY IN THE CITY--INSIDE THE PALACE, IN FACT.
OH, DADDY!
AT LEAST DON'T TRY TO BE A HERO.
DISCRETION SHALL BE MY WATCHWORD.

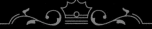

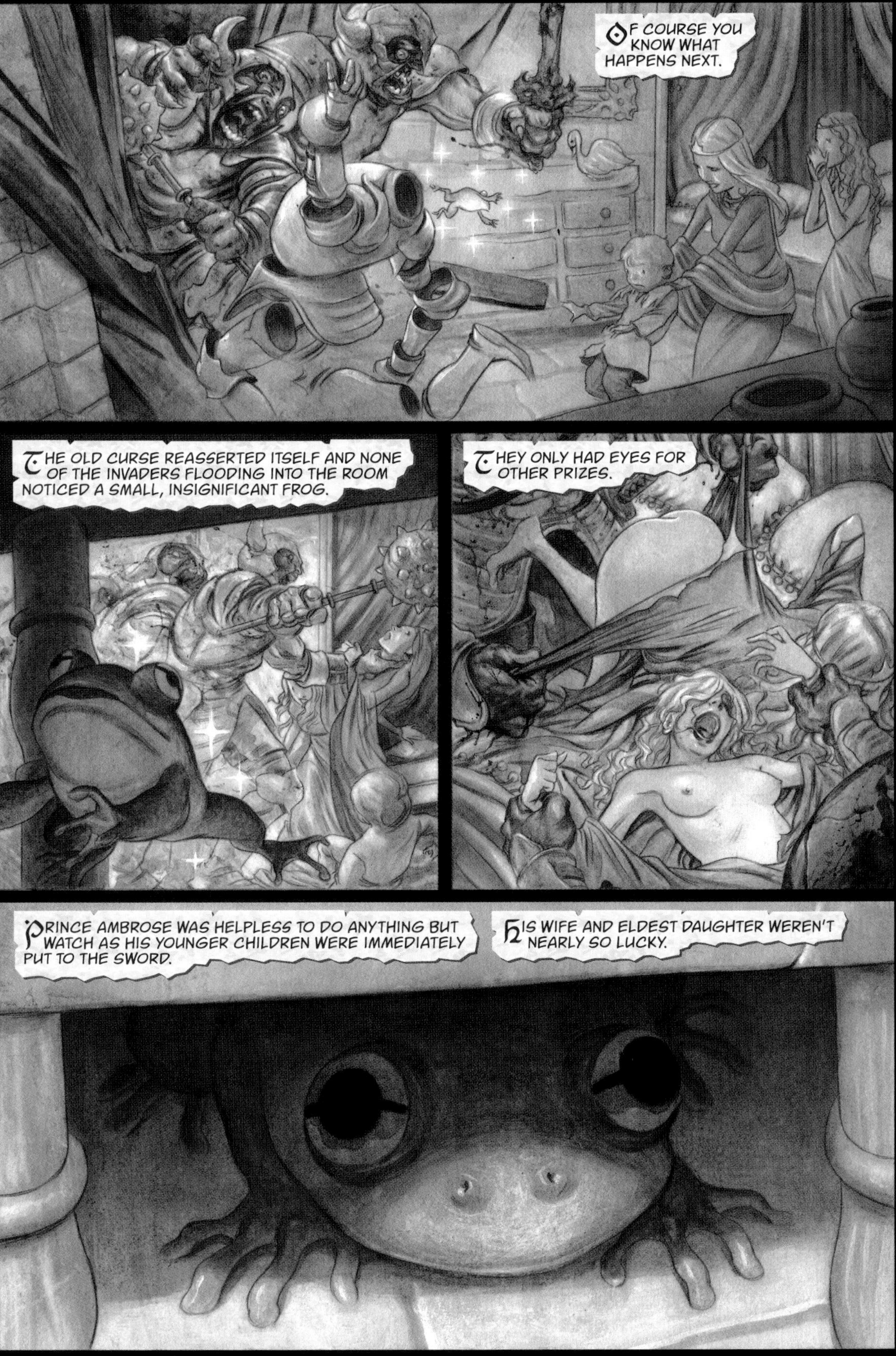
OF COURSE YOU KNOW WHAT HAPPENS NEXT.
THE OLD CURSE REASSERTED ITSELF AND NONE OF THE INVADERS FLOODING INTO THE ROOM NOTICED A SMALL, INSIGNIFICANT FROG.
THEY ONLY HAD EYES FOR OTHER PRIZES.
PRINCE AMBROSE WAS HELPLESS TO DO ANYTHING BUT WATCH AS HIS YOUNGER CHILDREN WERE IMMEDIATELY PUT TO THE SWORD.
HIS WIFE AND ELDEST DAUGHTER WEREN'T NEARLY SO LUCKY.

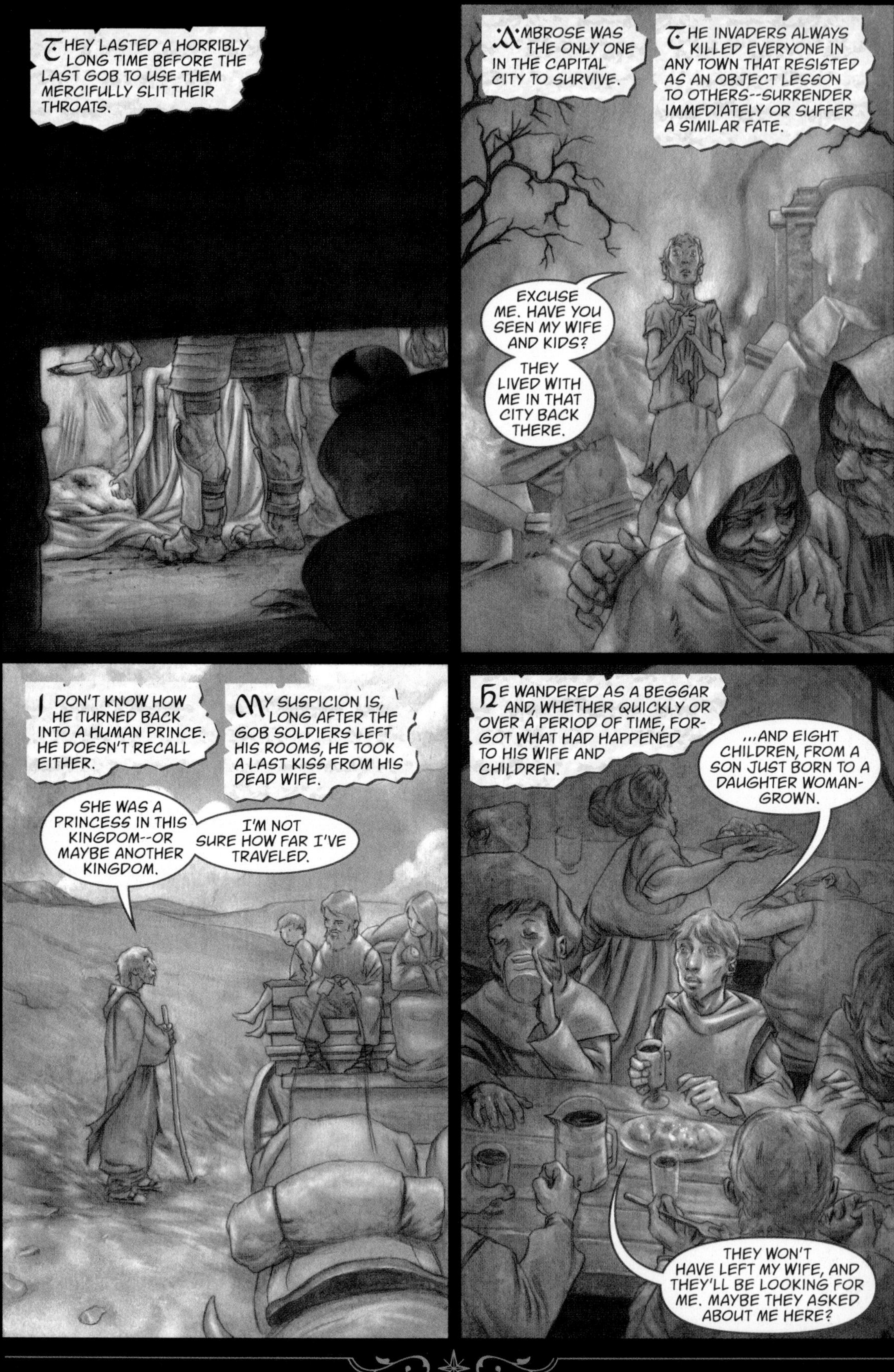
THEY LASTED A HORRIBLY LONG TIME BEFORE THE LAST GOB TO USE THEM MERCIFULLY SLIT THEIR THROATS.
AMBROSE WAS THE ONLY ONE IN THE CAPITAL CITY TO SURVIVE.
THE INVADERS ALWAYS KILLED EVERYONE IN ANY TOWN THAT RESISTED AS AN OBJECT LESSON TO OTHERS--SURRENDER IMMEDIATELY OR SUFFER A SIMILAR FATE.
EXCUSE ME. HAVE YOU SEEN MY WIFE AND KIDS?
THEY LIVED WITH ME IN THAT CITY BACK THERE.
I DON'T KNOW HOW HE TURNED BACK INTO A HUMAN PRINCE. HE DOESN'T RECALL EITHER.
MY SUSPICION IS, LONG AFTER THE GOB SOLDIERS LEFT HIS ROOMS, HE TOOK A LAST KISS FROM HIS DEAD WIFE.
SHE WAS A PRINCESS IN THIS KINGDOM--OR MAYBE ANOTHER KINGDOM.
I'M NOT SURE HOW FAR I'VE TRAVELED.
HE WANDERED AS A BEGGAR AND, WHETHER QUICKLY OR OVER A PERIOD OF TIME, FORGOT WHAT HAD HAPPENED TO HIS WIFE AND CHILDREN.
...AND EIGHT CHILDREN, FROM A SON JUST BORN TO A DAUGHTER WOMAN-GROWN.
THEY WON'T HAVE LEFT MY WIFE, AND THEY'LL BE LOOKING FOR ME. MAYBE THEY ASKED ABOUT ME HERE?

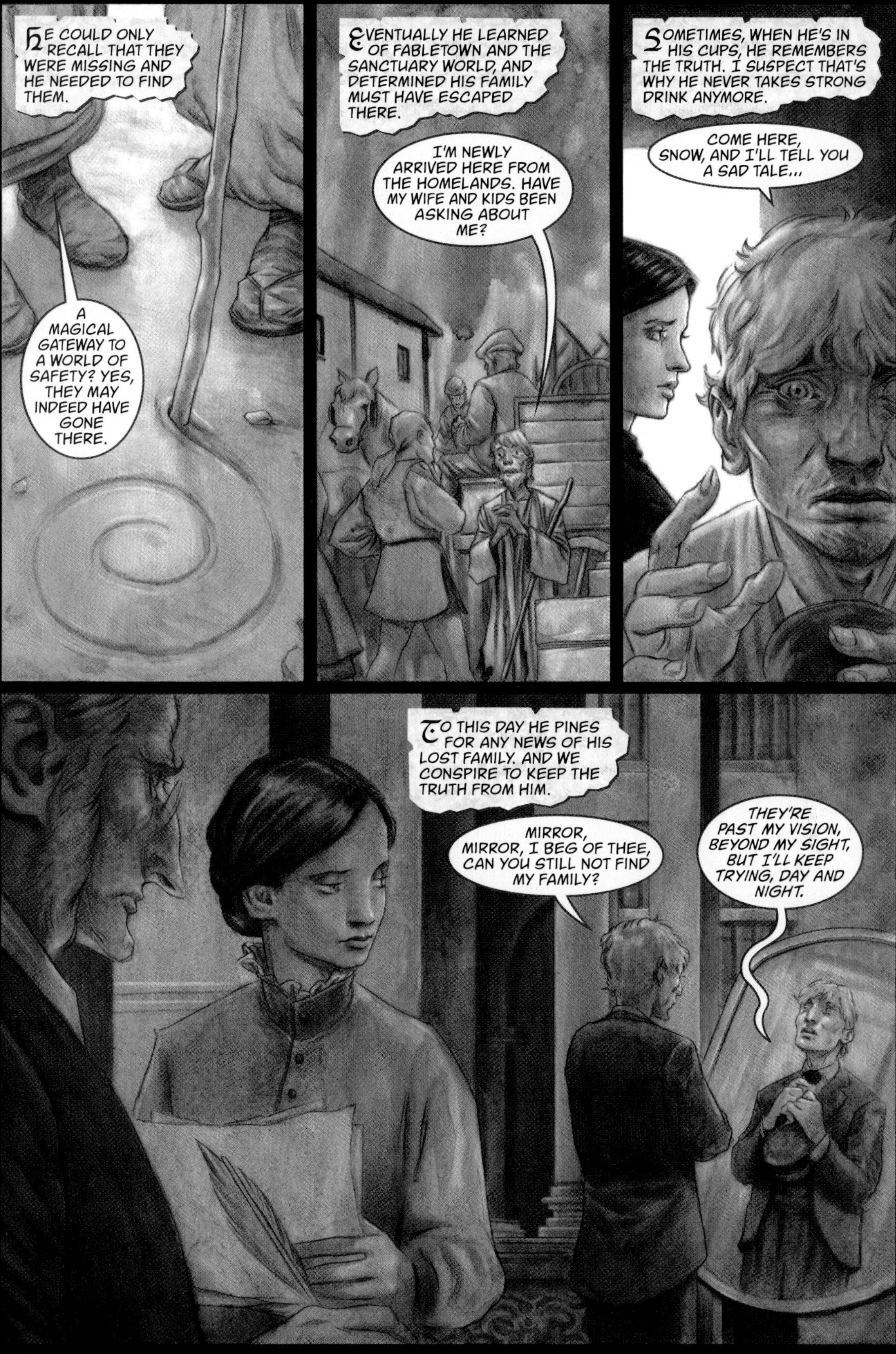

He could only recall that they were missing and he needed to find them.
A magical gateway to a world of safety? Yes, they may indeed have gone there.
Eventually he learned of Fabletown and the sanctuary world, and determined his family must have escaped there.
I'm newly arrived here from the Homelands. Have my wife and kids been asking about me?
Sometimes, when he's in his cups, he remembers the truth. I suspect that's why he never takes strong drink anymore.
Come here, Snow, and I'll tell you a sad tale...
To this day he pines for any news of his lost family. And we conspire to keep the truth from him.
Mirror, mirror, I beg of thee, can you still not find my family?
They're past my vision, beyond my sight, but I'll keep trying, day and night.

end

THE RUNT

In which the North Wind grows restless with his life and becomes something else for a time, and what happens as a result.

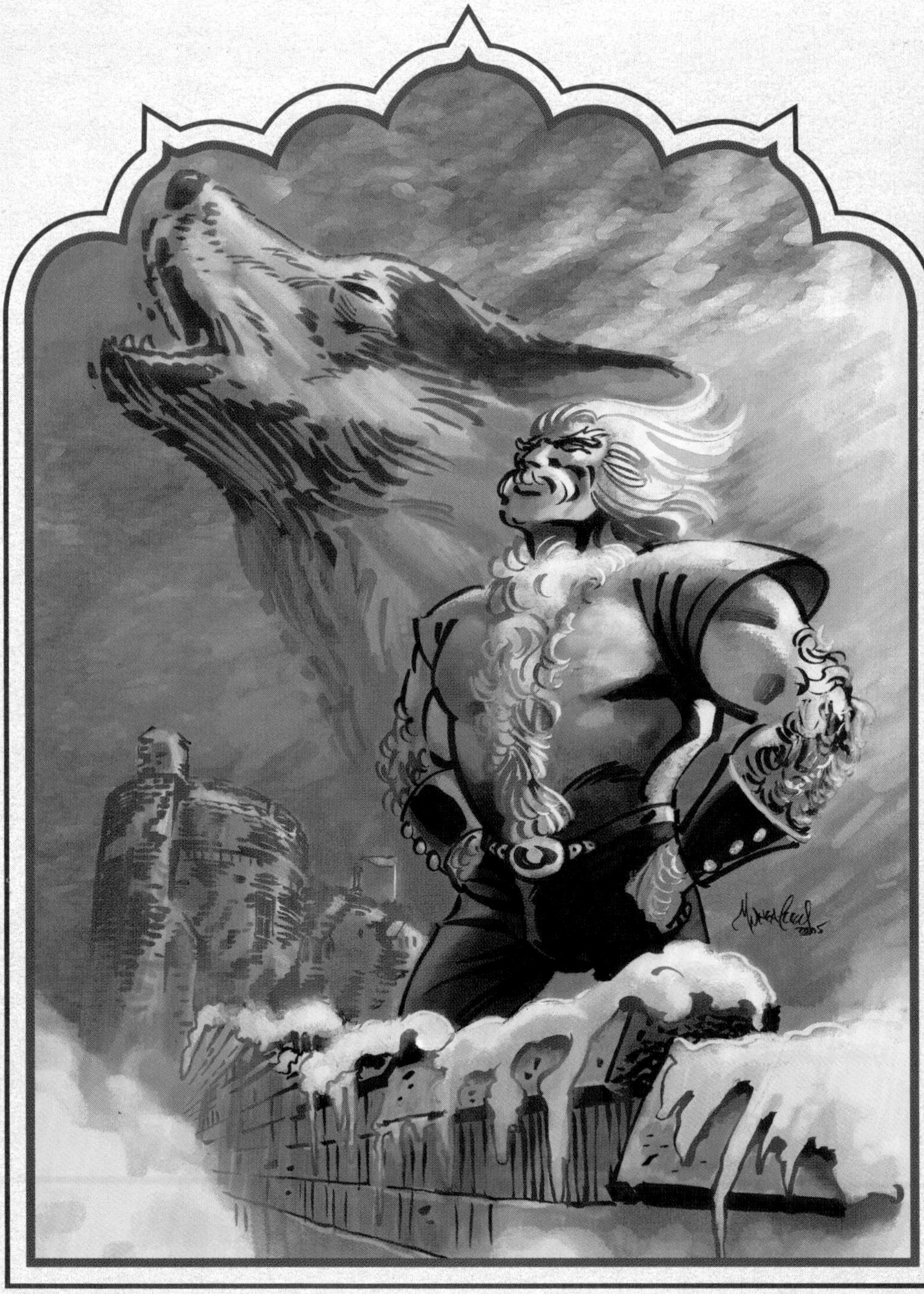

ILLUSTRATED BY MARK WHEATLEY

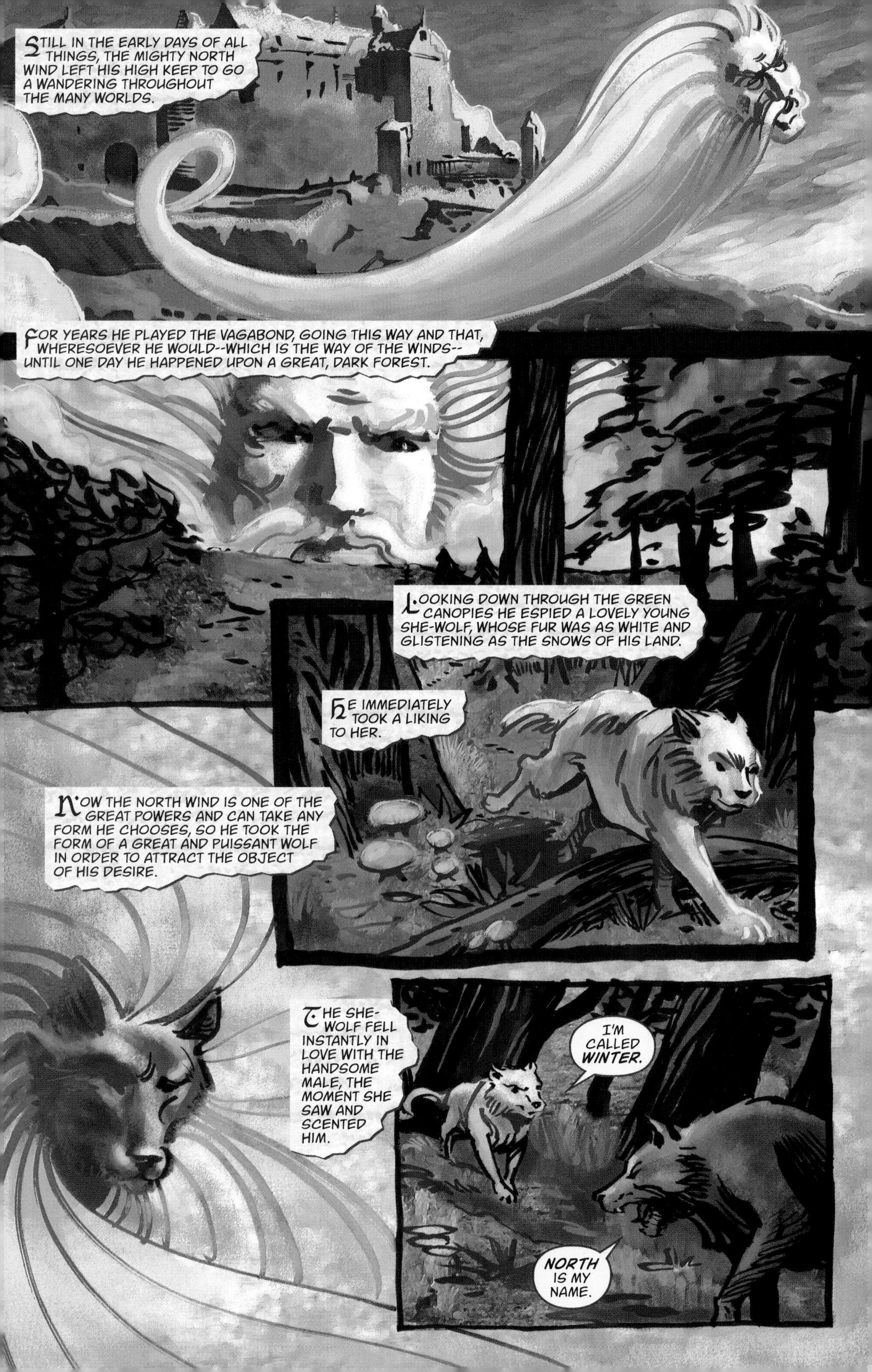
STILL IN THE EARLY DAYS OF ALL THINGS, THE MIGHTY NORTH WIND LEFT HIS HIGH KEEP TO GO A WANDERING THROUGHOUT THE MANY WORLDS.
FOR YEARS HE PLAYED THE VAGABOND, GOING THIS WAY AND THAT, WHERESOEVER HE WOULD--WHICH IS THE WAY OF THE WINDS--UNTIL ONE DAY HE HAPPENED UPON A GREAT, DARK FOREST.
LOOKING DOWN THROUGH THE GREEN CANOPIES HE ESPIED A LOVELY YOUNG SHE-WOLF, WHOSE FUR WAS AS WHITE AND GLISTENING AS THE SNOWS OF HIS LAND.
HE IMMEDIATELY TOOK A LIKING TO HER.
NOW THE NORTH WIND IS ONE OF THE GREAT POWERS AND CAN TAKE ANY FORM HE CHOOSES, SO HE TOOK THE FORM OF A GREAT AND PUISSANT WOLF IN ORDER TO ATTRACT THE OBJECT OF HIS DESIRE.
THE SHE-WOLF FELL INSTANTLY IN LOVE WITH THE HANDSOME MALE, THE MOMENT SHE SAW AND SCENTED HIM.
I'M CALLED *WINTER.*
NORTH IS MY NAME.

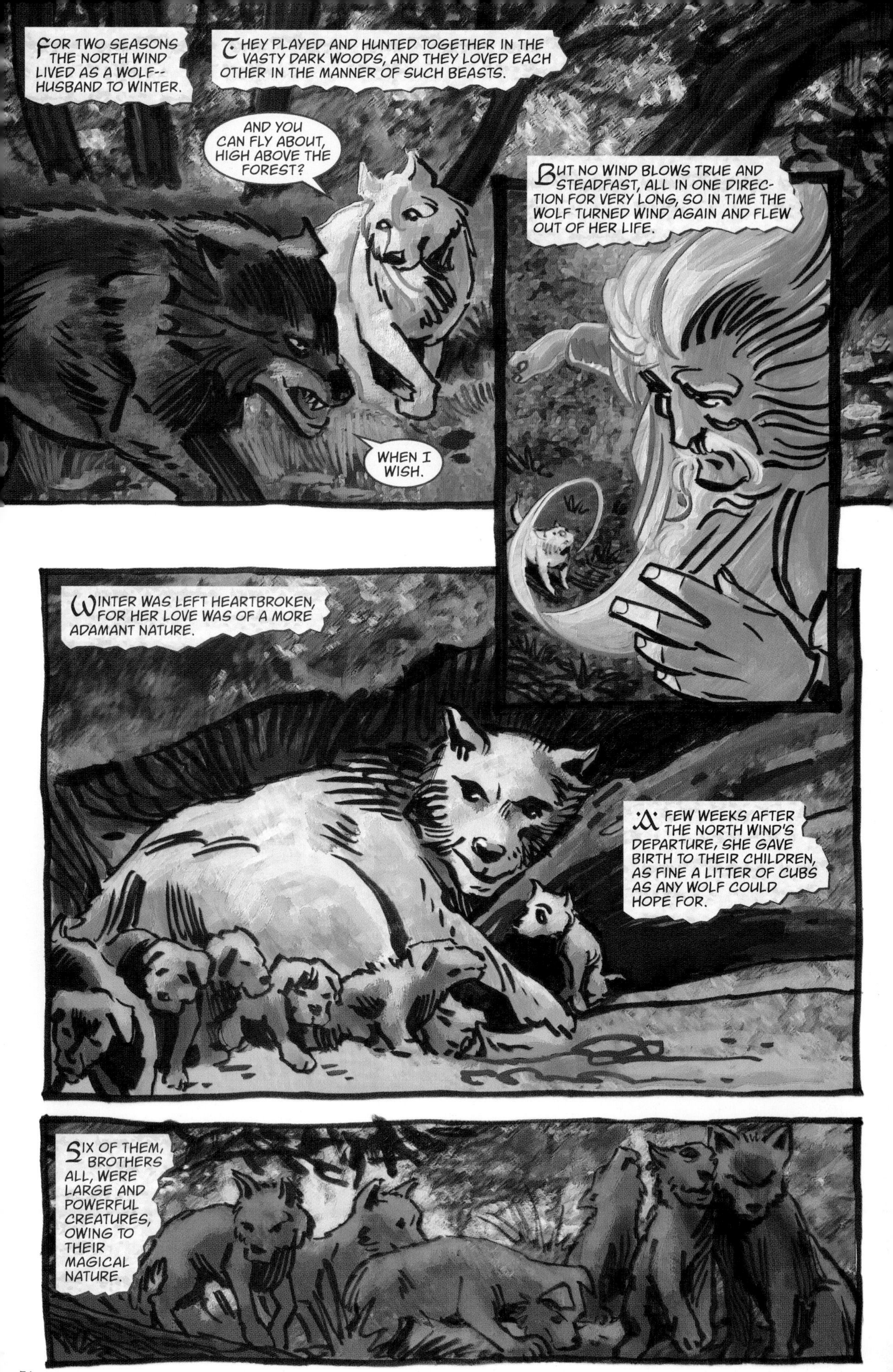
FOR TWO SEASONS THE NORTH WIND LIVED AS A WOLF-- HUSBAND TO WINTER.
THEY PLAYED AND HUNTED TOGETHER IN THE VASTY DARK WOODS, AND THEY LOVED EACH OTHER IN THE MANNER OF SUCH BEASTS.
AND YOU CAN FLY ABOUT, HIGH ABOVE THE FOREST?
WHEN I WISH.
BUT NO WIND BLOWS TRUE AND STEADFAST, ALL IN ONE DIRECTION FOR VERY LONG, SO IN TIME THE WOLF TURNED WIND AGAIN AND FLEW OUT OF HER LIFE.
WINTER WAS LEFT HEARTBROKEN, FOR HER LOVE WAS OF A MORE ADAMANT NATURE.
A FEW WEEKS AFTER THE NORTH WIND'S DEPARTURE, SHE GAVE BIRTH TO THEIR CHILDREN, AS FINE A LITTER OF CUBS AS ANY WOLF COULD HOPE FOR.
SIX OF THEM, BROTHERS ALL, WERE LARGE AND POWERFUL CREATURES, OWING TO THEIR MAGICAL NATURE.

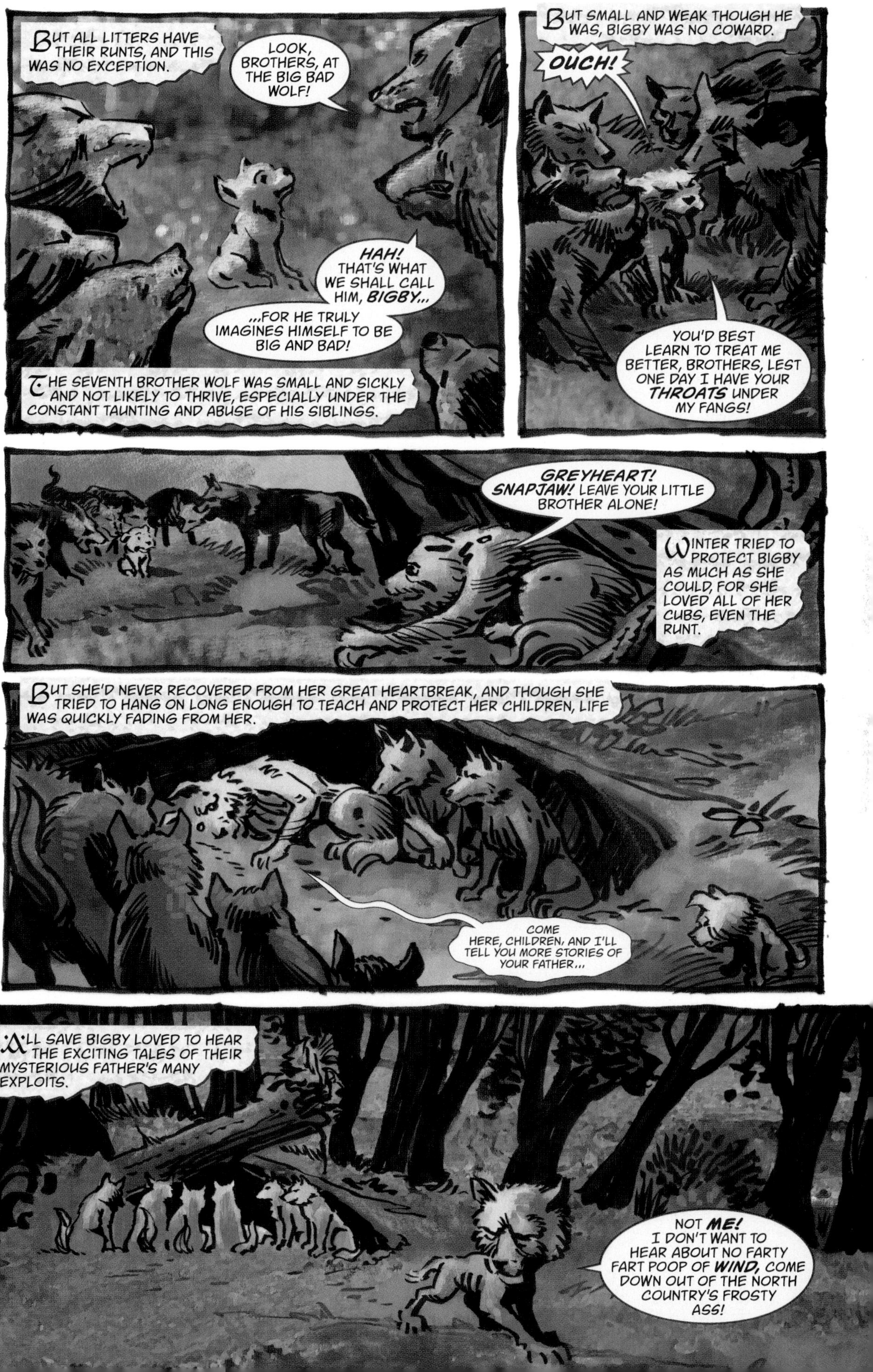

BUT ALL LITTERS HAVE THEIR RUNTS, AND THIS WAS NO EXCEPTION.
LOOK, BROTHERS, AT THE BIG BAD WOLF!
HAH! THAT'S WHAT WE SHALL CALL HIM, BIGBY...
...FOR HE TRULY IMAGINES HIMSELF TO BE BIG AND BAD!
THE SEVENTH BROTHER WOLF WAS SMALL AND SICKLY AND NOT LIKELY TO THRIVE, ESPECIALLY UNDER THE CONSTANT TAUNTING AND ABUSE OF HIS SIBLINGS.
BUT SMALL AND WEAK THOUGH HE WAS, BIGBY WAS NO COWARD.
OUCH!
YOU'D BEST LEARN TO TREAT ME BETTER, BROTHERS, LEST ONE DAY I HAVE YOUR THROATS UNDER MY FANGS!
GREYHEART! SNAPJAW! LEAVE YOUR LITTLE BROTHER ALONE!
WINTER TRIED TO PROTECT BIGBY AS MUCH AS SHE COULD, FOR SHE LOVED ALL OF HER CUBS, EVEN THE RUNT.
BUT SHE'D NEVER RECOVERED FROM HER GREAT HEARTBREAK, AND THOUGH SHE TRIED TO HANG ON LONG ENOUGH TO TEACH AND PROTECT HER CHILDREN, LIFE WAS QUICKLY FADING FROM HER.
COME HERE, CHILDREN, AND I'LL TELL YOU MORE STORIES OF YOUR FATHER...
ALL SAVE BIGBY LOVED TO HEAR THE EXCITING TALES OF THEIR MYSTERIOUS FATHER'S MANY EXPLOITS.
NOT ME! I DON'T WANT TO HEAR ABOUT NO FARTY FART POOP OF WIND, COME DOWN OUT OF THE NORTH COUNTRY'S FROSTY ASS!

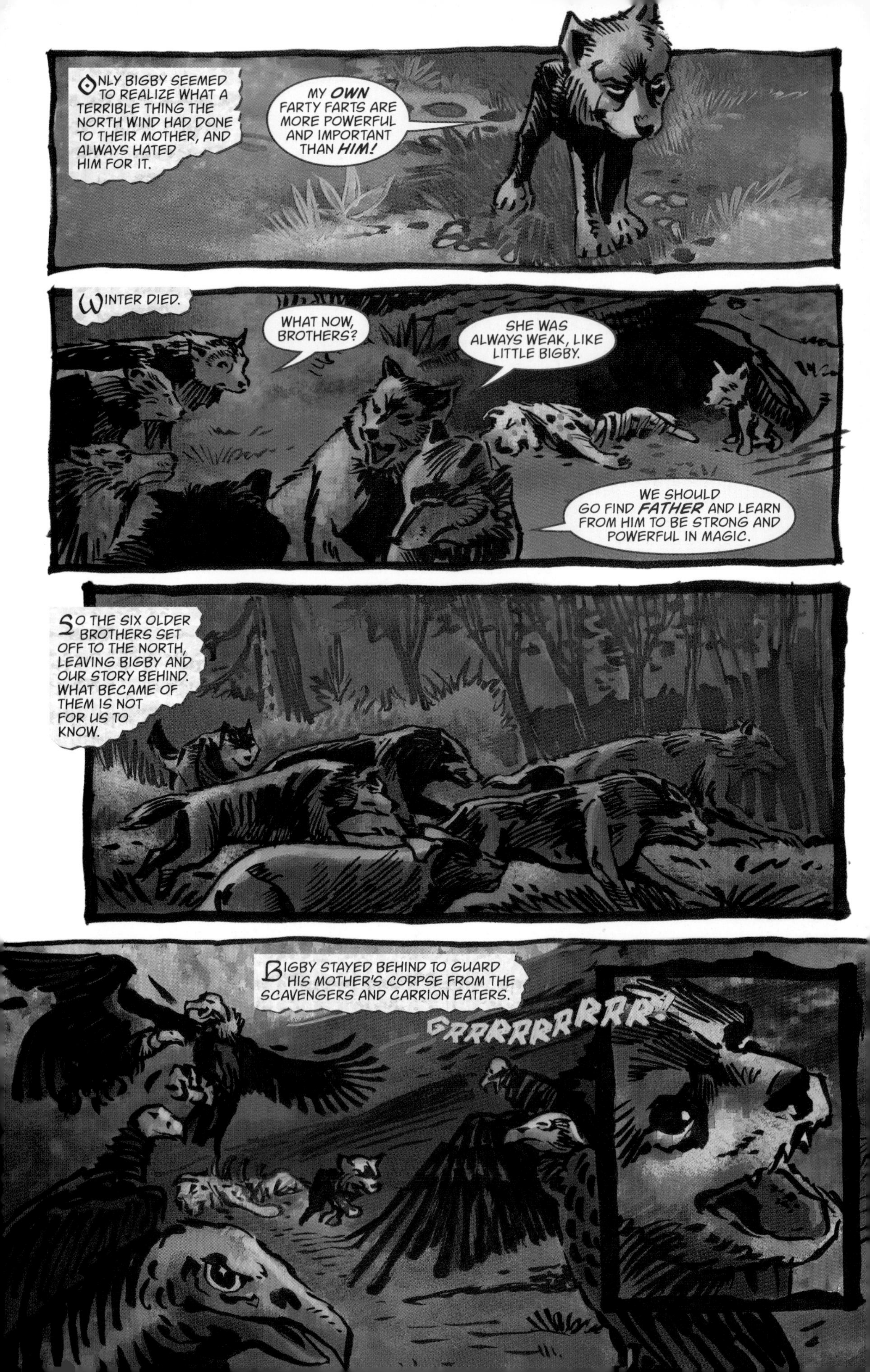
ONLY BIGBY SEEMED TO REALIZE WHAT A TERRIBLE THING THE NORTH WIND HAD DONE TO THEIR MOTHER, AND ALWAYS HATED HIM FOR IT.
MY OWN FARTY FARTS ARE MORE POWERFUL AND IMPORTANT THAN HIM!
WINTER DIED.
WHAT NOW, BROTHERS?
SHE WAS ALWAYS WEAK, LIKE LITTLE BIGBY.
WE SHOULD GO FIND FATHER AND LEARN FROM HIM TO BE STRONG AND POWERFUL IN MAGIC.
SO THE SIX OLDER BROTHERS SET OFF TO THE NORTH, LEAVING BIGBY AND OUR STORY BEHIND. WHAT BECAME OF THEM IS NOT FOR US TO KNOW.
BIGBY STAYED BEHIND TO GUARD HIS MOTHER'S CORPSE FROM THE SCAVENGERS AND CARRION EATERS.
GRRRRRRRRR!

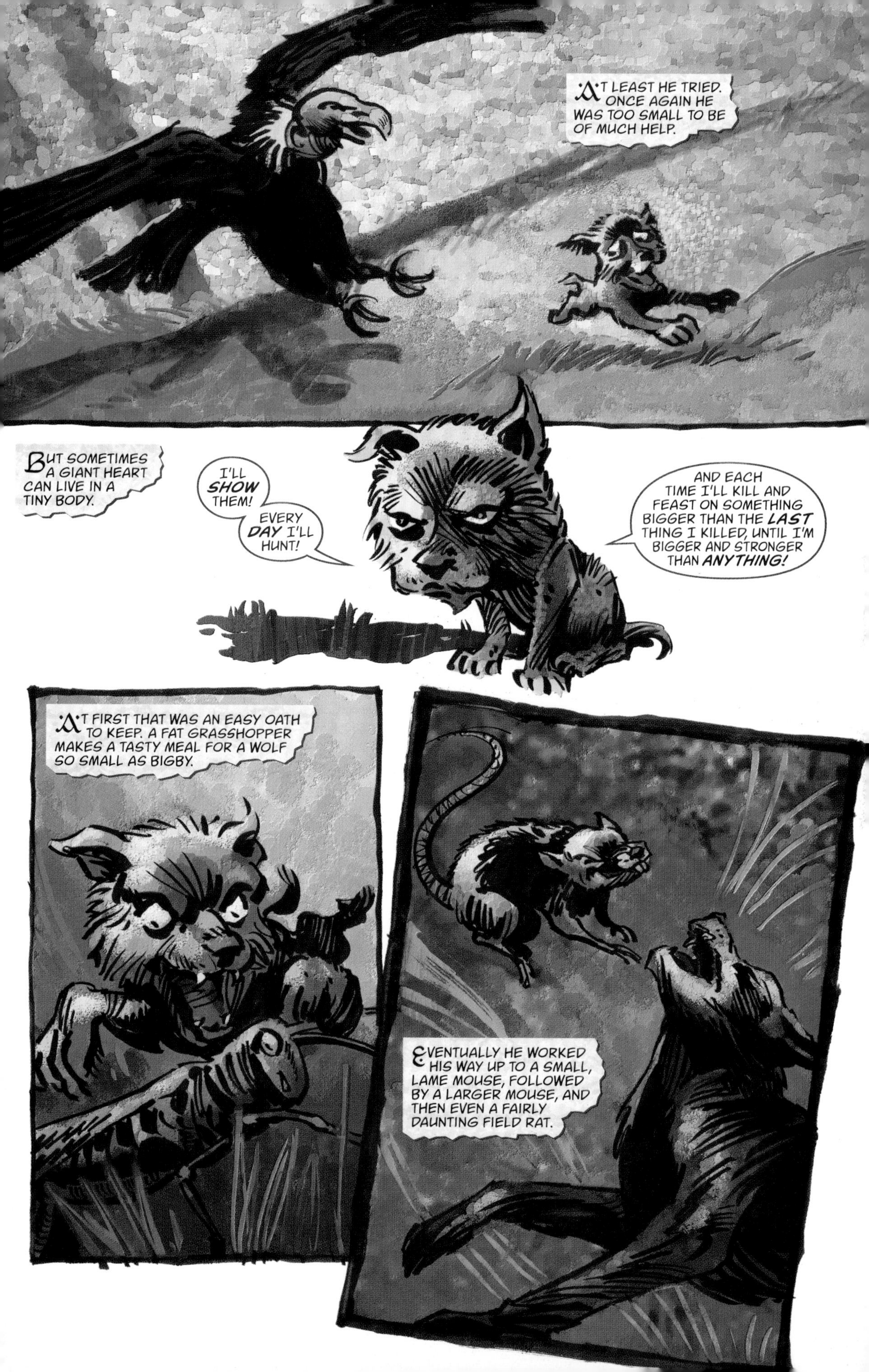
AT LEAST HE TRIED. ONCE AGAIN HE WAS TOO SMALL TO BE OF MUCH HELP.
BUT SOMETIMES A GIANT HEART CAN LIVE IN A TINY BODY.
I'LL SHOW THEM!
EVERY DAY I'LL HUNT!
AND EACH TIME I'LL KILL AND FEAST ON SOMETHING BIGGER THAN THE LAST THING I KILLED, UNTIL I'M BIGGER AND STRONGER THAN ANYTHING!
AT FIRST THAT WAS AN EASY OATH TO KEEP. A FAT GRASSHOPPER MAKES A TASTY MEAL FOR A WOLF SO SMALL AS BIGBY.
EVENTUALLY HE WORKED HIS WAY UP TO A SMALL, LAME MOUSE, FOLLOWED BY A LARGER MOUSE, AND THEN EVEN A FAIRLY DAUNTING FIELD RAT.

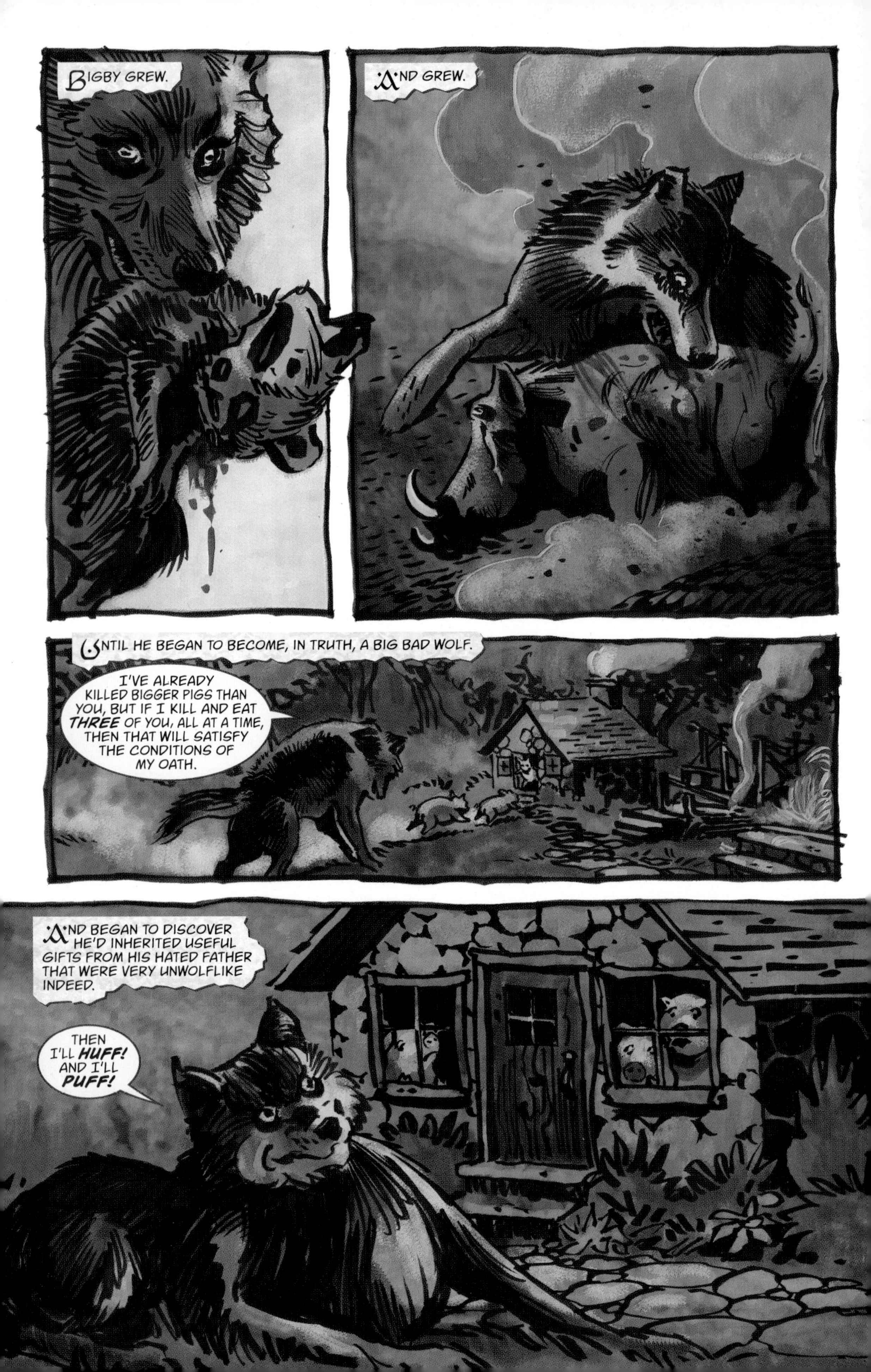
BIGBY GREW.
AND GREW.
UNTIL HE BEGAN TO BECOME, IN TRUTH, A BIG BAD WOLF.
I'VE ALREADY KILLED BIGGER PIGS THAN YOU, BUT IF I KILL AND EAT THREE OF YOU, ALL AT A TIME, THEN THAT WILL SATISFY THE CONDITIONS OF MY OATH.
AND BEGAN TO DISCOVER HE'D INHERITED USEFUL GIFTS FROM HIS HATED FATHER THAT WERE VERY UNWOLFLIKE INDEED.
THEN I'LL HUFF! AND I'LL PUFF!

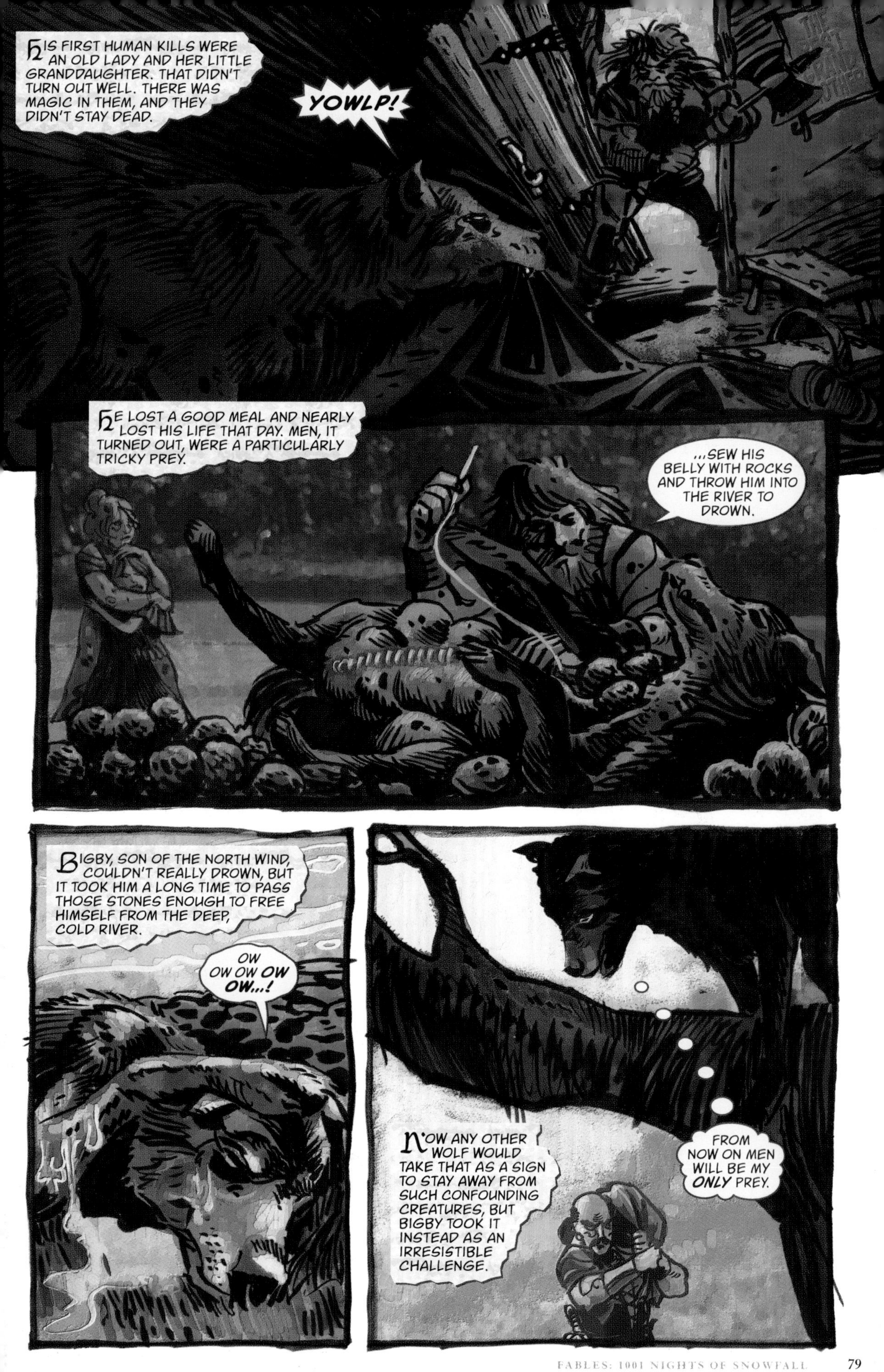
HIS FIRST HUMAN KILLS WERE AN OLD LADY AND HER LITTLE GRANDDAUGHTER. THAT DIDN'T TURN OUT WELL. THERE WAS MAGIC IN THEM, AND THEY DIDN'T STAY DEAD.
YOWLP!
HE LOST A GOOD MEAL AND NEARLY LOST HIS LIFE THAT DAY. MEN, IT TURNED OUT, WERE A PARTICULARLY TRICKY PREY.
...SEW HIS BELLY WITH ROCKS AND THROW HIM INTO THE RIVER TO DROWN.
BIGBY, SON OF THE NORTH WIND, COULDN'T REALLY DROWN, BUT IT TOOK HIM A LONG TIME TO PASS THOSE STONES ENOUGH TO FREE HIMSELF FROM THE DEEP, COLD RIVER.
OW OW OW OW OW...!
NOW ANY OTHER WOLF WOULD TAKE THAT AS A SIGN TO STAY AWAY FROM SUCH CONFOUNDING CREATURES, BUT BIGBY TOOK IT INSTEAD AS AN IRRESISTIBLE CHALLENGE.
FROM NOW ON MEN WILL BE MY ONLY PREY.

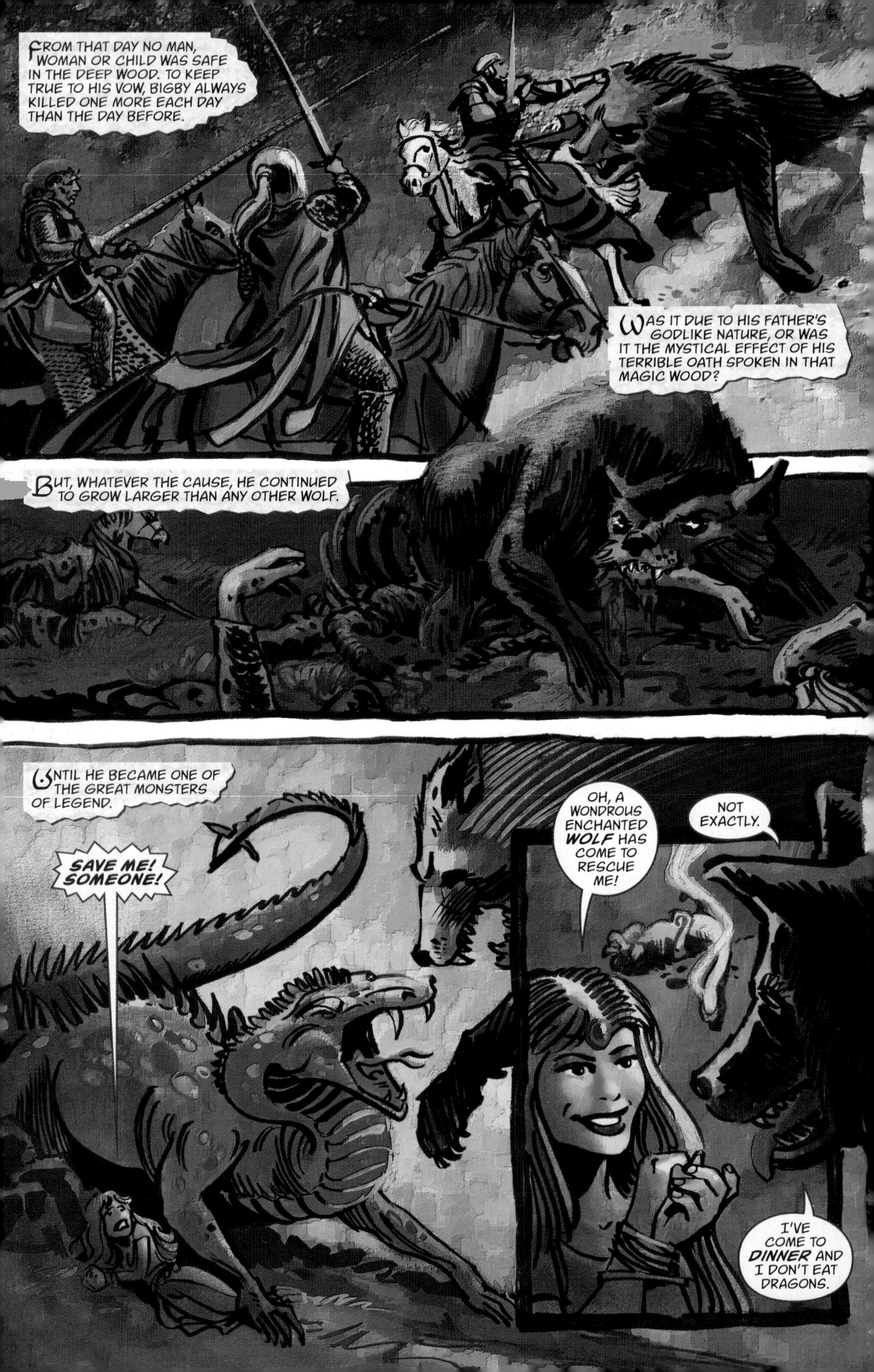
FROM THAT DAY NO MAN, WOMAN OR CHILD WAS SAFE IN THE DEEP WOOD. TO KEEP TRUE TO HIS VOW, BIGBY ALWAYS KILLED ONE MORE EACH DAY THAN THE DAY BEFORE.
WAS IT DUE TO HIS FATHER'S GODLIKE NATURE, OR WAS IT THE MYSTICAL EFFECT OF HIS TERRIBLE OATH SPOKEN IN THAT MAGIC WOOD?
BUT, WHATEVER THE CAUSE, HE CONTINUED TO GROW LARGER THAN ANY OTHER WOLF.
UNTIL HE BECAME ONE OF THE GREAT MONSTERS OF LEGEND.
SAVE ME! SOMEONE!
OH, A WONDROUS ENCHANTED WOLF HAS COME TO RESCUE ME!
NOT EXACTLY.
I'VE COME TO DINNER AND I DON'T EAT DRAGONS.

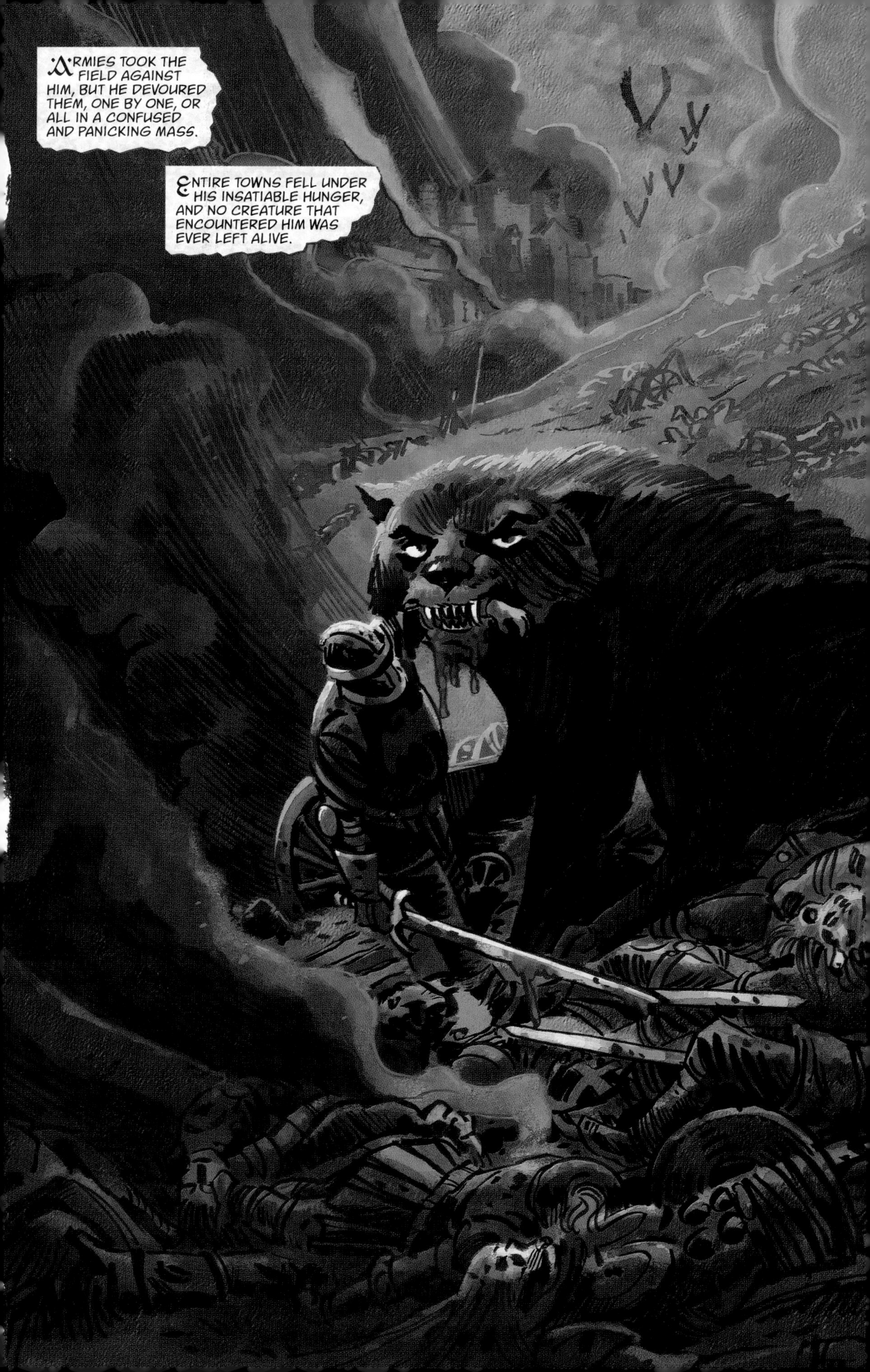
ARMIES TOOK THE FIELD AGAINST HIM, BUT HE DEVOURED THEM, ONE BY ONE, OR ALL IN A CONFUSED AND PANICKING MASS.
ENTIRE TOWNS FELL UNDER HIS INSATIABLE HUNGER, AND NO CREATURE THAT ENCOUNTERED HIM WAS EVER LEFT ALIVE.

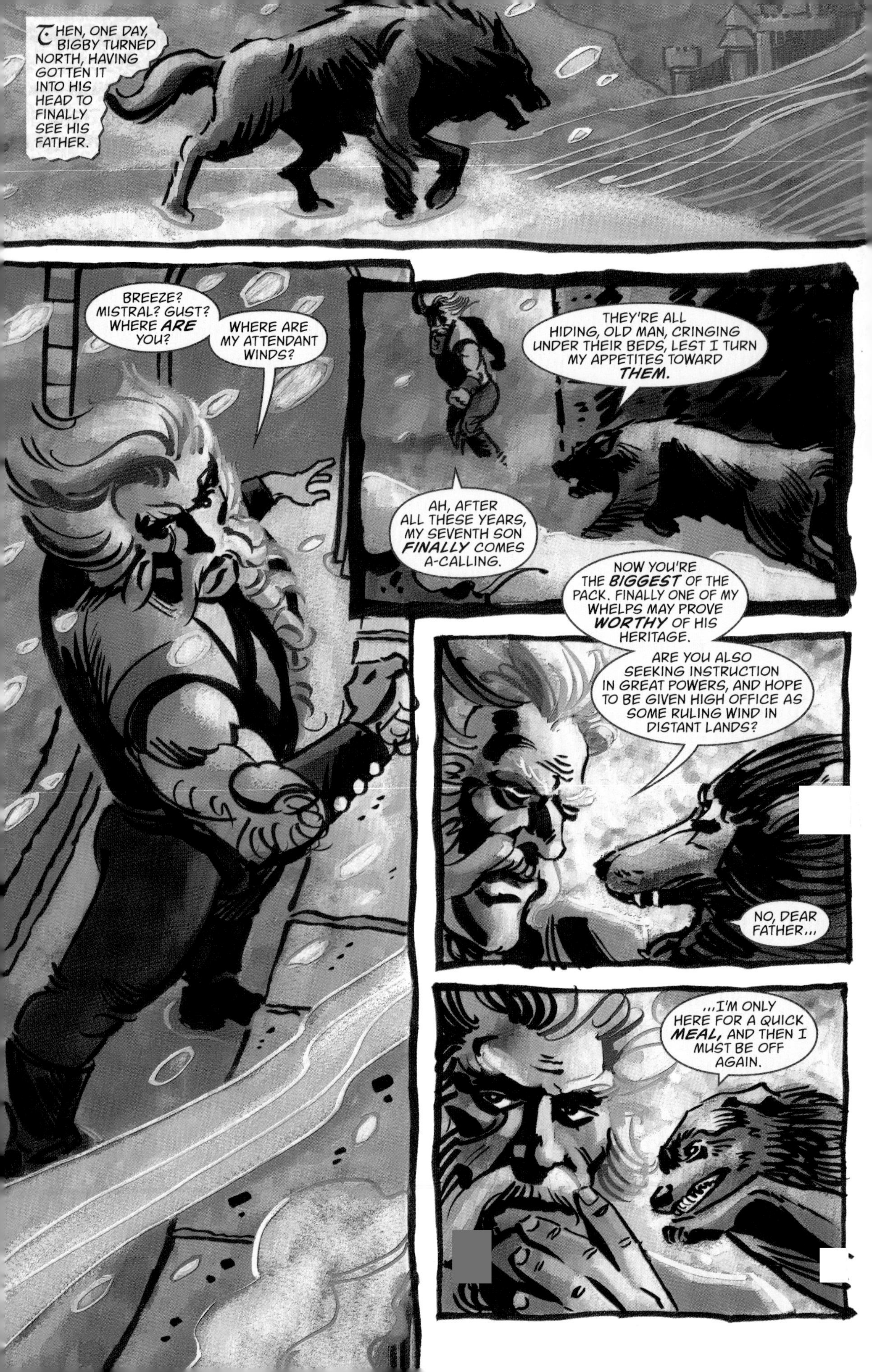
THEN, ONE DAY, BIGBY TURNED NORTH, HAVING GOTTEN IT INTO HIS HEAD TO FINALLY SEE HIS FATHER.
BREEZE? MISTRAL? GUST? WHERE ARE YOU?
WHERE ARE MY ATTENDANT WINDS?
THEY'RE ALL HIDING, OLD MAN, CRINGING UNDER THEIR BEDS, LEST I TURN MY APPETITES TOWARD THEM.
AH, AFTER ALL THESE YEARS, MY SEVENTH SON FINALLY COMES A-CALLING.
NOW YOU'RE THE BIGGEST OF THE PACK. FINALLY ONE OF MY WHELPS MAY PROVE WORTHY OF HIS HERITAGE.
ARE YOU ALSO SEEKING INSTRUCTION IN GREAT POWERS, AND HOPE TO BE GIVEN HIGH OFFICE AS SOME RULING WIND IN DISTANT LANDS?
NO, DEAR FATHER...
...I'M ONLY HERE FOR A QUICK MEAL, AND THEN I MUST BE OFF AGAIN.

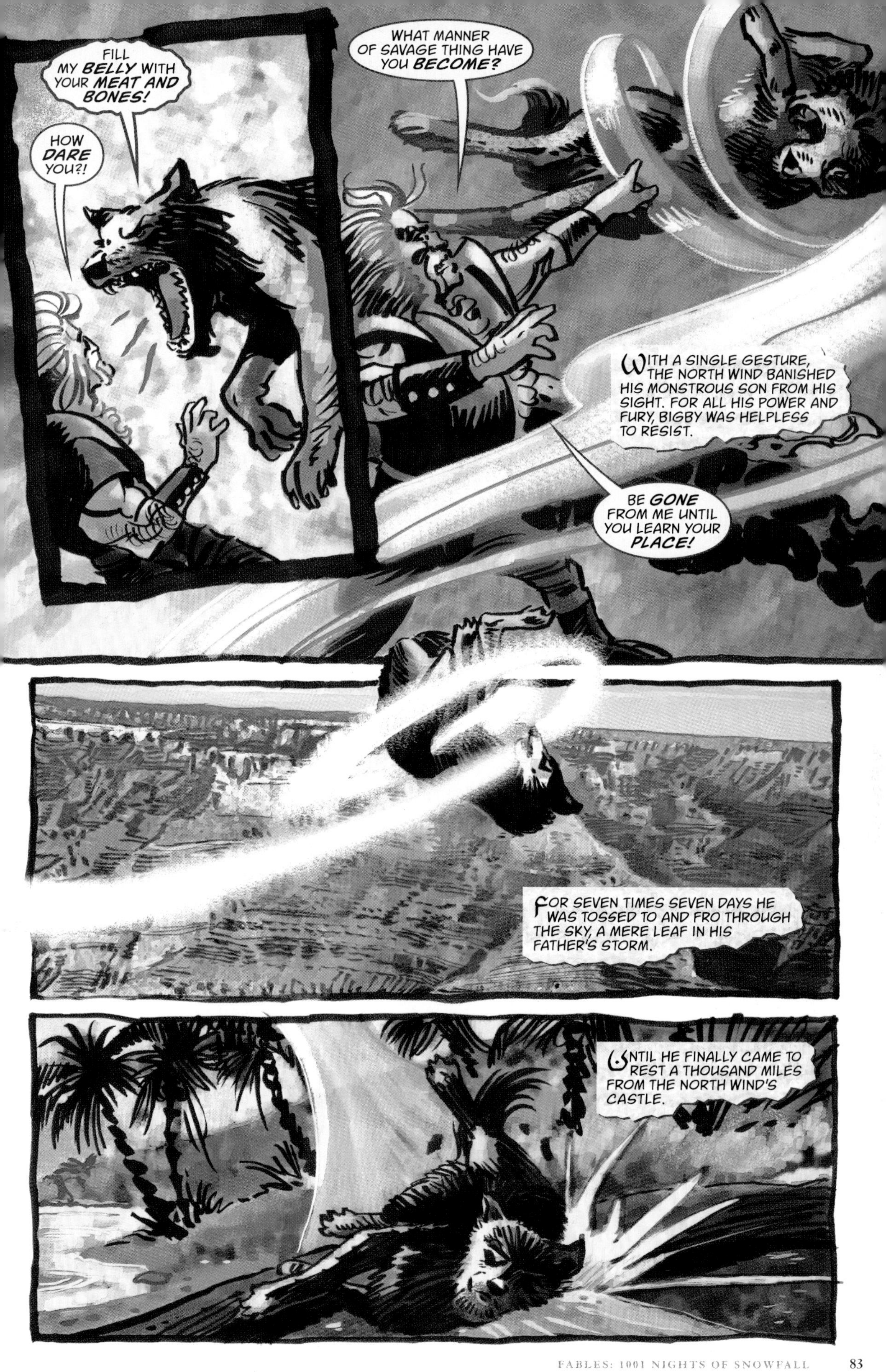
FILL MY BELLY WITH YOUR MEAT AND BONES!
HOW DARE YOU?!
WHAT MANNER OF SAVAGE THING HAVE YOU BECOME?
WITH A SINGLE GESTURE, THE NORTH WIND BANISHED HIS MONSTROUS SON FROM HIS SIGHT. FOR ALL HIS POWER AND FURY, BIGBY WAS HELPLESS TO RESIST.
BE GONE FROM ME UNTIL YOU LEARN YOUR PLACE!
FOR SEVEN TIMES SEVEN DAYS HE WAS TOSSED TO AND FRO THROUGH THE SKY, A MERE LEAF IN HIS FATHER'S STORM.
UNTIL HE FINALLY CAME TO REST A THOUSAND MILES FROM THE NORTH WIND'S CASTLE.

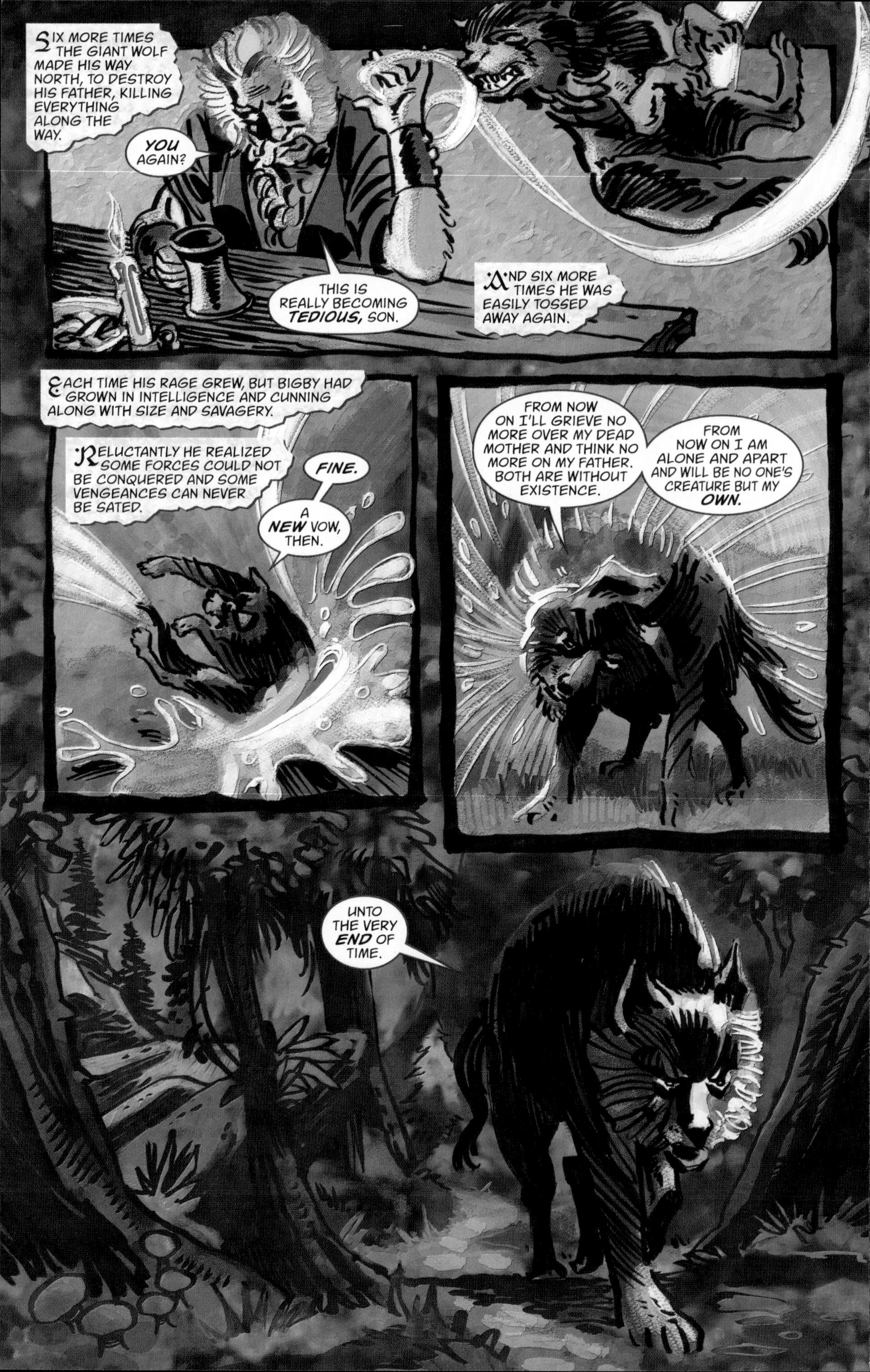
SIX MORE TIMES THE GIANT WOLF MADE HIS WAY NORTH, TO DESTROY HIS FATHER, KILLING EVERYTHING ALONG THE WAY.
YOU AGAIN?
THIS IS REALLY BECOMING TEDIOUS, SON.
AND SIX MORE TIMES HE WAS EASILY TOSSED AWAY AGAIN.
EACH TIME HIS RAGE GREW, BUT BIGBY HAD GROWN IN INTELLIGENCE AND CUNNING ALONG WITH SIZE AND SAVAGERY.
RELUCTANTLY HE REALIZED SOME FORCES COULD NOT BE CONQUERED AND SOME VENGEANCES CAN NEVER BE SATED.
FINE.
A NEW VOW, THEN.
FROM NOW ON I'LL GRIEVE NO MORE OVER MY DEAD MOTHER AND THINK NO MORE ON MY FATHER. BOTH ARE WITHOUT EXISTENCE.
FROM NOW ON I AM ALONE AND APART AND WILL BE NO ONE'S CREATURE BUT MY OWN.
UNTO THE VERY END OF TIME.

Such a grim story," the Sultan yawned, at the conclusion of that night's tale. The musicians were sleeping soundly in one corner of the chamber and the serving girls had not been seen in many an hour. The Sultan tasted one of the remaining sweet meats from a serving dish of alabaster, worked with carnelian inlays, but the tidbit was cold and had congealed. With a sour expression he carefully placed it back on the tray. "Was that also meant to be instructional?" he continued. "If so, I don't discern the lesson."

"There's no lesson to decipher, generous King," Snow White said, from behind her veil of sanguine gauze, "unless it's to point out that even the great wolf's many offenses could be forgiven in time. He is now a trusted and loyal member of our community in exile, and no citizen of Fabletown fears him any longer."

"Not one?"

"Well, perhaps one or two hold onto unvoiced cautions," Snow said, "but without cause. The wolf is reformed in full. And so you, too, could enter our compact with newly cleansed hands, for how so much worse the wolf's crimes were than yours."

"And what crimes have I done, that I need to be forgiven? I'm an unfaltering servant of Allah and submit to His will in all matters." The Sultan sat up from his recline and a dark look shadowed his features. Snow did not notice it, or if she did she was truly bolder than most women and paid his new countenance no heed, as she continued in a demure but firm voice.

"A new wife wed each evening and killed each morning?" she said.

"My Wazir was right!" the Sultan cried, and rose stamping and huffing to his feet. "You are a most infuriating woman!" And here it was that Snow White finally realized she should have spoken with more delicacy. Would his next words be a command for her swift execution?

But instead he only said, "Make sure tomorrow evening's tale is more pleasing to my ear." And then he took himself off to his carpet bed.

A Mother's Love

In which a bold commander of war suffers one of the prices of leadership.

Illustrated by Derek Kirk Kim

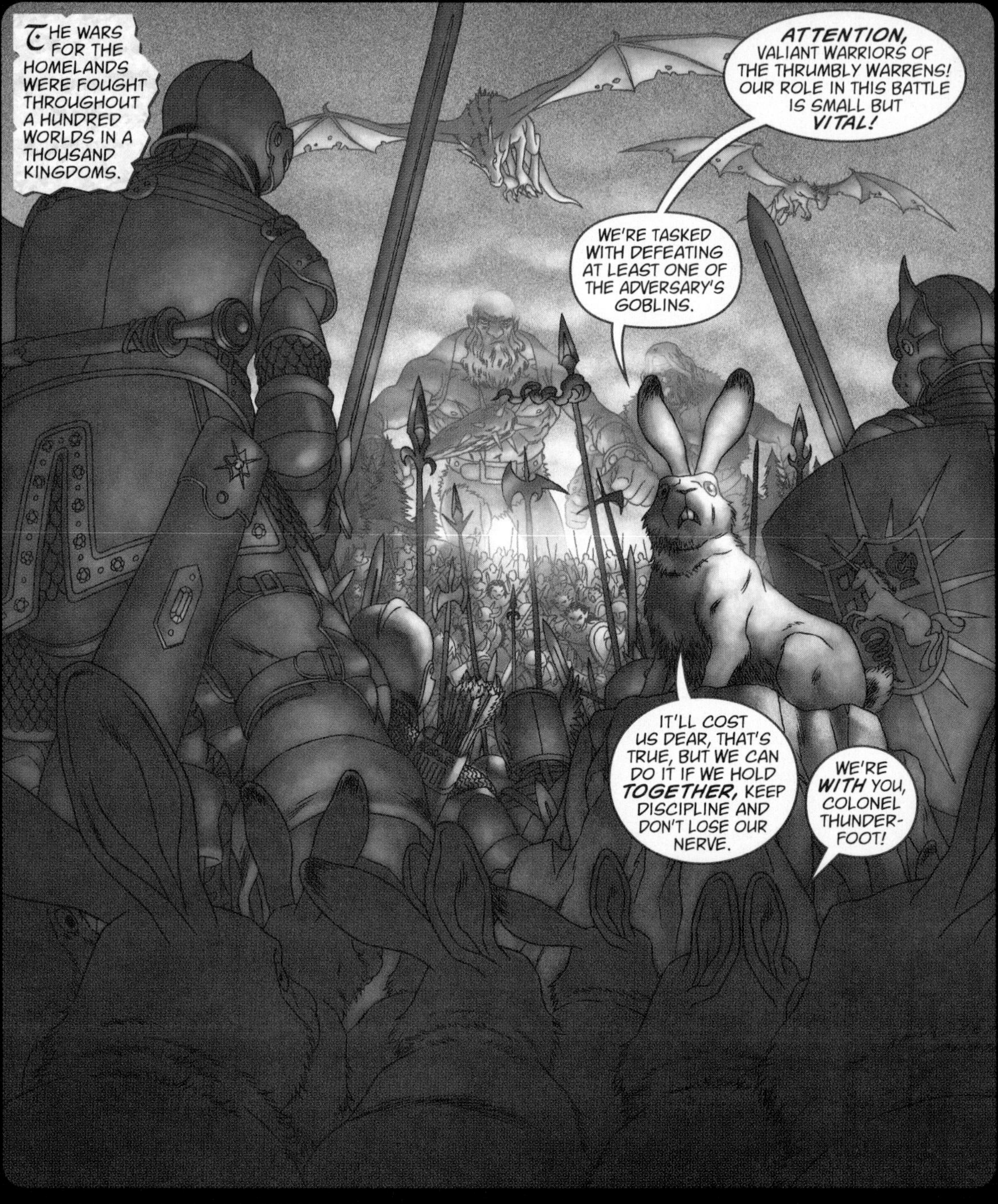
THE WARS FOR THE HOMELANDS WERE FOUGHT THROUGHOUT A HUNDRED WORLDS IN A THOUSAND KINGDOMS.
ATTENTION, VALIANT WARRIORS OF THE THRUMBLY WARRENS! OUR ROLE IN THIS BATTLE IS SMALL BUT VITAL!
WE'RE TASKED WITH DEFEATING AT LEAST ONE OF THE ADVERSARY'S GOBLINS.
IT'LL COST US DEAR, THAT'S TRUE, BUT WE CAN DO IT IF WE HOLD TOGETHER, KEEP DISCIPLINE AND DON'T LOSE OUR NERVE.
WE'RE WITH YOU, COLONEL THUNDERFOOT!

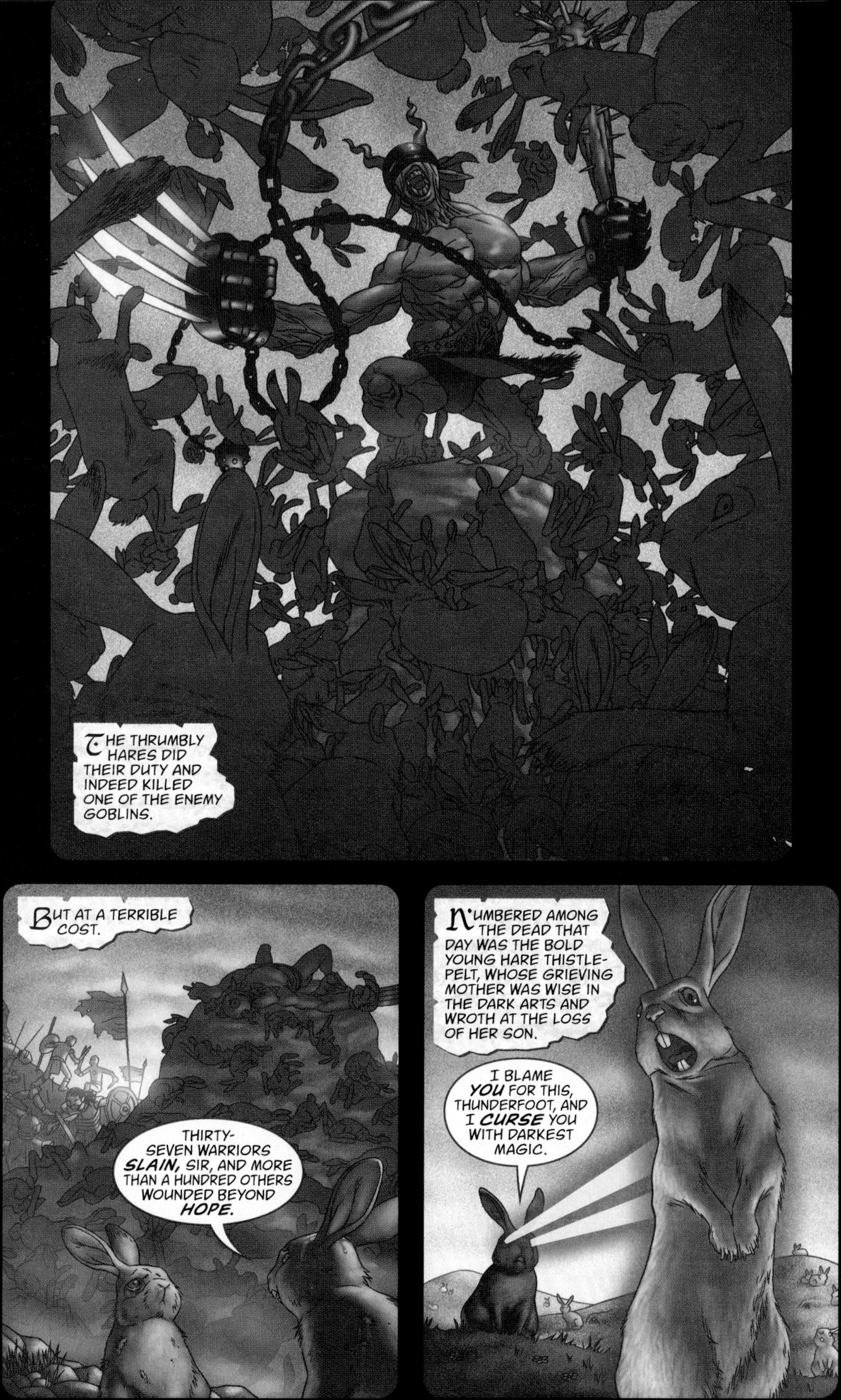
THE THRUMBLY HARES DID THEIR DUTY AND INDEED KILLED ONE OF THE ENEMY GOBLINS.
BUT AT A TERRIBLE COST.
THIRTY-SEVEN WARRIORS SLAIN, SIR, AND MORE THAN A HUNDRED OTHERS WOUNDED BEYOND HOPE.
NUMBERED AMONG THE DEAD THAT DAY WAS THE BOLD YOUNG HARE THISTLE-PELT, WHOSE GRIEVING MOTHER WAS WISE IN THE DARK ARTS AND WROTH AT THE LOSS OF HER SON.
I BLAME YOU FOR THIS, THUNDERFOOT, AND I CURSE YOU WITH DARKEST MAGIC.

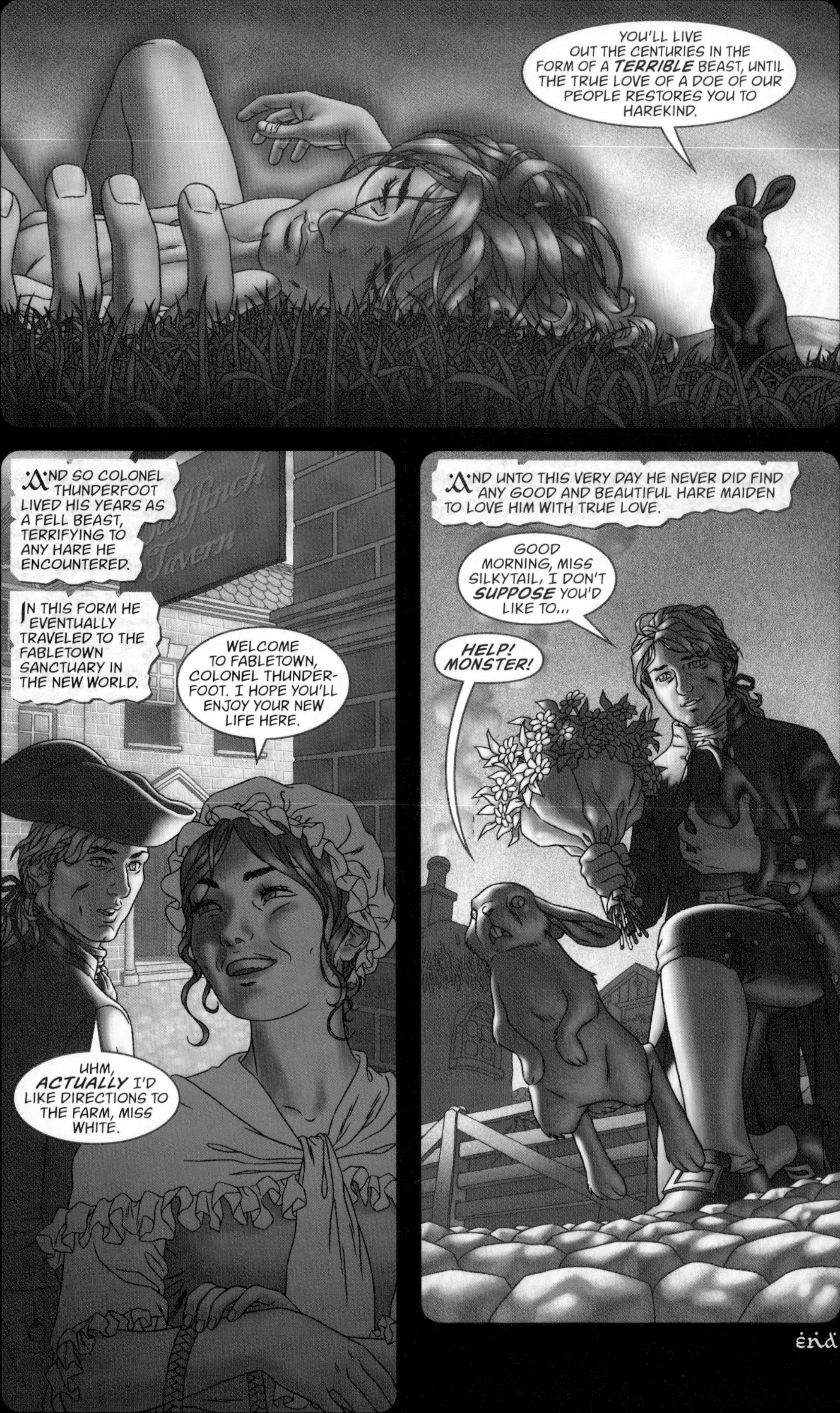
YOU'LL LIVE OUT THE CENTURIES IN THE FORM OF A TERRIBLE BEAST, UNTIL THE TRUE LOVE OF A DOE OF OUR PEOPLE RESTORES YOU TO HAREKIND.
AND SO COLONEL THUNDERFOOT LIVED HIS YEARS AS A FELL BEAST, TERRIFYING TO ANY HARE HE ENCOUNTERED.
IN THIS FORM HE EVENTUALLY TRAVELED TO THE FABLETOWN SANCTUARY IN THE NEW WORLD.
Tavern
WELCOME TO FABLETOWN, COLONEL THUNDERFOOT. I HOPE YOU'LL ENJOY YOUR NEW LIFE HERE.
UHM, ACTUALLY I'D LIKE DIRECTIONS TO THE FARM, MISS WHITE.
AND UNTO THIS VERY DAY HE NEVER DID FIND ANY GOOD AND BEAUTIFUL HARE MAIDEN TO LOVE HIM WITH TRUE LOVE.
GOOD MORNING, MISS SILKYTAIL, I DON'T SUPPOSE YOU'D LIKE TO...
HELP! MONSTER!
end

DIASPORA

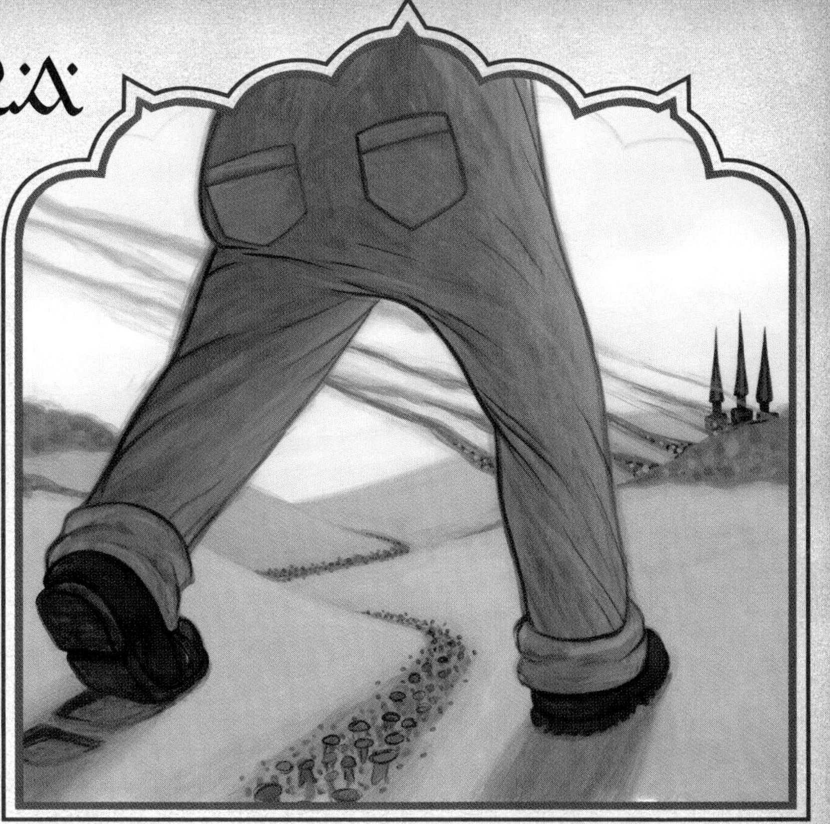

In which two sisters take refuge in a ruined cottage and what amazing things they find there.

ILLUSTRATED BY TARA McPHERSON

including THE WITCH'S TALE

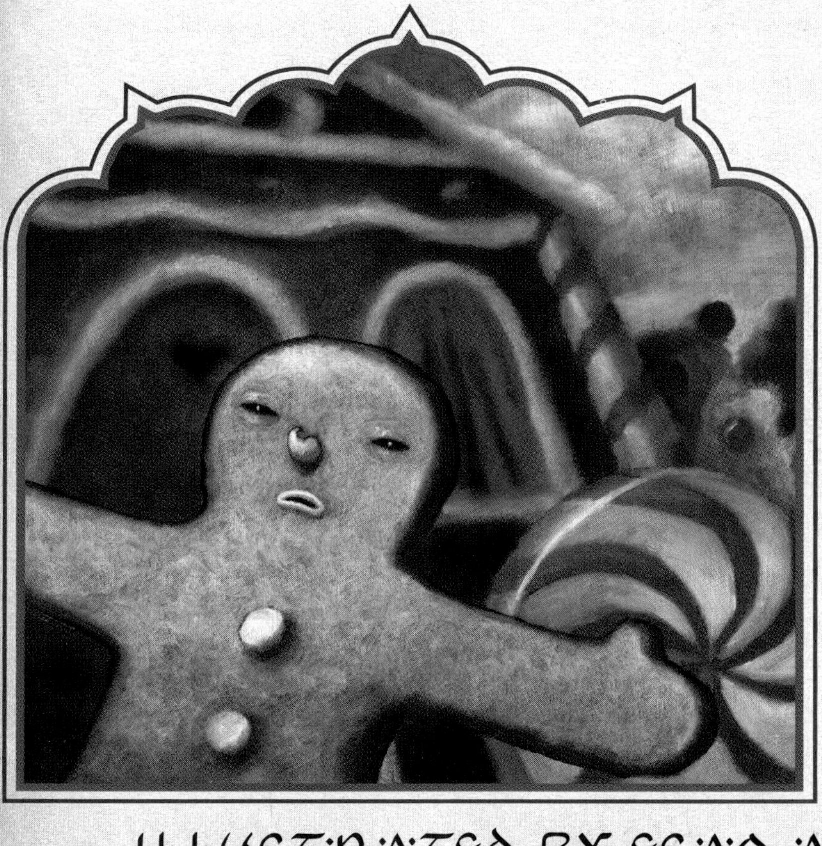

In which a witch tells her vasty life's story and we learn that acts of love and acts of revenge can often seem the same.

ILLUSTRATED BY ESAO ANDREWS

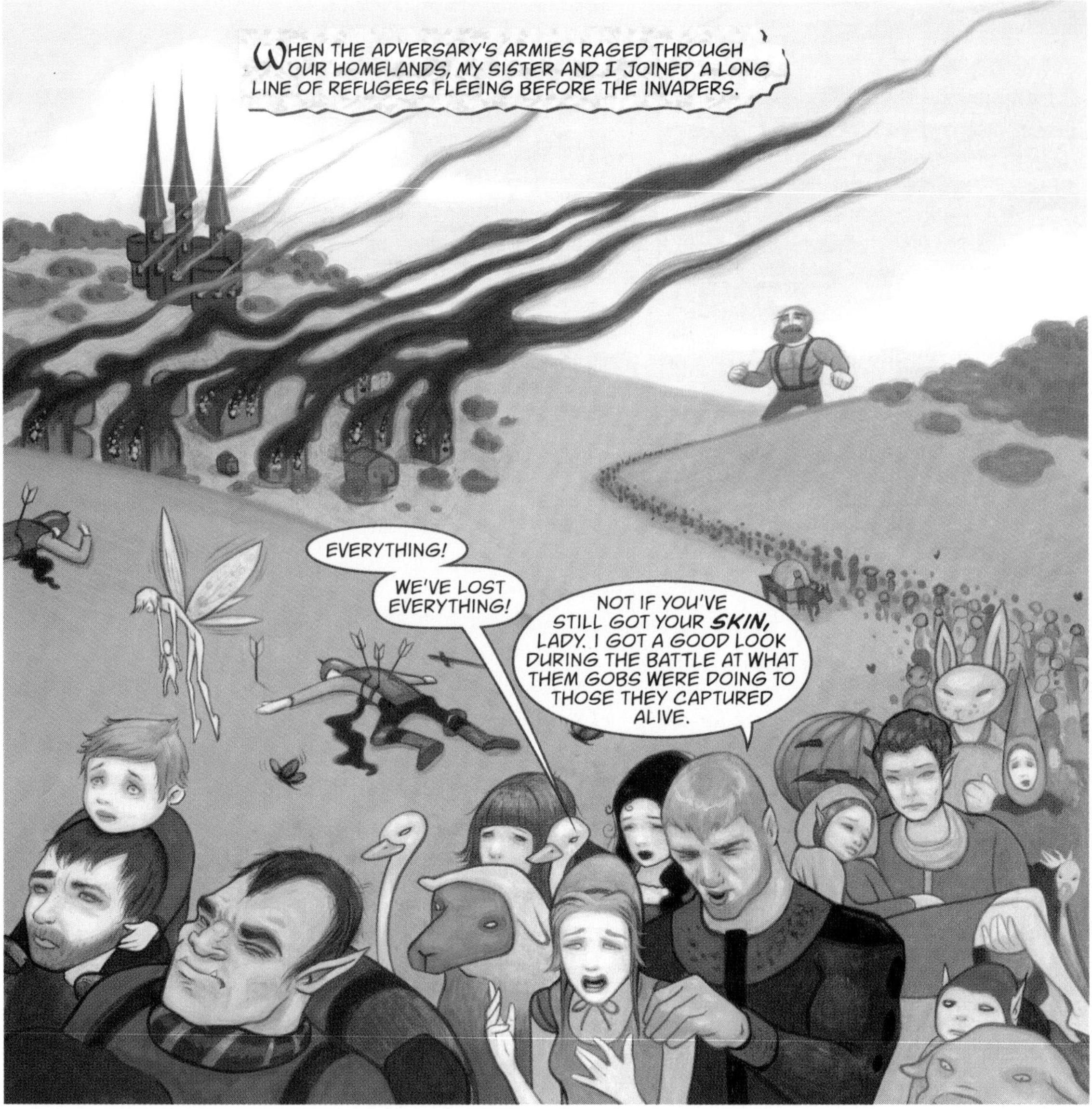
WHEN THE ADVERSARY'S ARMIES RAGED THROUGH OUR HOMELANDS, MY SISTER AND I JOINED A LONG LINE OF REFUGEES FLEEING BEFORE THE INVADERS.
EVERYTHING!
WE'VE LOST EVERYTHING!
NOT IF YOU'VE STILL GOT YOUR SKIN, LADY. I GOT A GOOD LOOK DURING THE BATTLE AT WHAT THEM GOBS WERE DOING TO THOSE THEY CAPTURED ALIVE.

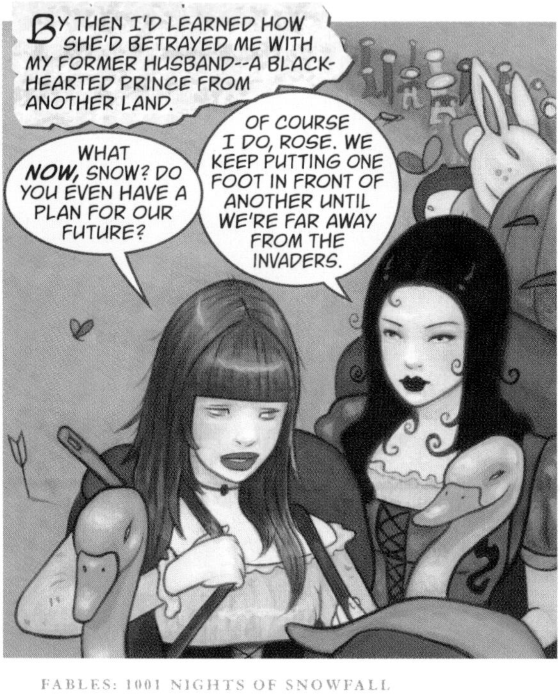
BY THEN I'D LEARNED HOW SHE'D BETRAYED ME WITH MY FORMER HUSBAND--A BLACK-HEARTED PRINCE FROM ANOTHER LAND.
WHAT NOW, SNOW? DO YOU EVEN HAVE A PLAN FOR OUR FUTURE?
OF COURSE I DO, ROSE. WE KEEP PUTTING ONE FOOT IN FRONT OF ANOTHER UNTIL WE'RE FAR AWAY FROM THE INVADERS.

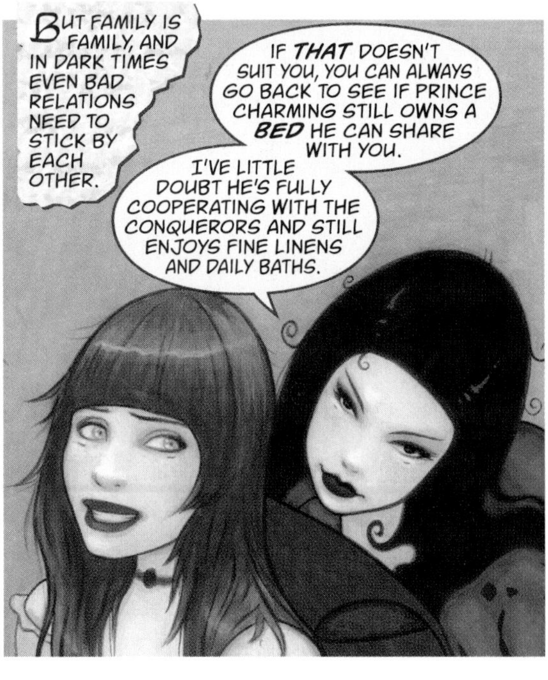
BUT FAMILY IS FAMILY, AND IN DARK TIMES EVEN BAD RELATIONS NEED TO STICK BY EACH OTHER.
IF THAT DOESN'T SUIT YOU, YOU CAN ALWAYS GO BACK TO SEE IF PRINCE CHARMING STILL OWNS A BED HE CAN SHARE WITH YOU.
I'VE LITTLE DOUBT HE'S FULLY COOPERATING WITH THE CONQUERORS AND STILL ENJOYS FINE LINENS AND DAILY BATHS.

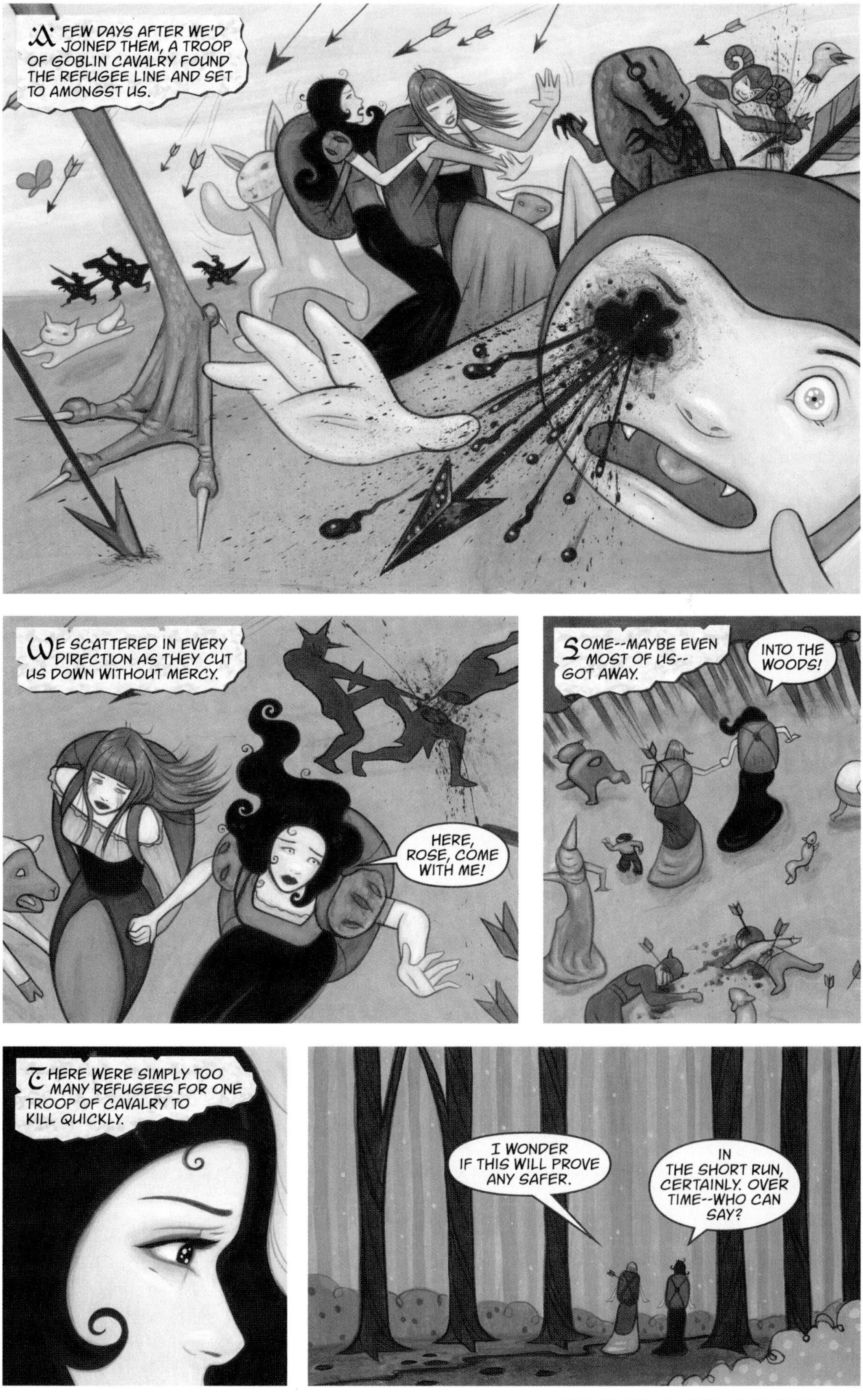
A FEW DAYS AFTER WE'D JOINED THEM, A TROOP OF GOBLIN CAVALRY FOUND THE REFUGEE LINE AND SET TO AMONGST US.
WE SCATTERED IN EVERY DIRECTION AS THEY CUT US DOWN WITHOUT MERCY.
HERE, ROSE, COME WITH ME!
SOME--MAYBE EVEN MOST OF US--GOT AWAY.
INTO THE WOODS!
THERE WERE SIMPLY TOO MANY REFUGEES FOR ONE TROOP OF CAVALRY TO KILL QUICKLY.
I WONDER IF THIS WILL PROVE ANY SAFER.
IN THE SHORT RUN, CERTAINLY. OVER TIME--WHO CAN SAY?

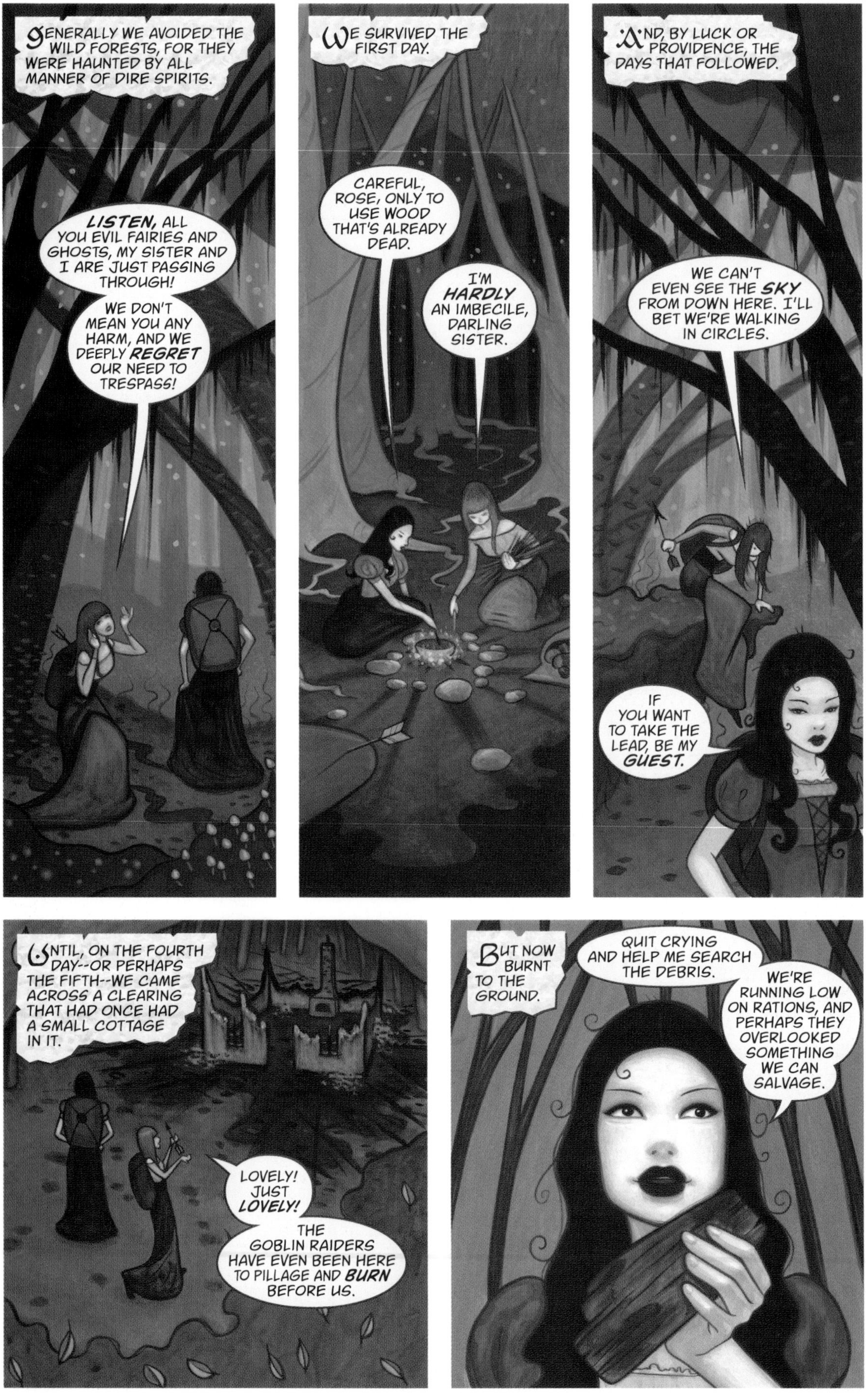
GENERALLY WE AVOIDED THE WILD FORESTS, FOR THEY WERE HAUNTED BY ALL MANNER OF DIRE SPIRITS.
LISTEN, ALL YOU EVIL FAIRIES AND GHOSTS, MY SISTER AND I ARE JUST PASSING THROUGH!
WE DON'T MEAN YOU ANY HARM, AND WE DEEPLY REGRET OUR NEED TO TRESPASS!
WE SURVIVED THE FIRST DAY.
CAREFUL, ROSE, ONLY TO USE WOOD THAT'S ALREADY DEAD.
I'M HARDLY AN IMBECILE, DARLING SISTER.
AND, BY LUCK OR PROVIDENCE, THE DAYS THAT FOLLOWED.
WE CAN'T EVEN SEE THE SKY FROM DOWN HERE. I'LL BET WE'RE WALKING IN CIRCLES.
IF YOU WANT TO TAKE THE LEAD, BE MY GUEST.
UNTIL, ON THE FOURTH DAY--OR PERHAPS THE FIFTH--WE CAME ACROSS A CLEARING THAT HAD ONCE HAD A SMALL COTTAGE IN IT.
LOVELY! JUST LOVELY!
THE GOBLIN RAIDERS HAVE EVEN BEEN HERE TO PILLAGE AND BURN BEFORE US.
BUT NOW BURNT TO THE GROUND.
QUIT CRYING AND HELP ME SEARCH THE DEBRIS.
WE'RE RUNNING LOW ON RATIONS, AND PERHAPS THEY OVERLOOKED SOMETHING WE CAN SALVAGE.

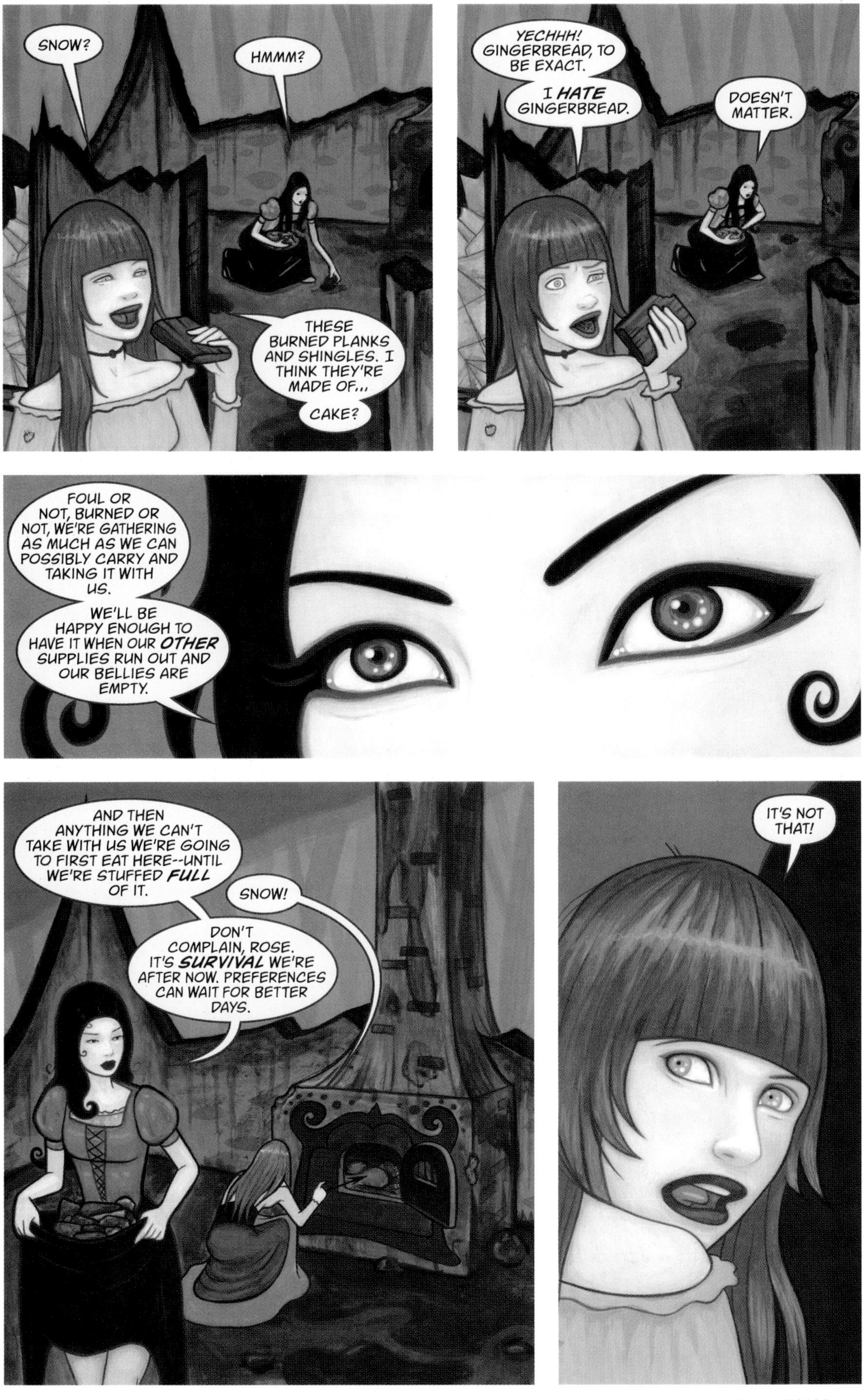
SNOW?
HMMM?
THESE BURNED PLANKS AND SHINGLES. I THINK THEY'RE MADE OF...
CAKE?
YECHHH! GINGERBREAD, TO BE EXACT.
I HATE GINGERBREAD.
DOESN'T MATTER.
FOUL OR NOT, BURNED OR NOT, WE'RE GATHERING AS MUCH AS WE CAN POSSIBLY CARRY AND TAKING IT WITH US.
WE'LL BE HAPPY ENOUGH TO HAVE IT WHEN OUR OTHER SUPPLIES RUN OUT AND OUR BELLIES ARE EMPTY.
AND THEN ANYTHING WE CAN'T TAKE WITH US WE'RE GOING TO FIRST EAT HERE--UNTIL WE'RE STUFFED FULL OF IT.
SNOW!
DON'T COMPLAIN, ROSE. IT'S SURVIVAL WE'RE AFTER NOW. PREFERENCES CAN WAIT FOR BETTER DAYS.
IT'S NOT THAT!

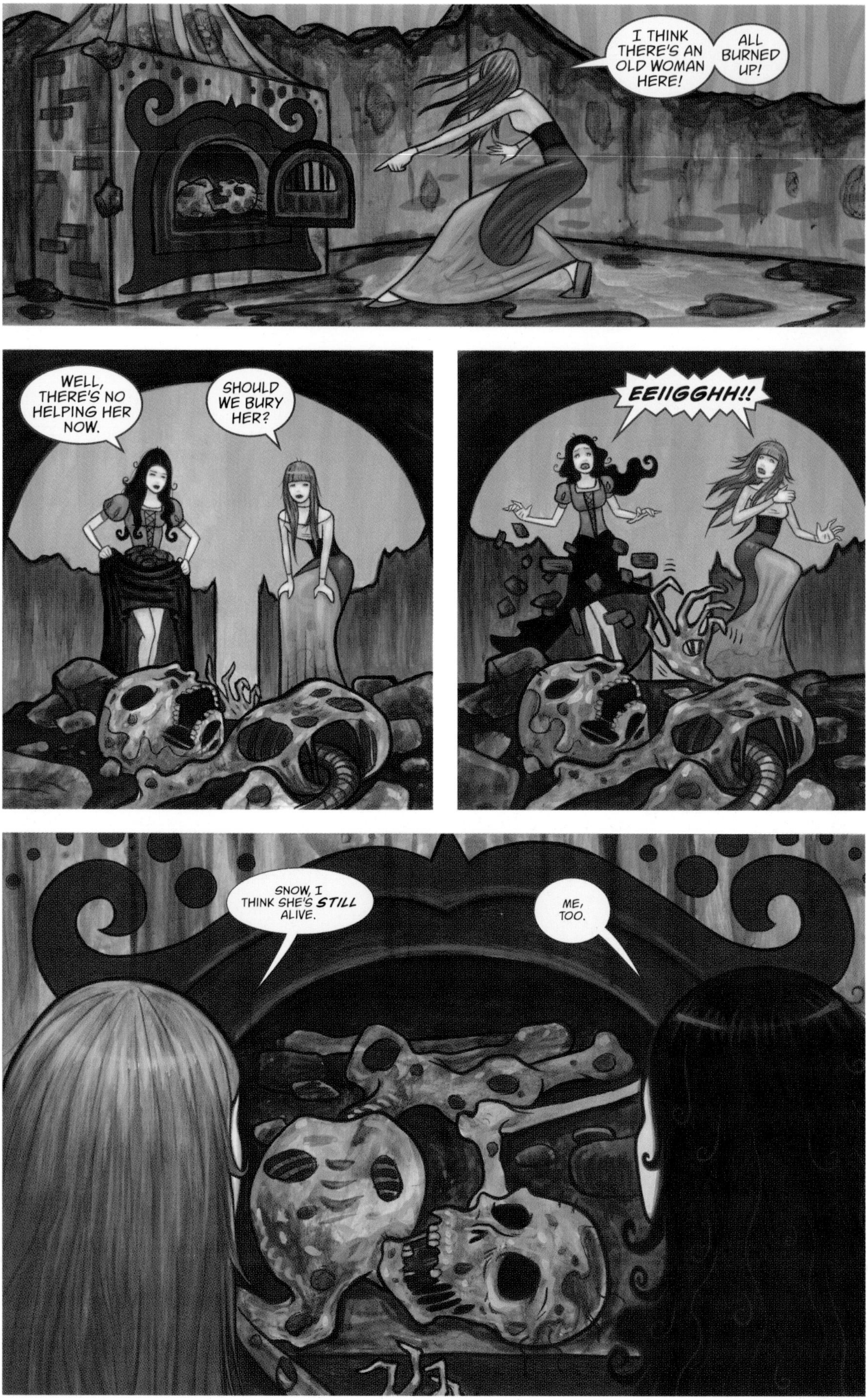
I THINK THERE'S AN OLD WOMAN HERE!
ALL BURNED UP!
WELL, THERE'S NO HELPING HER NOW.
SHOULD WE BURY HER?
EEIIGGHH!!
SNOW, I THINK SHE'S STILL ALIVE.
ME, TOO.

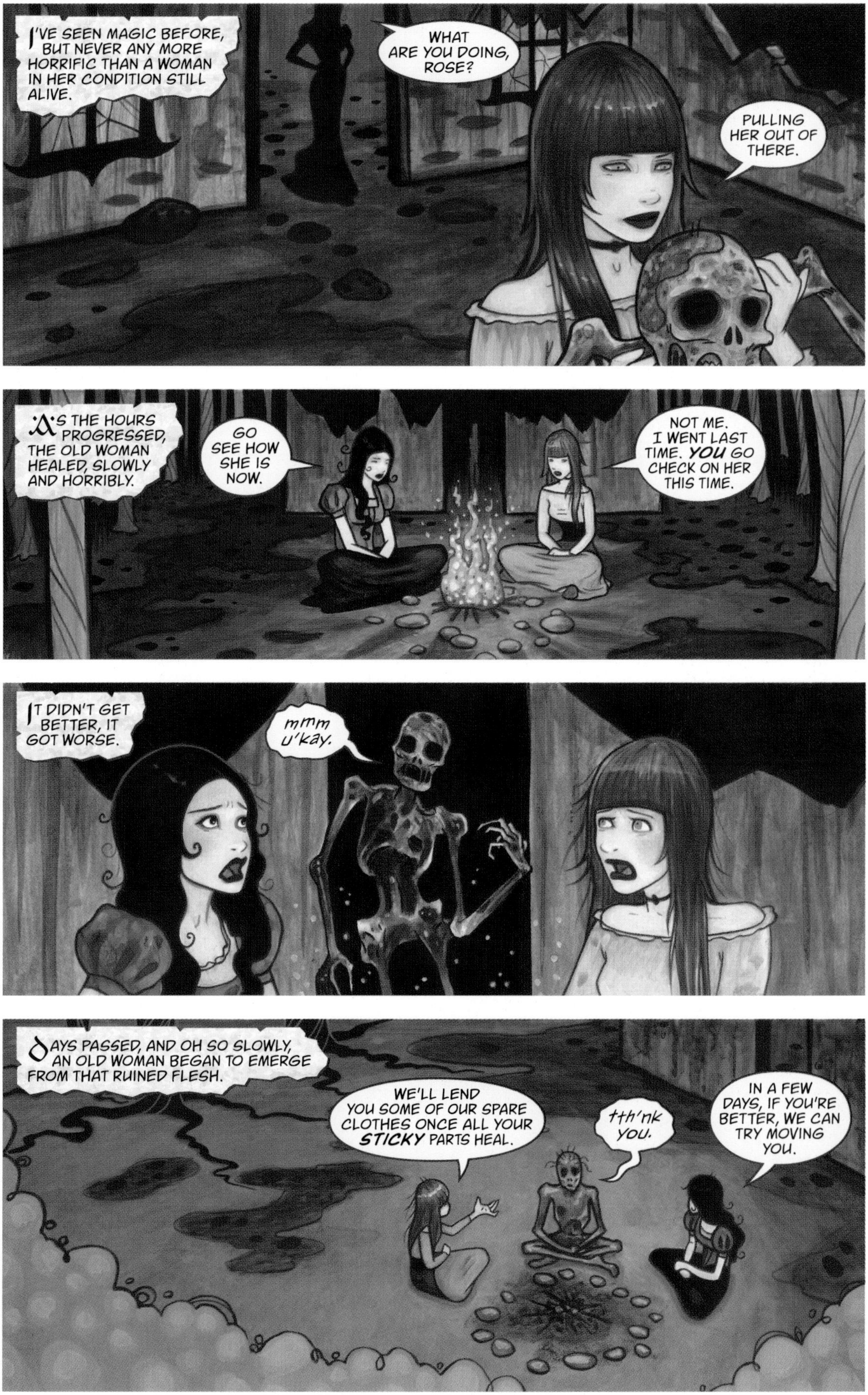
I'VE SEEN MAGIC BEFORE, BUT NEVER ANY MORE HORRIFIC THAN A WOMAN IN HER CONDITION STILL ALIVE.
WHAT ARE YOU DOING, ROSE?
PULLING HER OUT OF THERE.
AS THE HOURS PROGRESSED, THE OLD WOMAN HEALED, SLOWLY AND HORRIBLY.
GO SEE HOW SHE IS NOW.
NOT ME. I WENT LAST TIME. YOU GO CHECK ON HER THIS TIME.
IT DIDN'T GET BETTER, IT GOT WORSE.
mmm u'kay.
DAYS PASSED, AND OH SO SLOWLY, AN OLD WOMAN BEGAN TO EMERGE FROM THAT RUINED FLESH.
WE'LL LEND YOU SOME OF OUR SPARE CLOTHES ONCE ALL YOUR STICKY PARTS HEAL.
tth'nk you.
IN A FEW DAYS, IF YOU'RE BETTER, WE CAN TRY MOVING YOU.

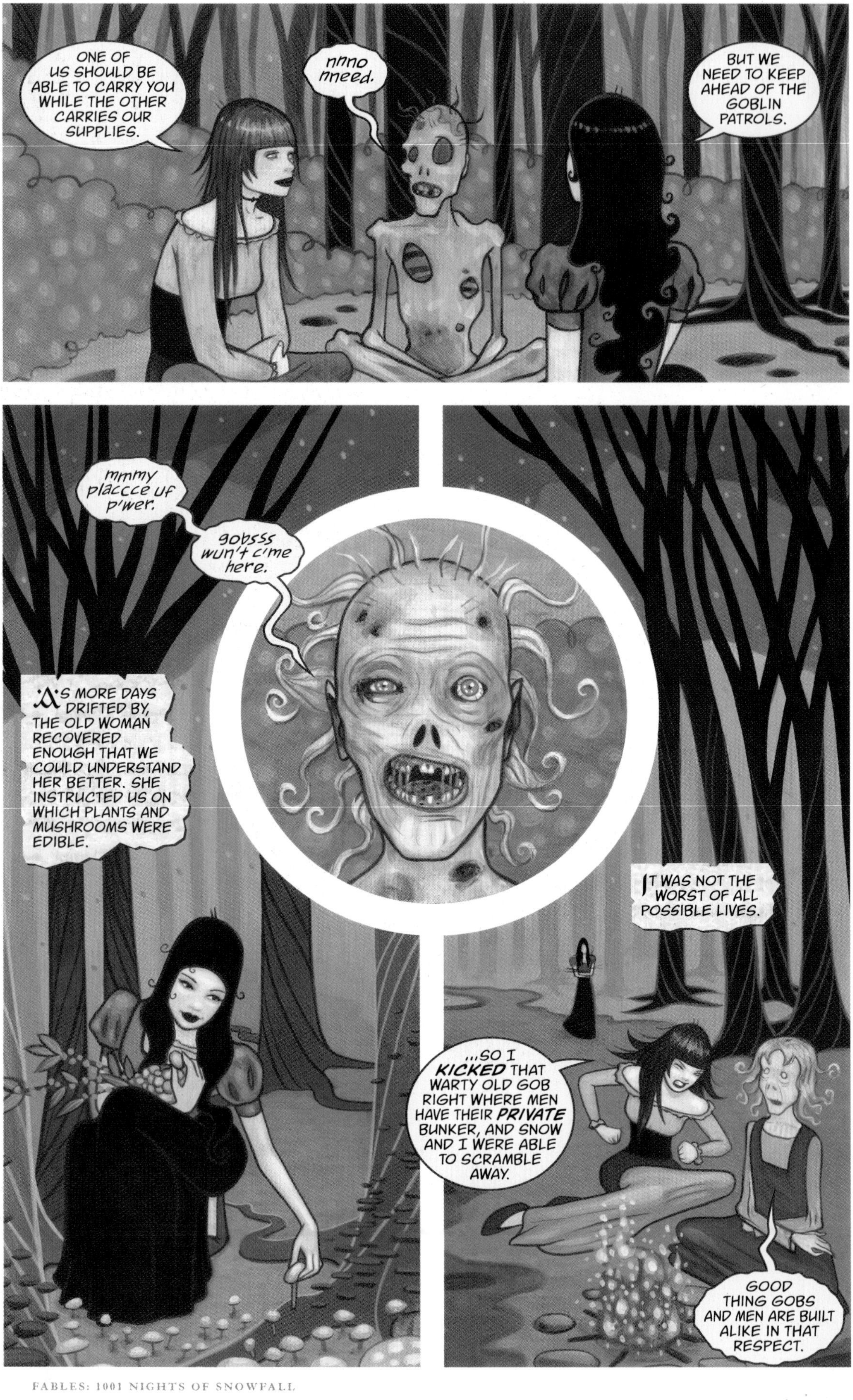
ONE OF US SHOULD BE ABLE TO CARRY YOU WHILE THE OTHER CARRIES OUR SUPPLIES.
nnno nneed.
BUT WE NEED TO KEEP AHEAD OF THE GOBLIN PATROLS.
mmmy placcce uf p'wer.
gobsss wun't c'me here.
AS MORE DAYS DRIFTED BY, THE OLD WOMAN RECOVERED ENOUGH THAT WE COULD UNDERSTAND HER BETTER. SHE INSTRUCTED US ON WHICH PLANTS AND MUSHROOMS WERE EDIBLE.
IT WAS NOT THE WORST OF ALL POSSIBLE LIVES.
...SO I KICKED THAT WARTY OLD GOB RIGHT WHERE MEN HAVE THEIR PRIVATE BUNKER, AND SNOW AND I WERE ABLE TO SCRAMBLE AWAY.
GOOD THING GOBS AND MEN ARE BUILT ALIKE IN THAT RESPECT.

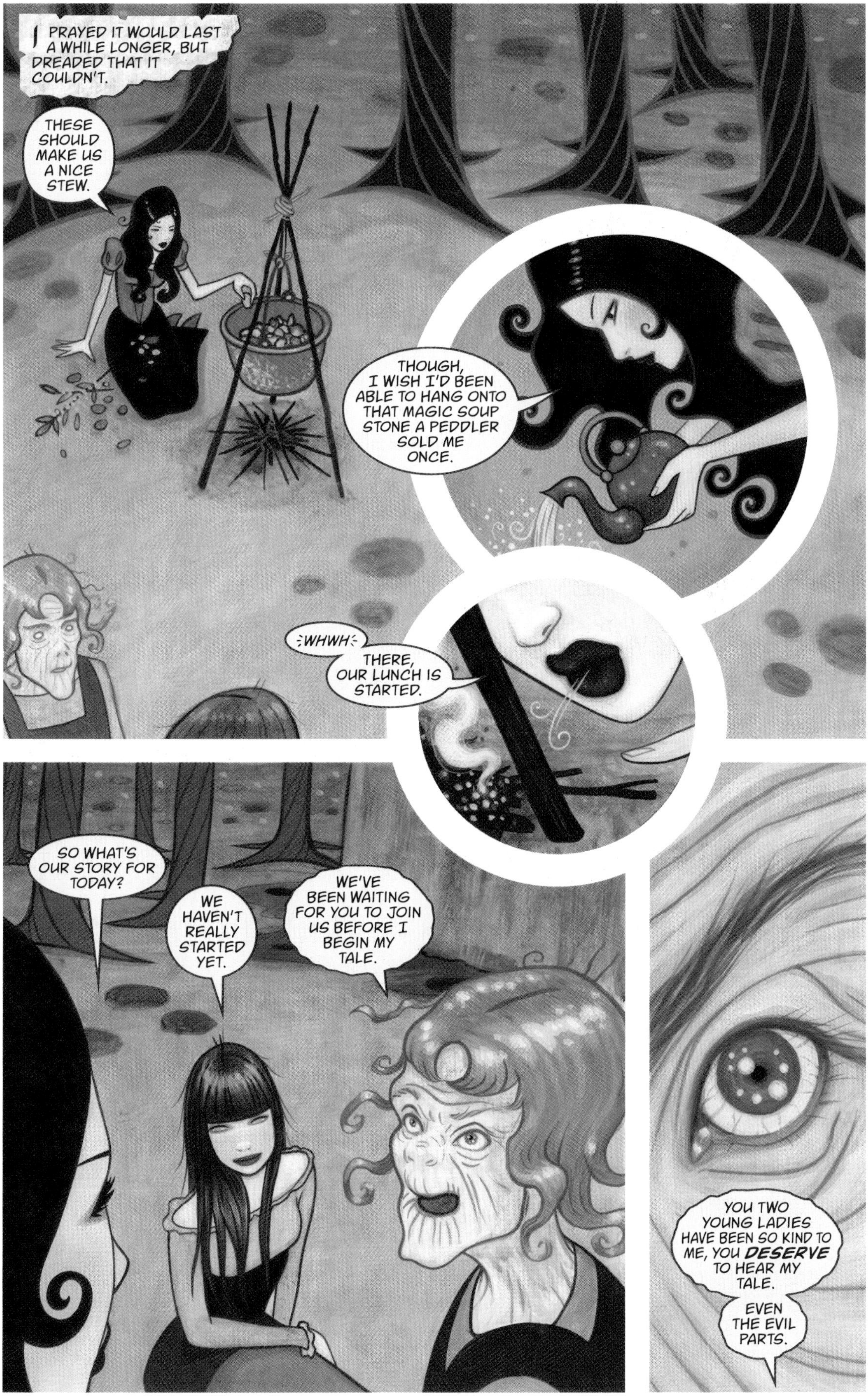
I PRAYED IT WOULD LAST A WHILE LONGER, BUT DREADED THAT IT COULDN'T.
THESE SHOULD MAKE US A NICE STEW.
THOUGH, I WISH I'D BEEN ABLE TO HANG ONTO THAT MAGIC SOUP STONE A PEDDLER SOLD ME ONCE.
WHWH
THERE, OUR LUNCH IS STARTED.
SO WHAT'S OUR STORY FOR TODAY?
WE HAVEN'T REALLY STARTED YET.
WE'VE BEEN WAITING FOR YOU TO JOIN US BEFORE I BEGIN MY TALE.
YOU TWO YOUNG LADIES HAVE BEEN SO KIND TO ME, YOU ***DESERVE*** TO HEAR MY TALE.
EVEN THE EVIL PARTS.

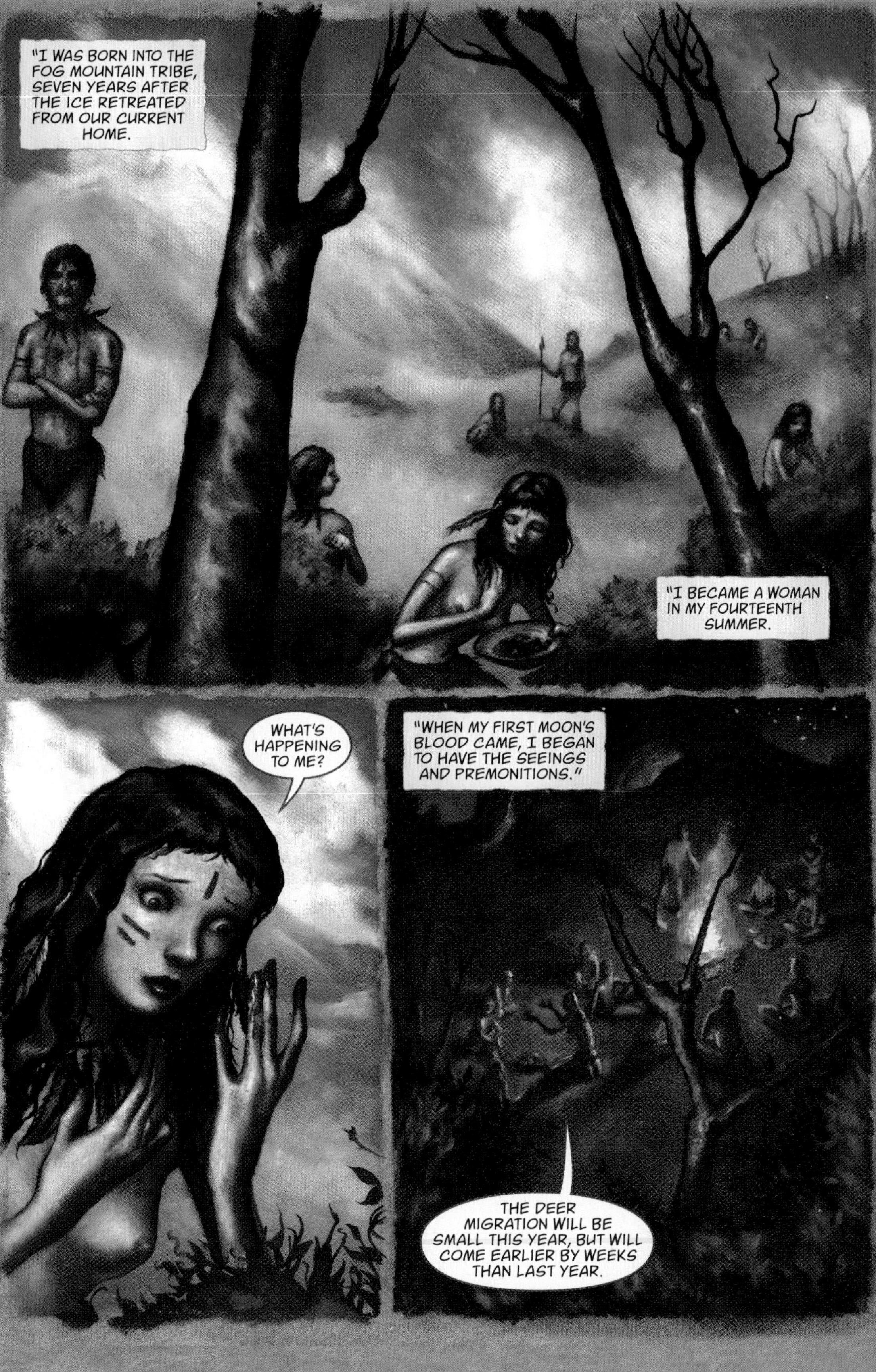
"I WAS BORN INTO THE FOG MOUNTAIN TRIBE, SEVEN YEARS AFTER THE ICE RETREATED FROM OUR CURRENT HOME.
"I BECAME A WOMAN IN MY FOURTEENTH SUMMER.
WHAT'S HAPPENING TO ME?
"WHEN MY FIRST MOON'S BLOOD CAME, I BEGAN TO HAVE THE SEEINGS AND PREMONITIONS."
THE DEER MIGRATION WILL BE SMALL THIS YEAR, BUT WILL COME EARLIER BY WEEKS THAN LAST YEAR.

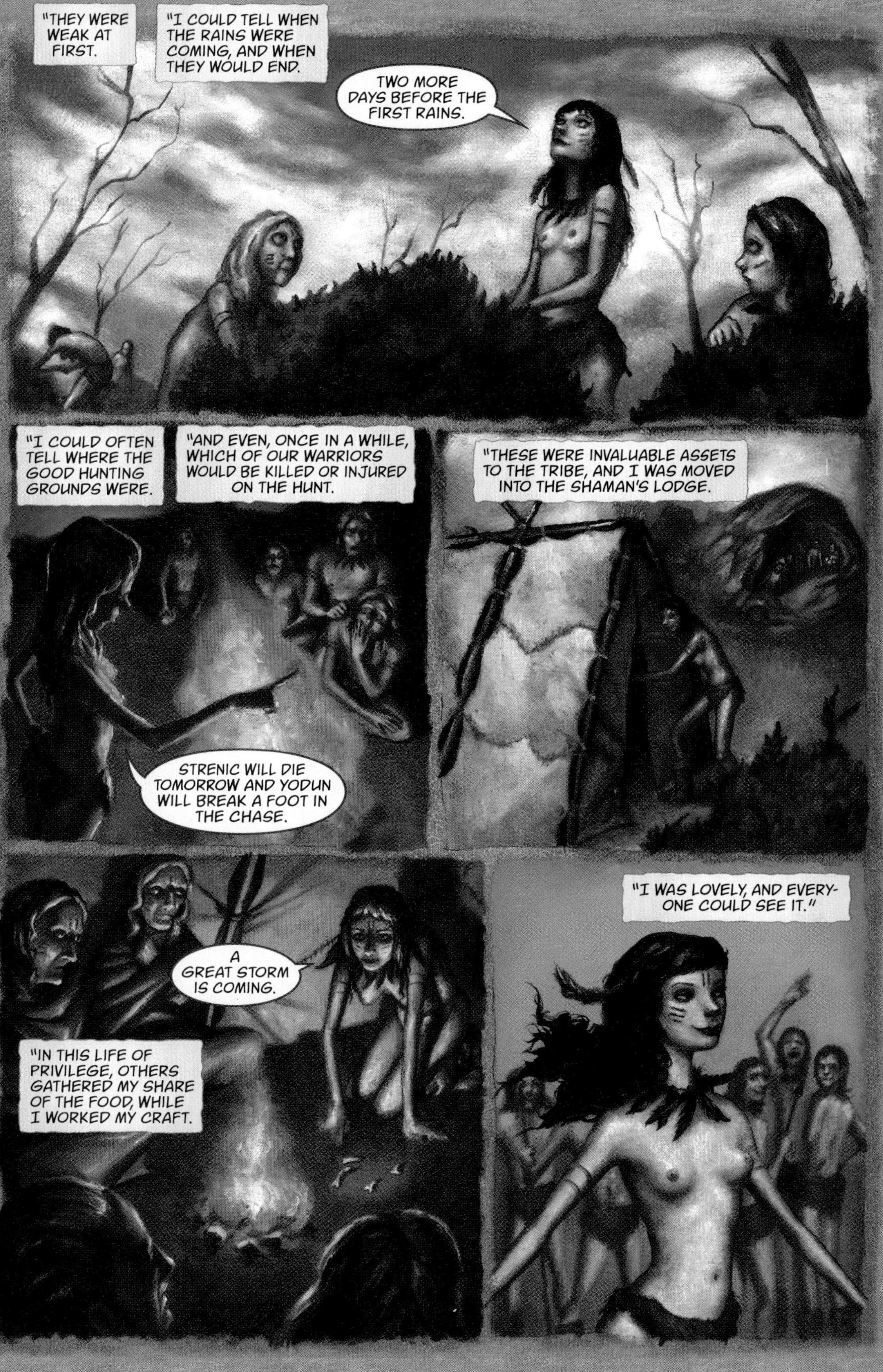

"THEY WERE WEAK AT FIRST.
"I COULD TELL WHEN THE RAINS WERE COMING, AND WHEN THEY WOULD END.
TWO MORE DAYS BEFORE THE FIRST RAINS.
"I COULD OFTEN TELL WHERE THE GOOD HUNTING GROUNDS WERE.
"AND EVEN, ONCE IN A WHILE, WHICH OF OUR WARRIORS WOULD BE KILLED OR INJURED ON THE HUNT.
STRENIC WILL DIE TOMORROW AND YODUN WILL BREAK A FOOT IN THE CHASE.
"THESE WERE INVALUABLE ASSETS TO THE TRIBE, AND I WAS MOVED INTO THE SHAMAN'S LODGE.
A GREAT STORM IS COMING.
"IN THIS LIFE OF PRIVILEGE, OTHERS GATHERED MY SHARE OF THE FOOD, WHILE I WORKED MY CRAFT.
"I WAS LOVELY, AND EVERY-ONE COULD SEE IT."

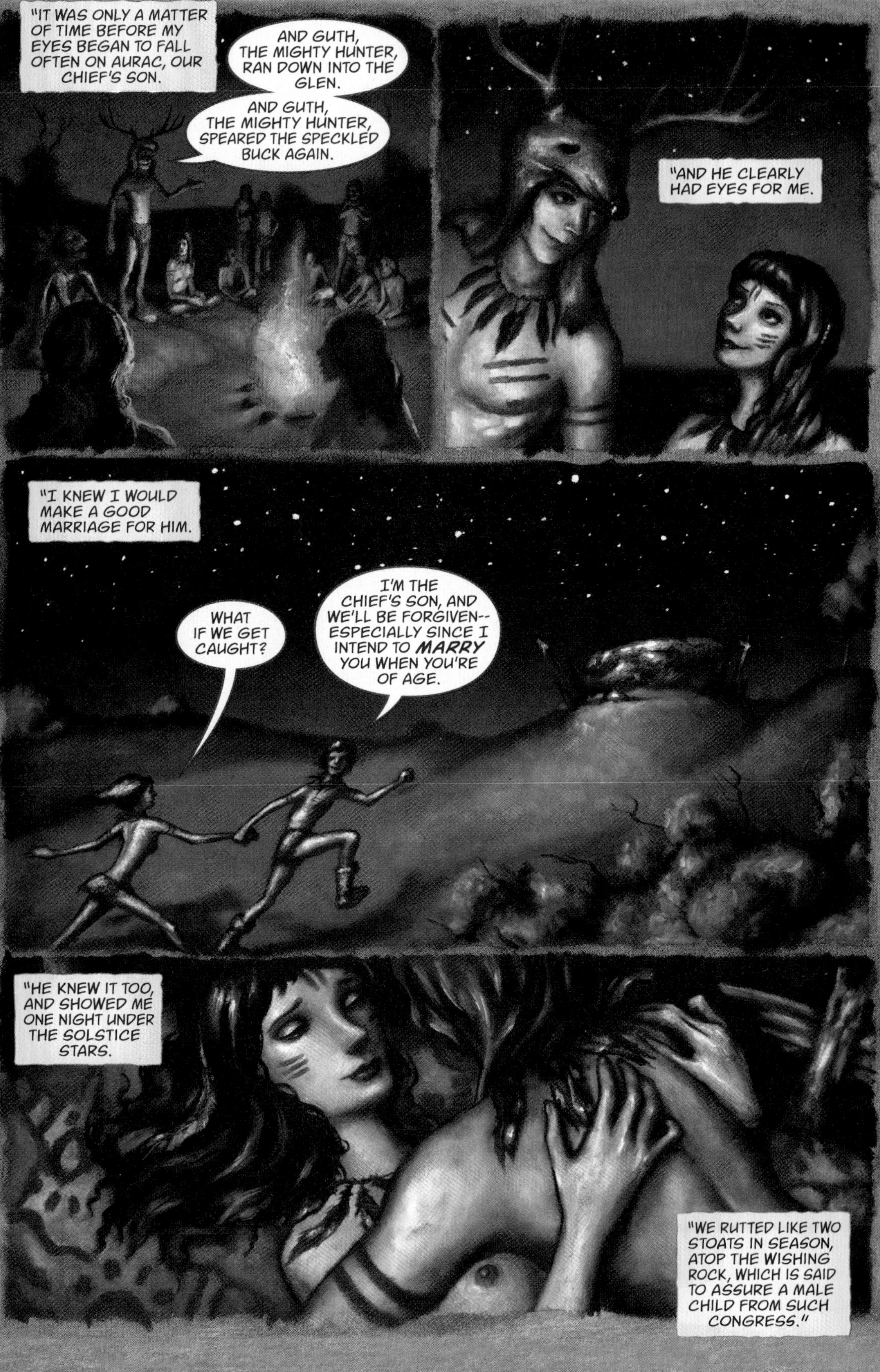
"IT WAS ONLY A MATTER OF TIME BEFORE MY EYES BEGAN TO FALL OFTEN ON AURAC, OUR CHIEF'S SON.
AND GUTH, THE MIGHTY HUNTER, RAN DOWN INTO THE GLEN.
AND GUTH, THE MIGHTY HUNTER, SPEARED THE SPECKLED BUCK AGAIN.
"AND HE CLEARLY HAD EYES FOR ME.
"I KNEW I WOULD MAKE A GOOD MARRIAGE FOR HIM.
WHAT IF WE GET CAUGHT?
I'M THE CHIEF'S SON, AND WE'LL BE FORGIVEN-- ESPECIALLY SINCE I INTEND TO MARRY YOU WHEN YOU'RE OF AGE.
"HE KNEW IT TOO, AND SHOWED ME ONE NIGHT UNDER THE SOLSTICE STARS.
"WE RUTTED LIKE TWO STOATS IN SEASON, ATOP THE WISHING ROCK, WHICH IS SAID TO ASSURE A MALE CHILD FROM SUCH CONGRESS."

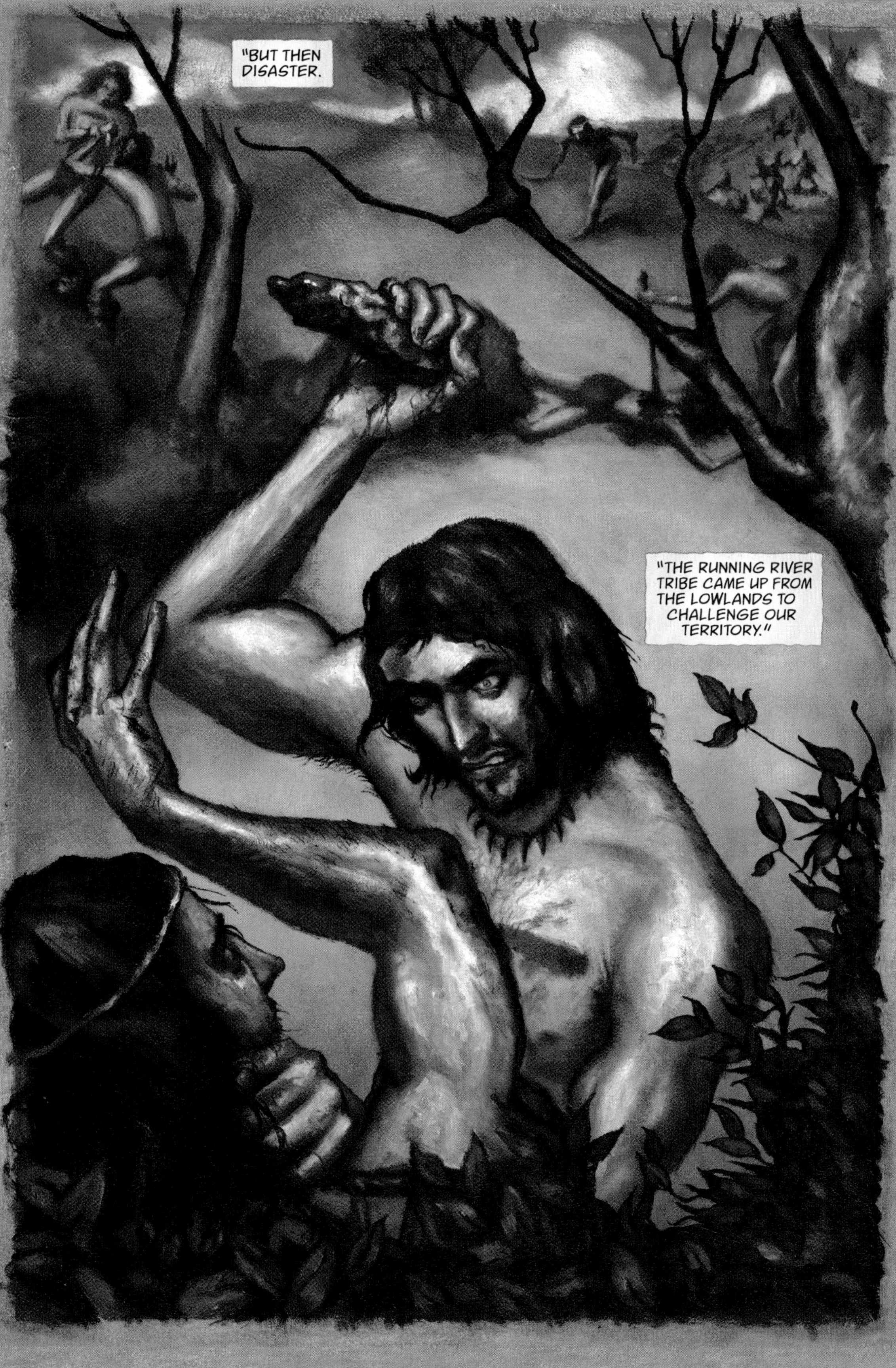
"BUT THEN DISASTER.
"THE RUNNING RIVER TRIBE CAME UP FROM THE LOWLANDS TO CHALLENGE OUR TERRITORY."

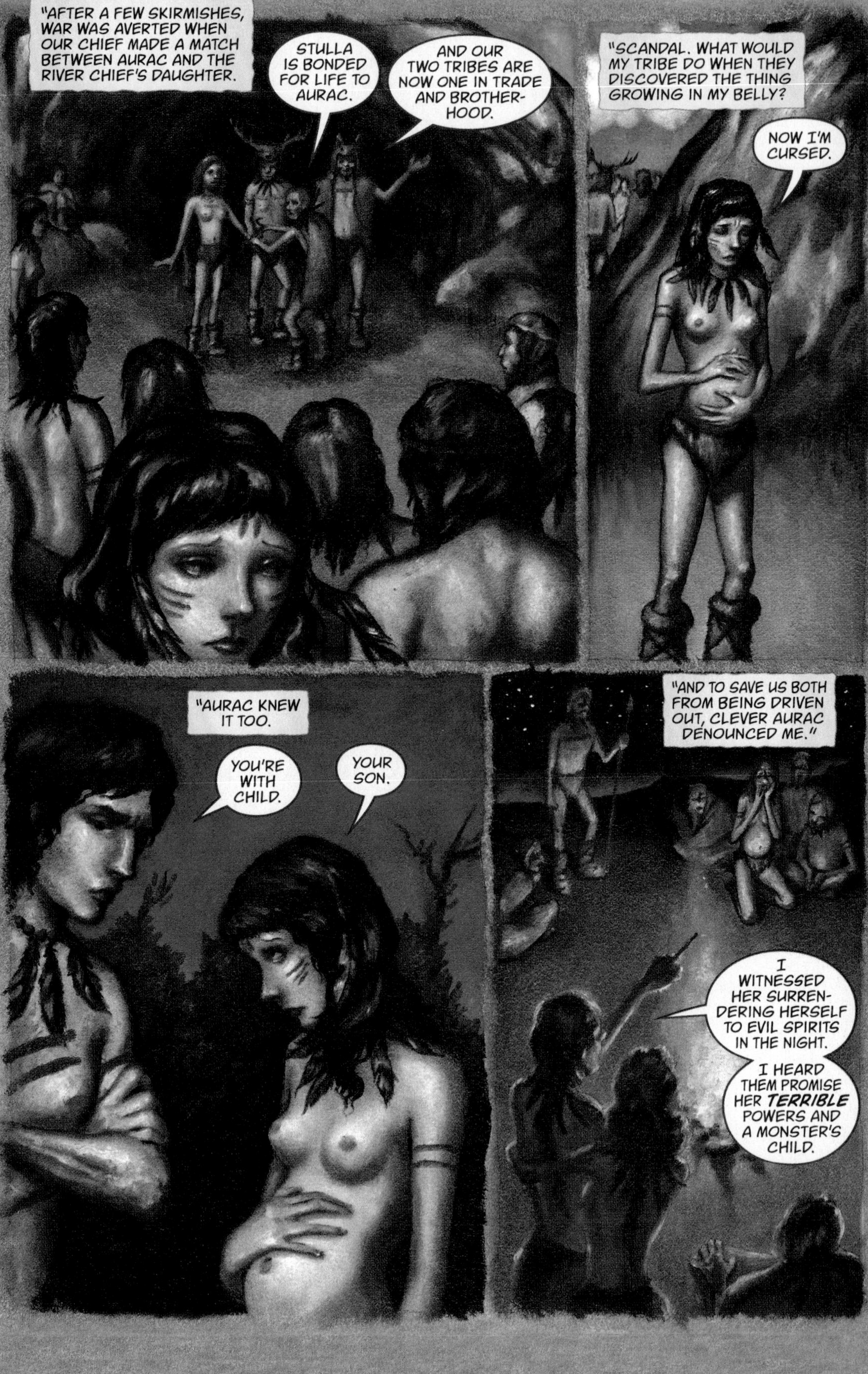
"AFTER A FEW SKIRMISHES, WAR WAS AVERTED WHEN OUR CHIEF MADE A MATCH BETWEEN AURAC AND THE RIVER CHIEF'S DAUGHTER.
STULLA IS BONDED FOR LIFE TO AURAC.
AND OUR TWO TRIBES ARE NOW ONE IN TRADE AND BROTHER-HOOD.
"SCANDAL. WHAT WOULD MY TRIBE DO WHEN THEY DISCOVERED THE THING GROWING IN MY BELLY?
NOW I'M CURSED.
"AURAC KNEW IT TOO.
YOU'RE WITH CHILD.
YOUR SON.
"AND TO SAVE US BOTH FROM BEING DRIVEN OUT, CLEVER AURAC DENOUNCED ME."
I WITNESSED HER SURREN-DERING HERSELF TO EVIL SPIRITS IN THE NIGHT.
I HEARD THEM PROMISE HER *TERRIBLE* POWERS AND A MONSTER'S CHILD.

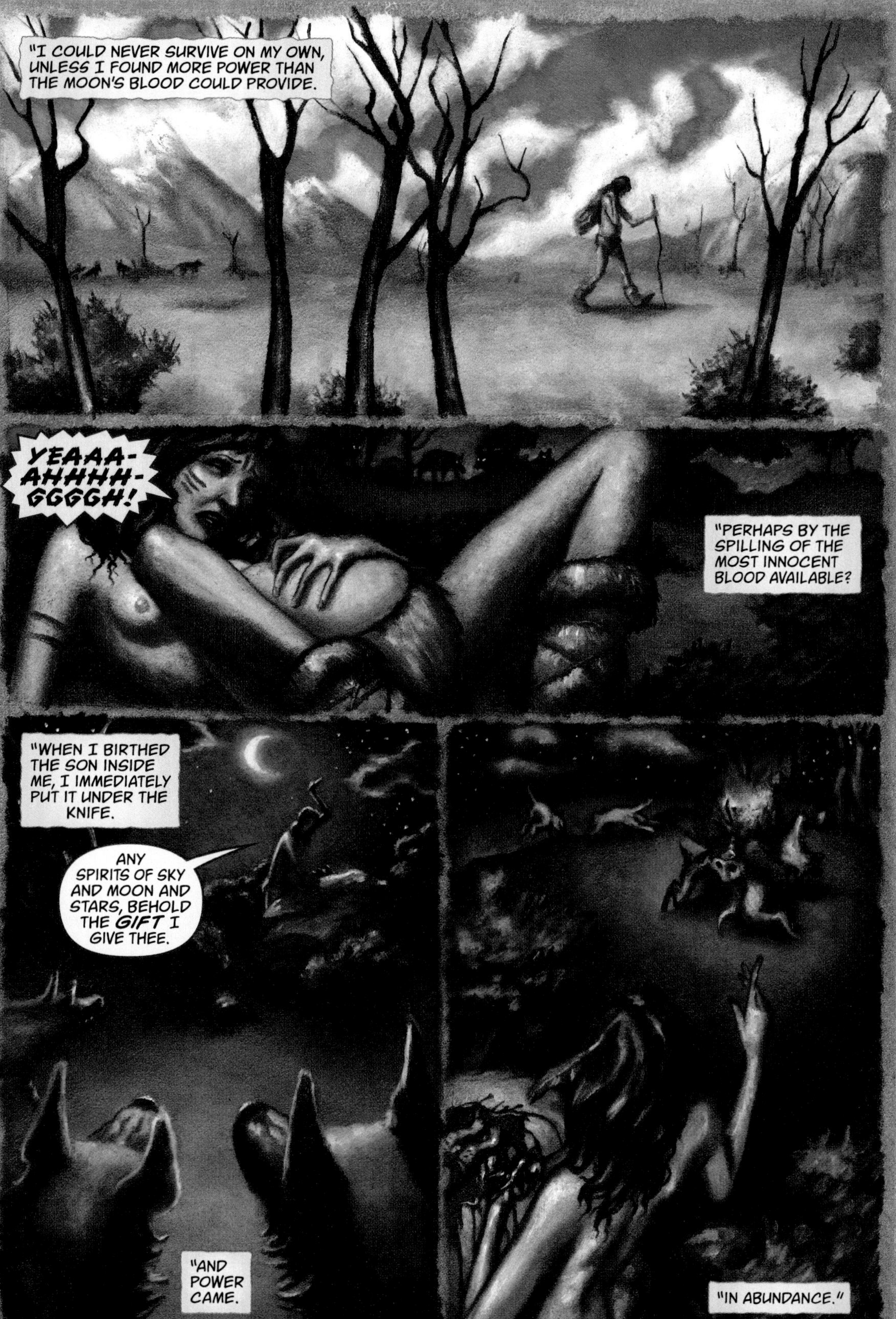
"I COULD NEVER SURVIVE ON MY OWN, UNLESS I FOUND MORE POWER THAN THE MOON'S BLOOD COULD PROVIDE.
YEAAAA-AHHHH-GGGGH!
"PERHAPS BY THE SPILLING OF THE MOST INNOCENT BLOOD AVAILABLE?
"WHEN I BIRTHED THE SON INSIDE ME, I IMMEDIATELY PUT IT UNDER THE KNIFE.
ANY SPIRITS OF SKY AND MOON AND STARS, BEHOLD THE GIFT I GIVE THEE.
"AND POWER CAME.
"IN ABUNDANCE."

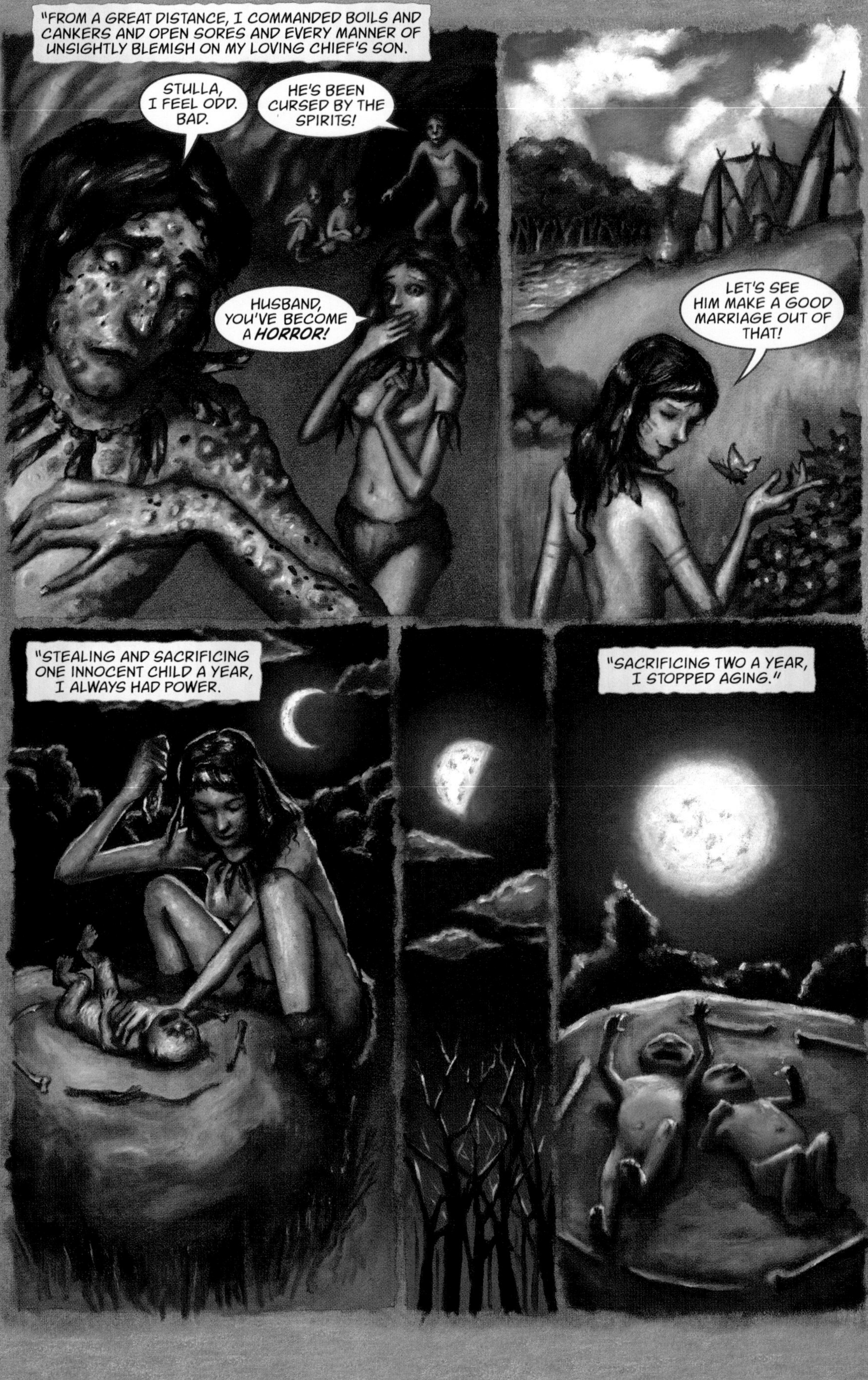
"FROM A GREAT DISTANCE, I COMMANDED BOILS AND CANKERS AND OPEN SORES AND EVERY MANNER OF UNSIGHTLY BLEMISH ON MY LOVING CHIEF'S SON.
STULLA, I FEEL ODD. BAD.
HE'S BEEN CURSED BY THE SPIRITS!
HUSBAND, YOU'VE BECOME A **HORROR!**
LET'S SEE HIM MAKE A GOOD MARRIAGE OUT OF THAT!
"STEALING AND SACRIFICING ONE INNOCENT CHILD A YEAR, I ALWAYS HAD POWER.
"SACRIFICING TWO A YEAR, I STOPPED AGING."

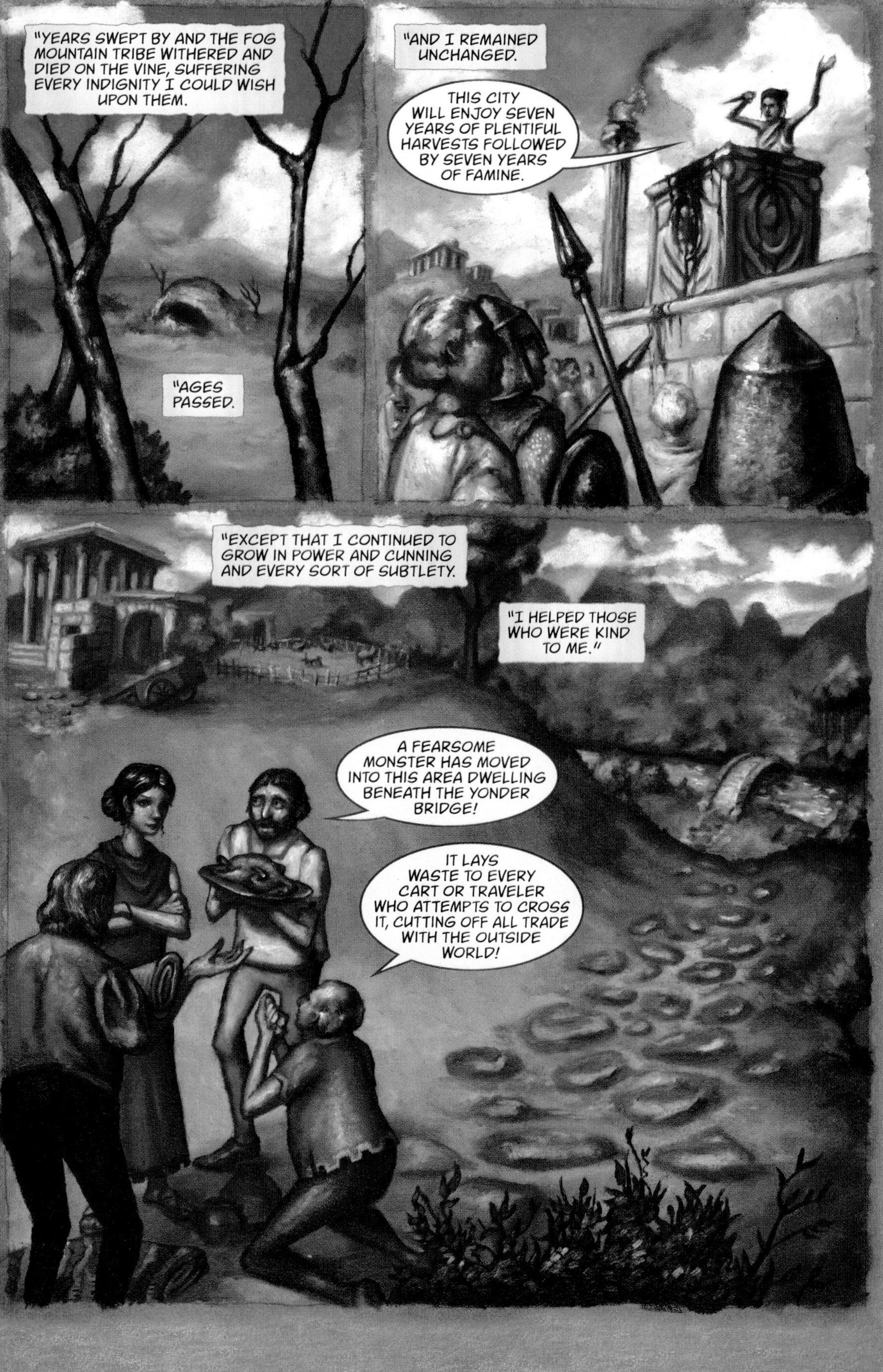
"YEARS SWEPT BY AND THE FOG MOUNTAIN TRIBE WITHERED AND DIED ON THE VINE, SUFFERING EVERY INDIGNITY I COULD WISH UPON THEM.
"AGES PASSED.
"AND I REMAINED UNCHANGED.
THIS CITY WILL ENJOY SEVEN YEARS OF PLENTIFUL HARVESTS FOLLOWED BY SEVEN YEARS OF FAMINE.
"EXCEPT THAT I CONTINUED TO GROW IN POWER AND CUNNING AND EVERY SORT OF SUBTLETY.
"I HELPED THOSE WHO WERE KIND TO ME."
A FEARSOME MONSTER HAS MOVED INTO THIS AREA DWELLING BENEATH THE YONDER BRIDGE!
IT LAYS WASTE TO EVERY CART OR TRAVELER WHO ATTEMPTS TO CROSS IT, CUTTING OFF ALL TRADE WITH THE OUTSIDE WORLD!

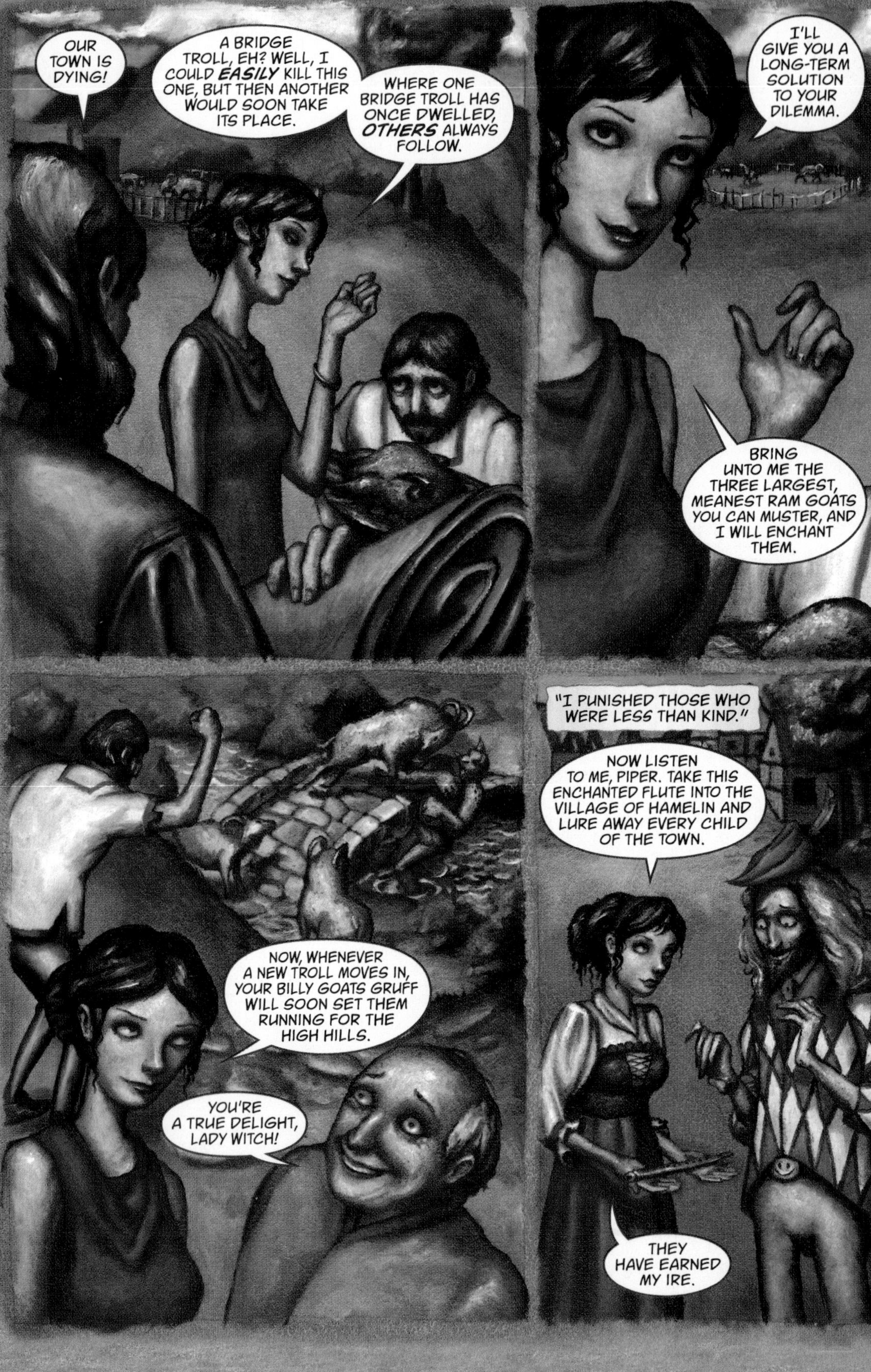
OUR TOWN IS DYING!
A BRIDGE TROLL, EH? WELL, I COULD EASILY KILL THIS ONE, BUT THEN ANOTHER WOULD SOON TAKE ITS PLACE.
WHERE ONE BRIDGE TROLL HAS ONCE DWELLED, OTHERS ALWAYS FOLLOW.
I'LL GIVE YOU A LONG-TERM SOLUTION TO YOUR DILEMMA.
BRING UNTO ME THE THREE LARGEST, MEANEST RAM GOATS YOU CAN MUSTER, AND I WILL ENCHANT THEM.
NOW, WHENEVER A NEW TROLL MOVES IN, YOUR BILLY GOATS GRUFF WILL SOON SET THEM RUNNING FOR THE HIGH HILLS.
YOU'RE A TRUE DELIGHT, LADY WITCH!
"I PUNISHED THOSE WHO WERE LESS THAN KIND."
NOW LISTEN TO ME, PIPER. TAKE THIS ENCHANTED FLUTE INTO THE VILLAGE OF HAMELIN AND LURE AWAY EVERY CHILD OF THE TOWN.
THEY HAVE EARNED MY IRE.

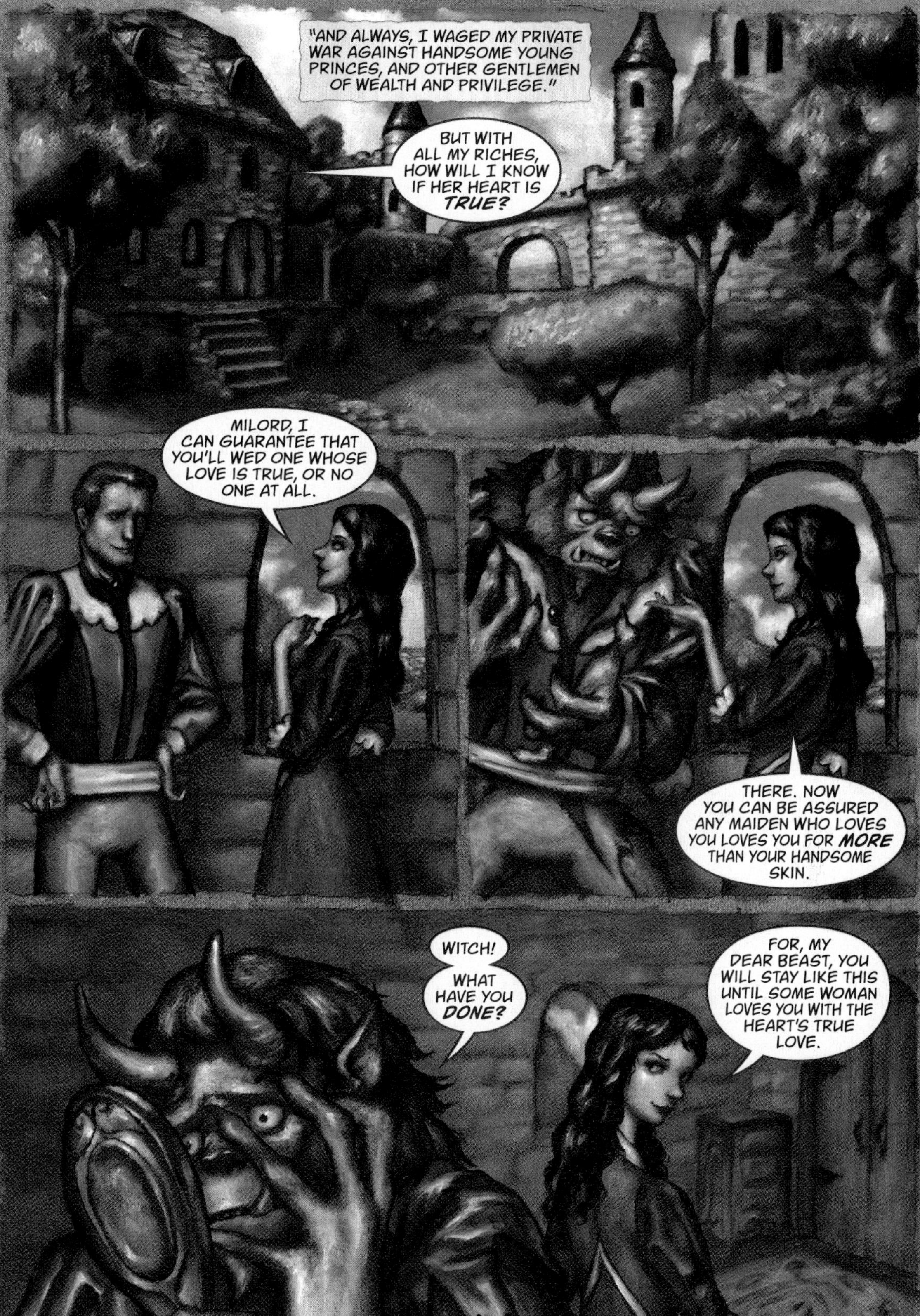
"AND ALWAYS, I WAGED MY PRIVATE WAR AGAINST HANDSOME YOUNG PRINCES, AND OTHER GENTLEMEN OF WEALTH AND PRIVILEGE."
BUT WITH ALL MY RICHES, HOW WILL I KNOW IF HER HEART IS *TRUE?*
MILORD, I CAN GUARANTEE THAT YOU'LL WED ONE WHOSE LOVE IS TRUE, OR NO ONE AT ALL.
THERE. NOW YOU CAN BE ASSURED ANY MAIDEN WHO LOVES YOU LOVES YOU FOR *MORE* THAN YOUR HANDSOME SKIN.
WITCH!
WHAT HAVE YOU *DONE?*
FOR, MY DEAR BEAST, YOU WILL STAY LIKE THIS UNTIL SOME WOMAN LOVES YOU WITH THE HEART'S TRUE LOVE.

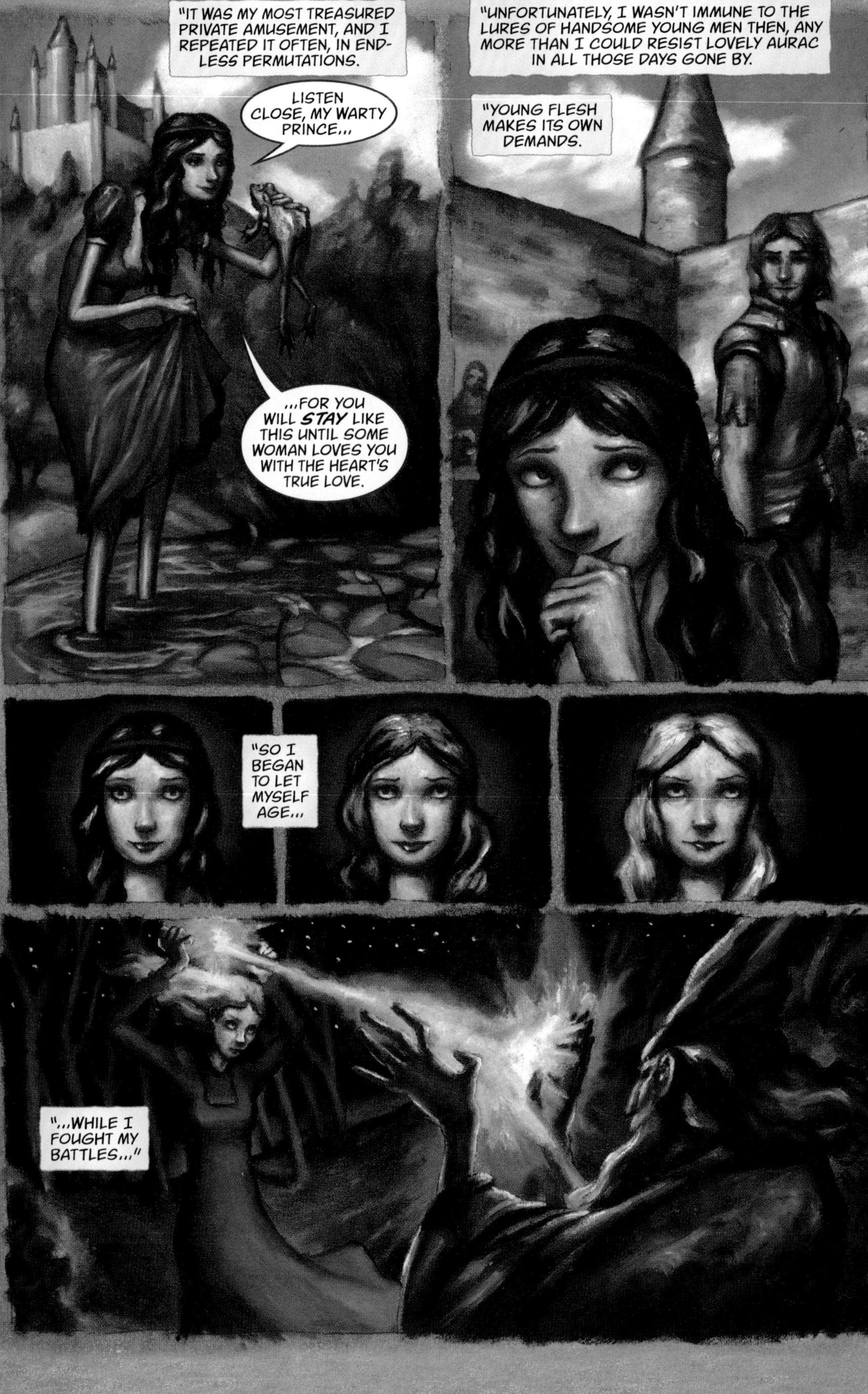
"IT WAS MY MOST TREASURED PRIVATE AMUSEMENT, AND I REPEATED IT OFTEN, IN END-LESS PERMUTATIONS.
LISTEN CLOSE, MY WARTY PRINCE...
...FOR YOU WILL STAY LIKE THIS UNTIL SOME WOMAN LOVES YOU WITH THE HEART'S TRUE LOVE.
"UNFORTUNATELY, I WASN'T IMMUNE TO THE LURES OF HANDSOME YOUNG MEN THEN, ANY MORE THAN I COULD RESIST LOVELY AURAC IN ALL THOSE DAYS GONE BY.
"YOUNG FLESH MAKES ITS OWN DEMANDS.
"SO I BEGAN TO LET MYSELF AGE...
"...WHILE I FOUGHT MY BATTLES..."

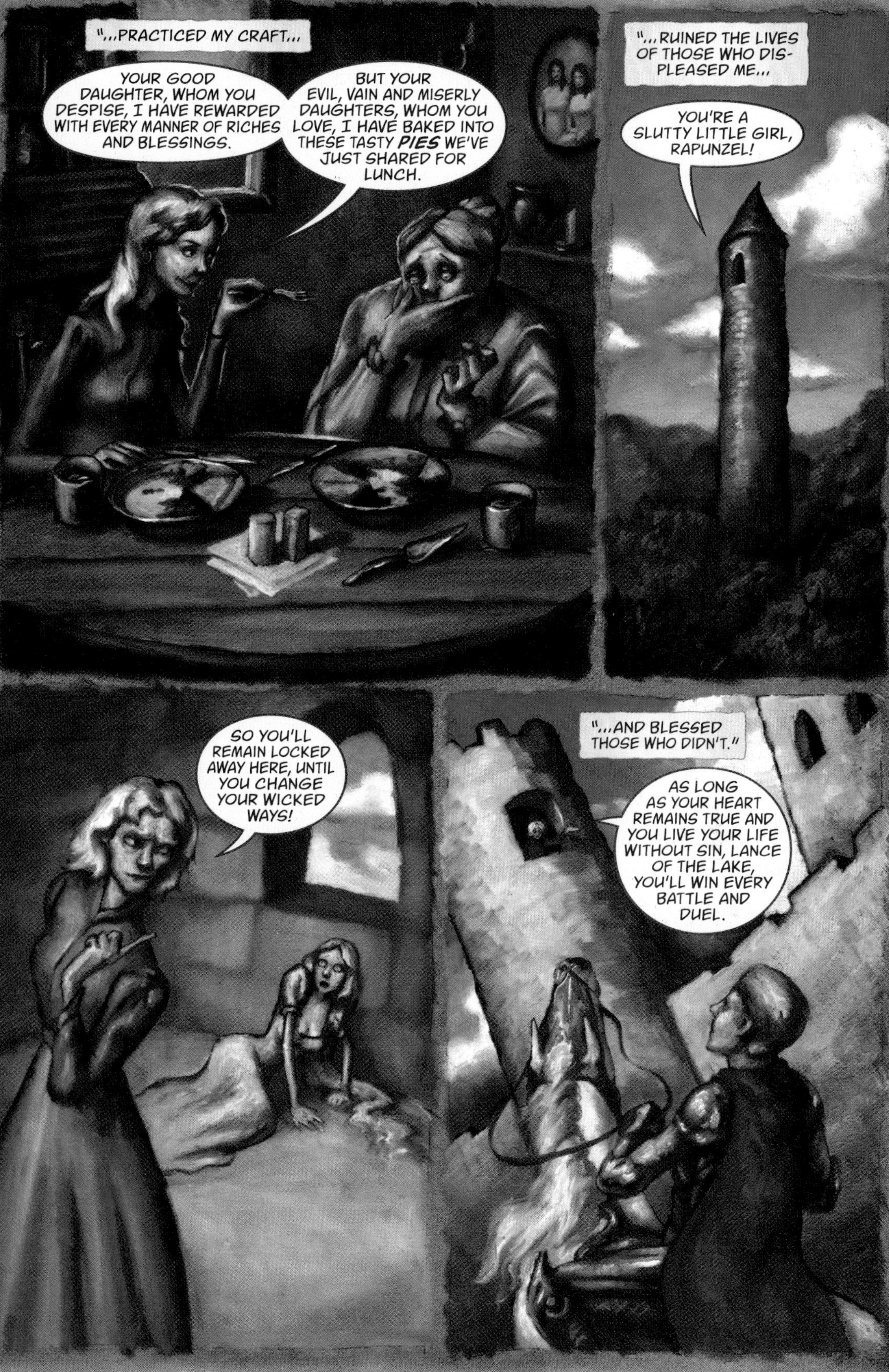
"...PRACTICED MY CRAFT...
YOUR GOOD DAUGHTER, WHOM YOU DESPISE, I HAVE REWARDED WITH EVERY MANNER OF RICHES AND BLESSINGS.
BUT YOUR EVIL, VAIN AND MISERLY DAUGHTERS, WHOM YOU LOVE, I HAVE BAKED INTO THESE TASTY PIES WE'VE JUST SHARED FOR LUNCH.
"...RUINED THE LIVES OF THOSE WHO DISPLEASED ME...
YOU'RE A SLUTTY LITTLE GIRL, RAPUNZEL!
SO YOU'LL REMAIN LOCKED AWAY HERE, UNTIL YOU CHANGE YOUR WICKED WAYS!
"...AND BLESSED THOSE WHO DIDN'T."
AS LONG AS YOUR HEART REMAINS TRUE AND YOU LIVE YOUR LIFE WITHOUT SIN, LANCE OF THE LAKE, YOU'LL WIN EVERY BATTLE AND DUEL.

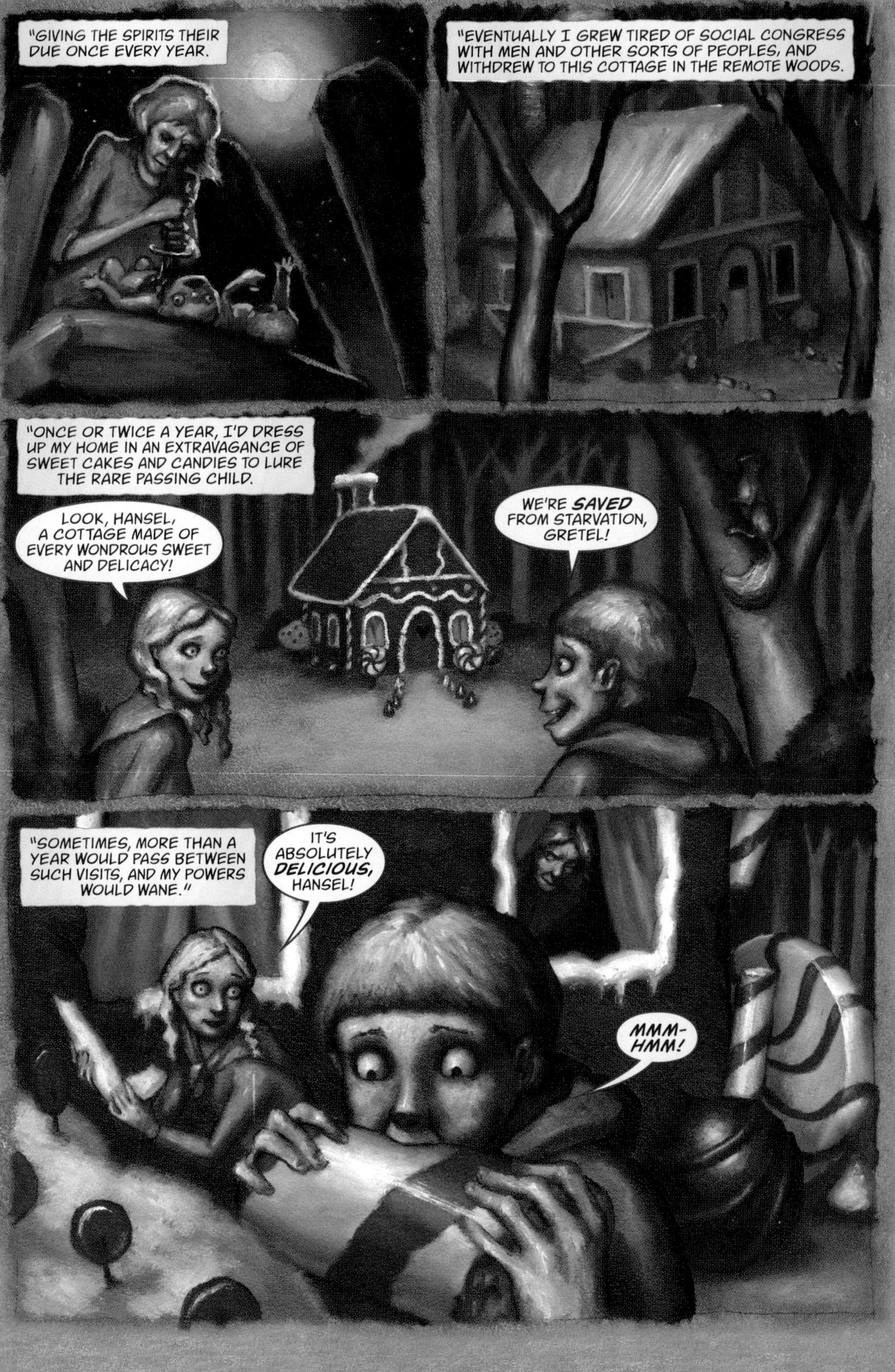
"GIVING THE SPIRITS THEIR DUE ONCE EVERY YEAR.
"EVENTUALLY I GREW TIRED OF SOCIAL CONGRESS WITH MEN AND OTHER SORTS OF PEOPLES, AND WITHDREW TO THIS COTTAGE IN THE REMOTE WOODS.
"ONCE OR TWICE A YEAR, I'D DRESS UP MY HOME IN AN EXTRAVAGANCE OF SWEET CAKES AND CANDIES TO LURE THE RARE PASSING CHILD.
LOOK, HANSEL, A COTTAGE MADE OF EVERY WONDROUS SWEET AND DELICACY!
WE'RE SAVED FROM STARVATION, GRETEL!
"SOMETIMES, MORE THAN A YEAR WOULD PASS BETWEEN SUCH VISITS, AND MY POWERS WOULD WANE."
IT'S ABSOLUTELY DELICIOUS, HANSEL!
MMM-HMM!

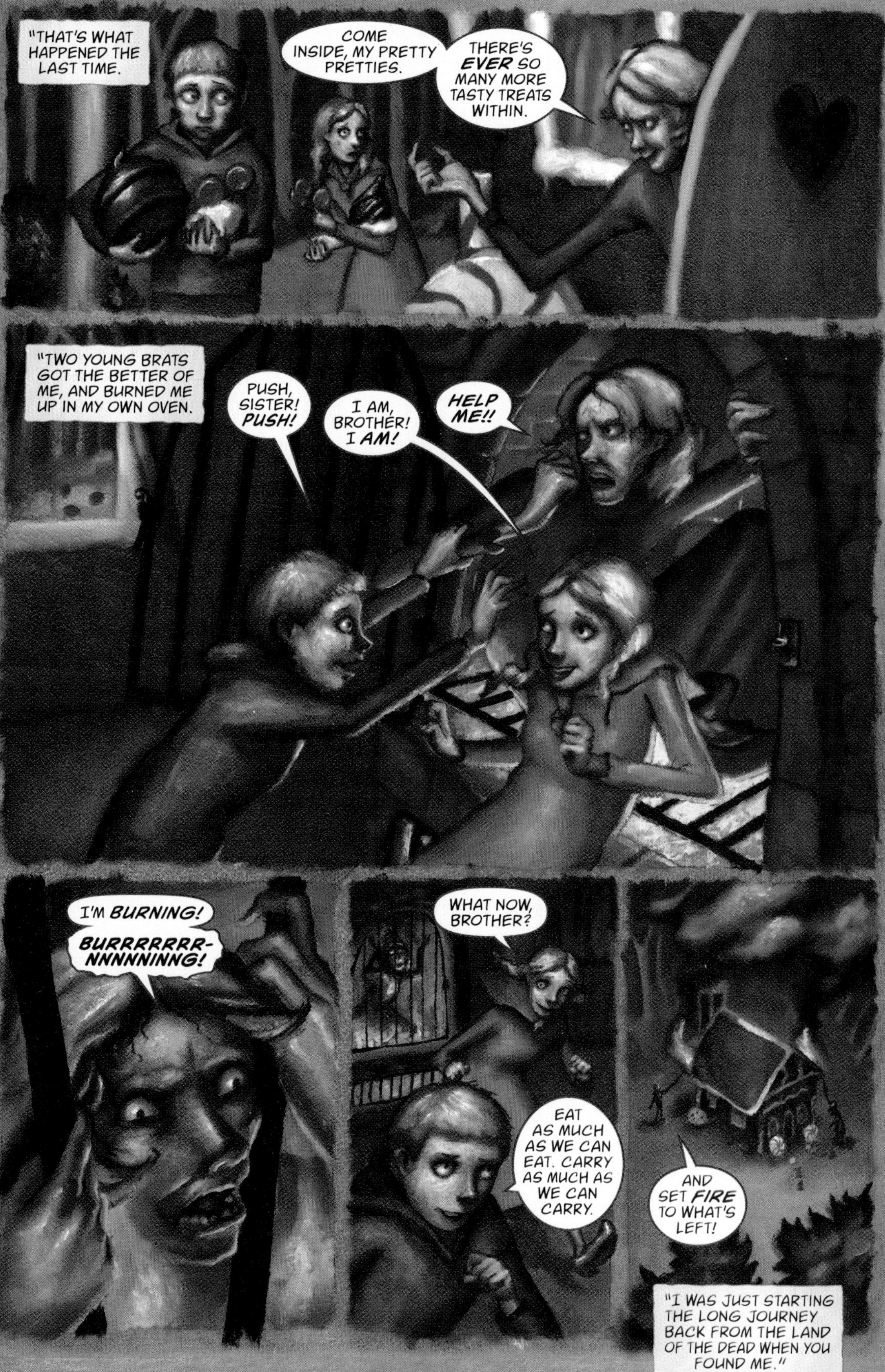
"THAT'S WHAT HAPPENED THE LAST TIME.
COME INSIDE, MY PRETTY PRETTIES.
THERE'S EVER SO MANY MORE TASTY TREATS WITHIN.
"TWO YOUNG BRATS GOT THE BETTER OF ME, AND BURNED ME UP IN MY OWN OVEN.
PUSH, SISTER! PUSH!
I AM, BROTHER! I AM!
HELP ME!!
I'M BURNING!
BURRRRRRR-NNNNNINNG!
WHAT NOW, BROTHER?
EAT AS MUCH AS WE CAN EAT. CARRY AS MUCH AS WE CAN CARRY.
AND SET FIRE TO WHAT'S LEFT!
"I WAS JUST STARTING THE LONG JOURNEY BACK FROM THE LAND OF THE DEAD WHEN YOU FOUND ME."

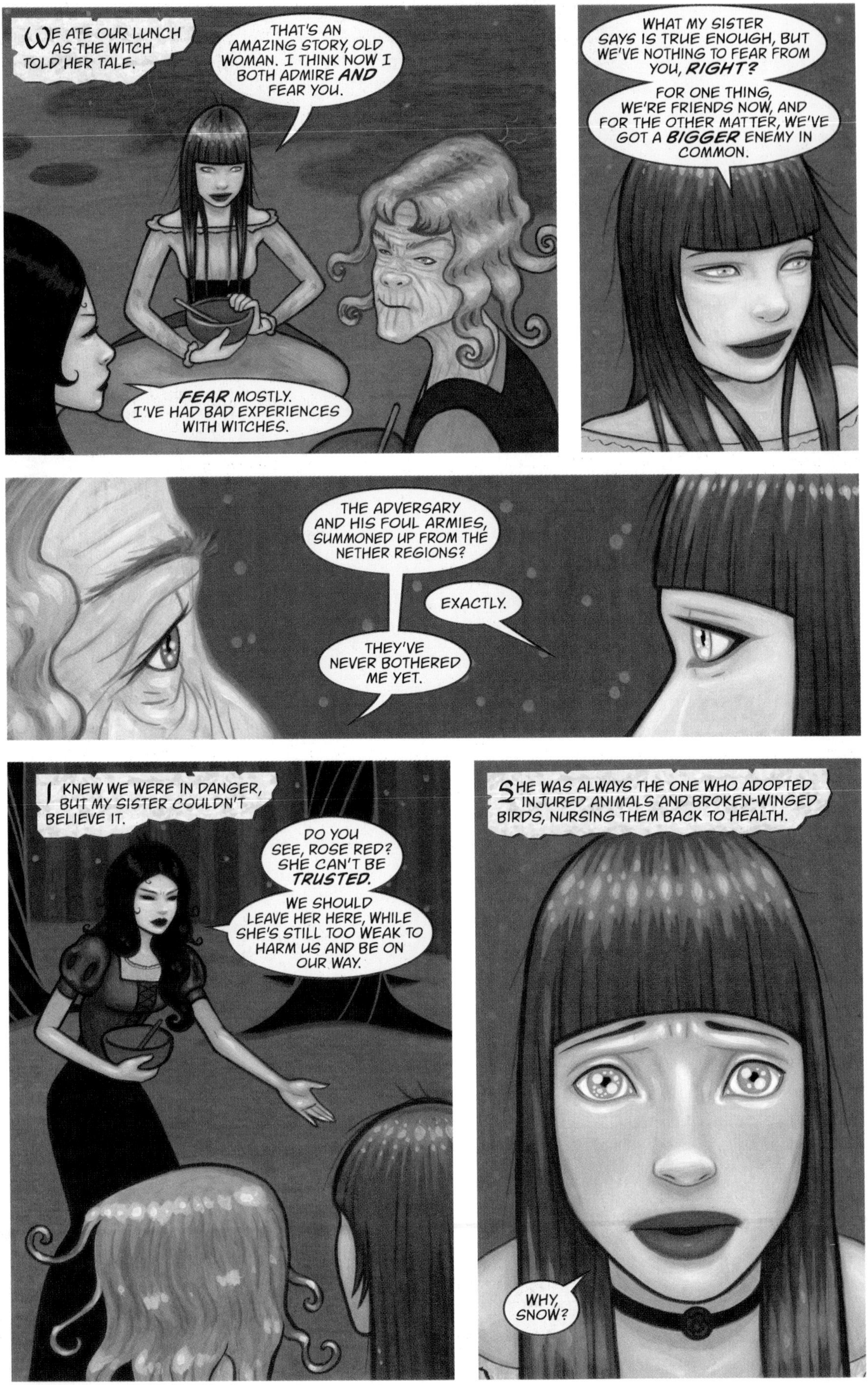
WE ATE OUR LUNCH AS THE WITCH TOLD HER TALE.
THAT'S AN AMAZING STORY, OLD WOMAN. I THINK NOW I BOTH ADMIRE AND FEAR YOU.
FEAR MOSTLY. I'VE HAD BAD EXPERIENCES WITH WITCHES.
WHAT MY SISTER SAYS IS TRUE ENOUGH, BUT WE'VE NOTHING TO FEAR FROM YOU, RIGHT?
FOR ONE THING, WE'RE FRIENDS NOW, AND FOR THE OTHER MATTER, WE'VE GOT A BIGGER ENEMY IN COMMON.
THE ADVERSARY AND HIS FOUL ARMIES, SUMMONED UP FROM THE NETHER REGIONS?
EXACTLY.
THEY'VE NEVER BOTHERED ME YET.
I KNEW WE WERE IN DANGER, BUT MY SISTER COULDN'T BELIEVE IT.
DO YOU SEE, ROSE RED? SHE CAN'T BE TRUSTED.
WE SHOULD LEAVE HER HERE, WHILE SHE'S STILL TOO WEAK TO HARM US AND BE ON OUR WAY.
SHE WAS ALWAYS THE ONE WHO ADOPTED INJURED ANIMALS AND BROKEN-WINGED BIRDS, NURSING THEM BACK TO HEALTH.
WHY, SNOW?

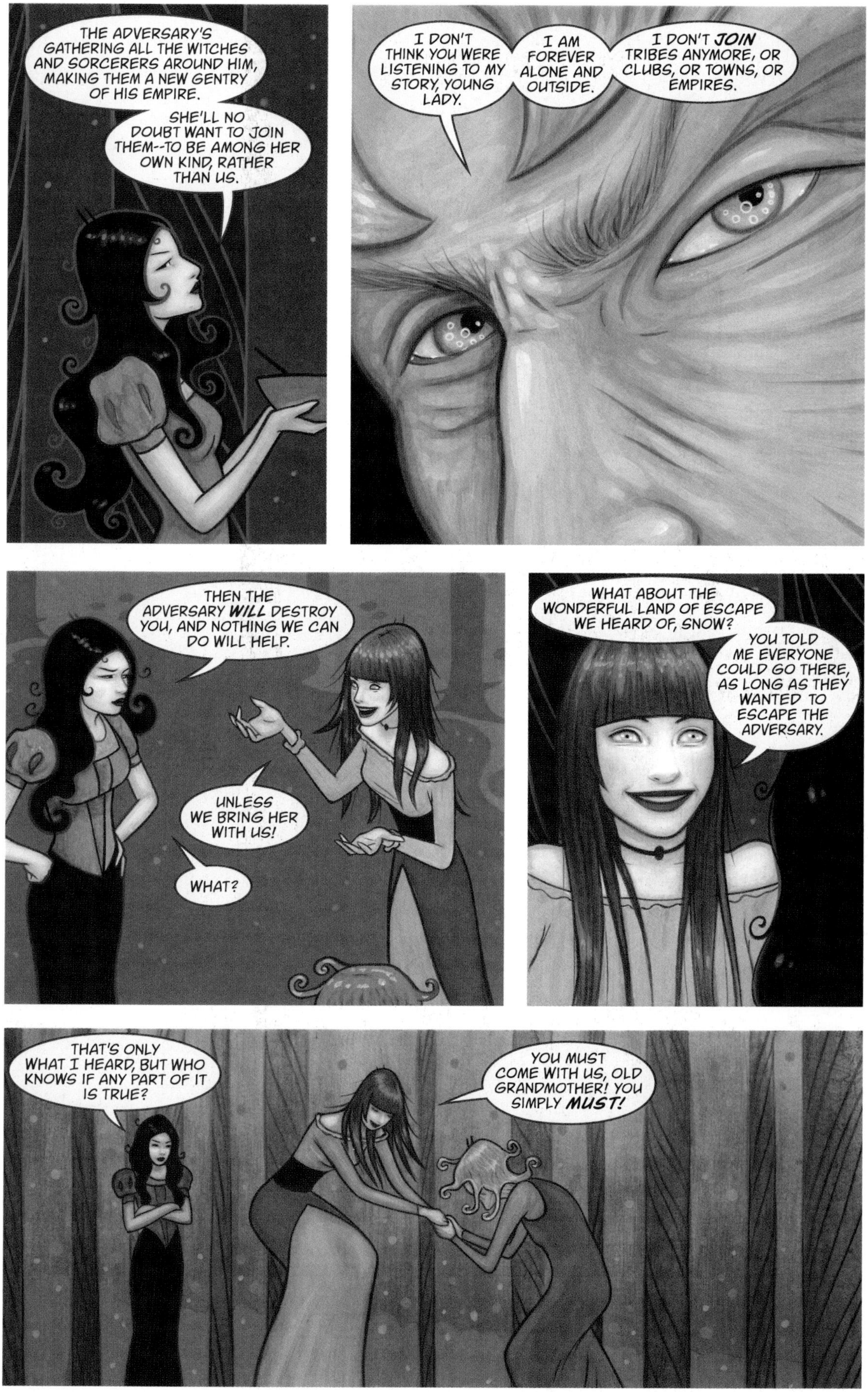
THE ADVERSARY'S GATHERING ALL THE WITCHES AND SORCERERS AROUND HIM, MAKING THEM A NEW GENTRY OF HIS EMPIRE.
SHE'LL NO DOUBT WANT TO JOIN THEM--TO BE AMONG HER OWN KIND, RATHER THAN US.
I DON'T THINK YOU WERE LISTENING TO MY STORY, YOUNG LADY.
I AM FOREVER ALONE AND OUTSIDE.
I DON'T JOIN TRIBES ANYMORE, OR CLUBS, OR TOWNS, OR EMPIRES.
THEN THE ADVERSARY WILL DESTROY YOU, AND NOTHING WE CAN DO WILL HELP.
UNLESS WE BRING HER WITH US!
WHAT?
WHAT ABOUT THE WONDERFUL LAND OF ESCAPE WE HEARD OF, SNOW?
YOU TOLD ME EVERYONE COULD GO THERE, AS LONG AS THEY WANTED TO ESCAPE THE ADVERSARY.
THAT'S ONLY WHAT I HEARD, BUT WHO KNOWS IF ANY PART OF IT IS TRUE?
YOU MUST COME WITH US, OLD GRANDMOTHER! YOU SIMPLY MUST!

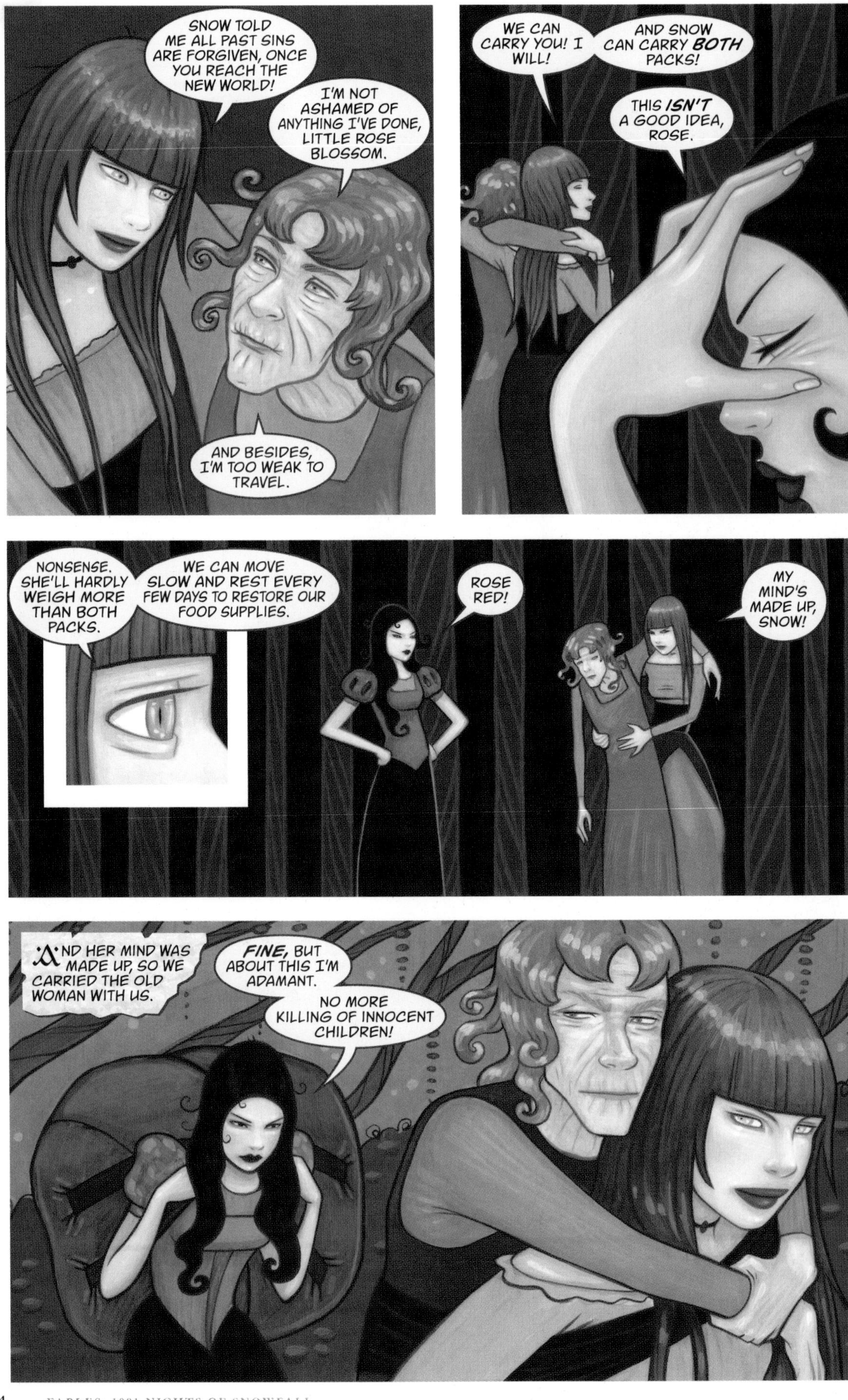
SNOW TOLD ME ALL PAST SINS ARE FORGIVEN, ONCE YOU REACH THE NEW WORLD!
I'M NOT ASHAMED OF ANYTHING I'VE DONE, LITTLE ROSE BLOSSOM.
AND BESIDES, I'M TOO WEAK TO TRAVEL.
WE CAN CARRY YOU! I WILL!
AND SNOW CAN CARRY BOTH PACKS!
THIS ISN'T A GOOD IDEA, ROSE.
NONSENSE. SHE'LL HARDLY WEIGH MORE THAN BOTH PACKS.
WE CAN MOVE SLOW AND REST EVERY FEW DAYS TO RESTORE OUR FOOD SUPPLIES.
ROSE RED!
MY MIND'S MADE UP, SNOW!
AND HER MIND WAS MADE UP, SO WE CARRIED THE OLD WOMAN WITH US.
FINE, BUT ABOUT THIS I'M ADAMANT.
NO MORE KILLING OF INNOCENT CHILDREN!

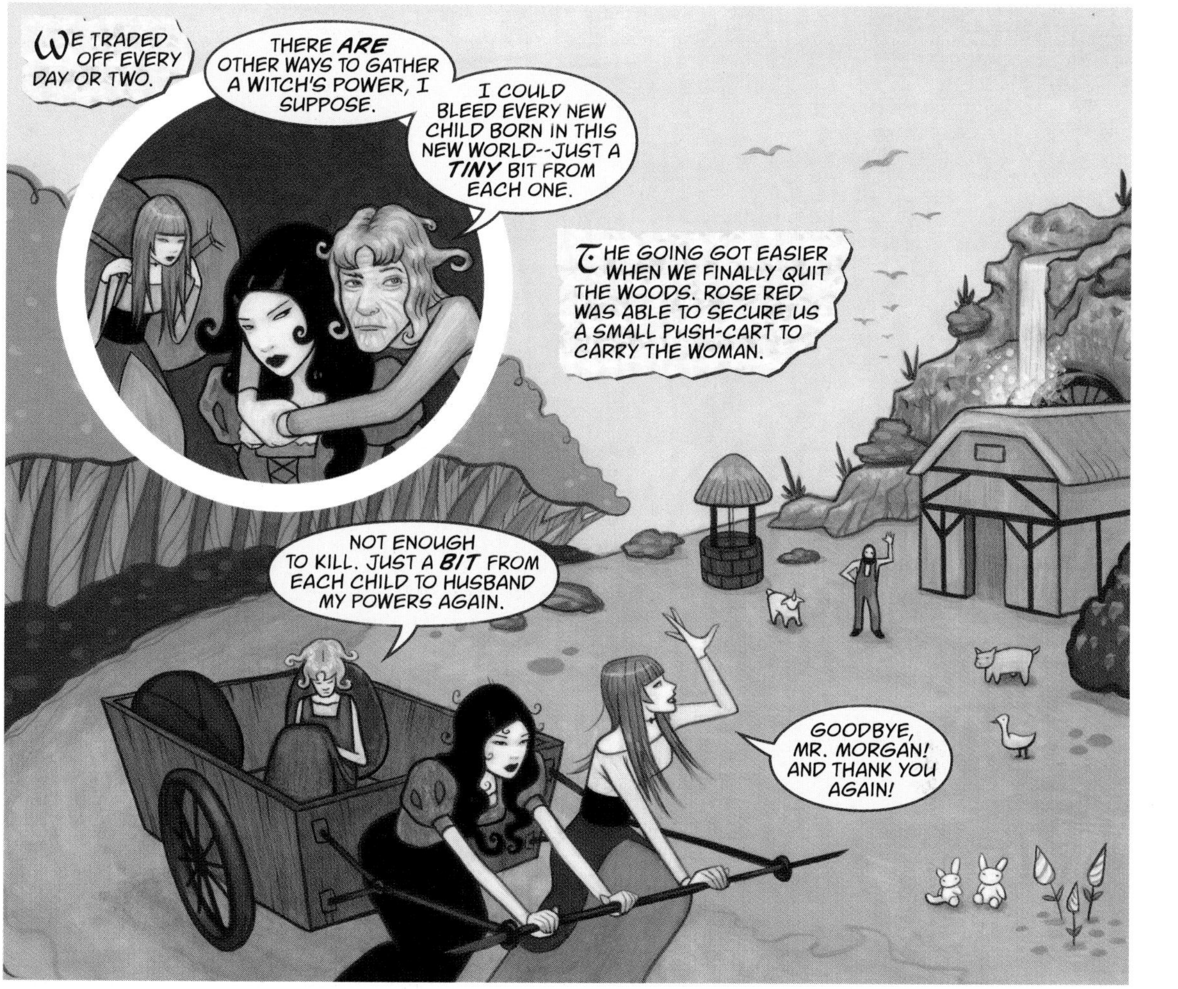
WE TRADED OFF EVERY DAY OR TWO.
THERE ARE OTHER WAYS TO GATHER A WITCH'S POWER, I SUPPOSE.
I COULD BLEED EVERY NEW CHILD BORN IN THIS NEW WORLD--JUST A TINY BIT FROM EACH ONE.
THE GOING GOT EASIER WHEN WE FINALLY QUIT THE WOODS. ROSE RED WAS ABLE TO SECURE US A SMALL PUSH-CART TO CARRY THE WOMAN.
NOT ENOUGH TO KILL. JUST A BIT FROM EACH CHILD TO HUSBAND MY POWERS AGAIN.
GOODBYE, MR. MORGAN! AND THANK YOU AGAIN!

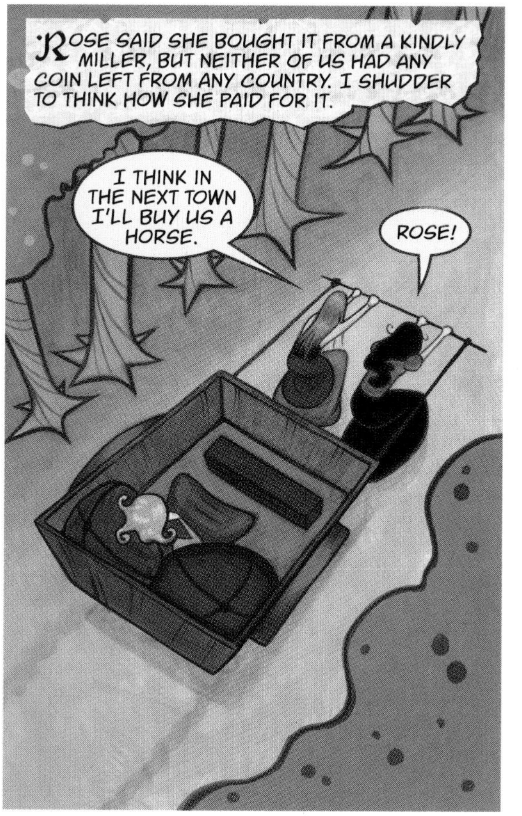
ROSE SAID SHE BOUGHT IT FROM A KINDLY MILLER, BUT NEITHER OF US HAD ANY COIN LEFT FROM ANY COUNTRY. I SHUDDER TO THINK HOW SHE PAID FOR IT.
I THINK IN THE NEXT TOWN I'LL BUY US A HORSE.
ROSE!

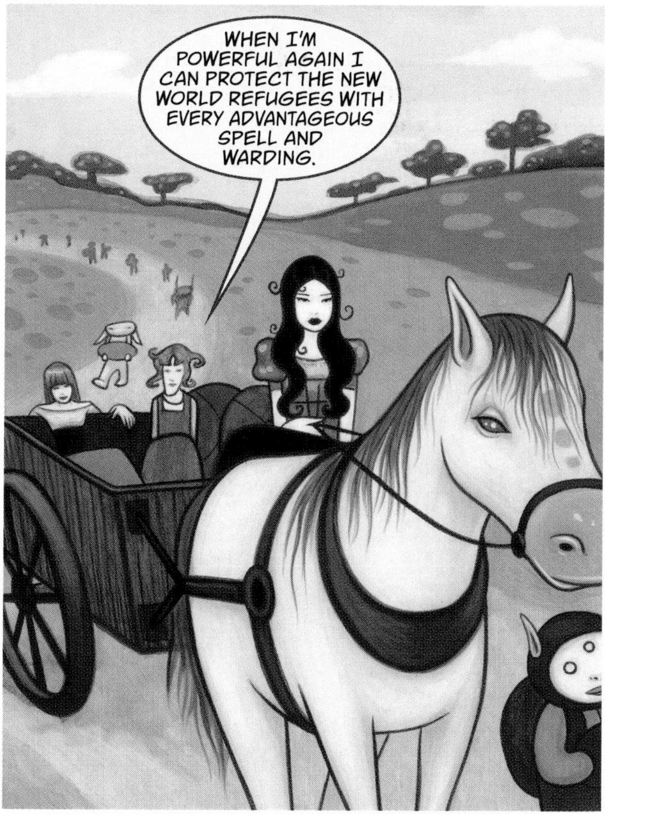
WHEN I'M POWERFUL AGAIN I CAN PROTECT THE NEW WORLD REFUGEES WITH EVERY ADVANTAGEOUS SPELL AND WARDING.

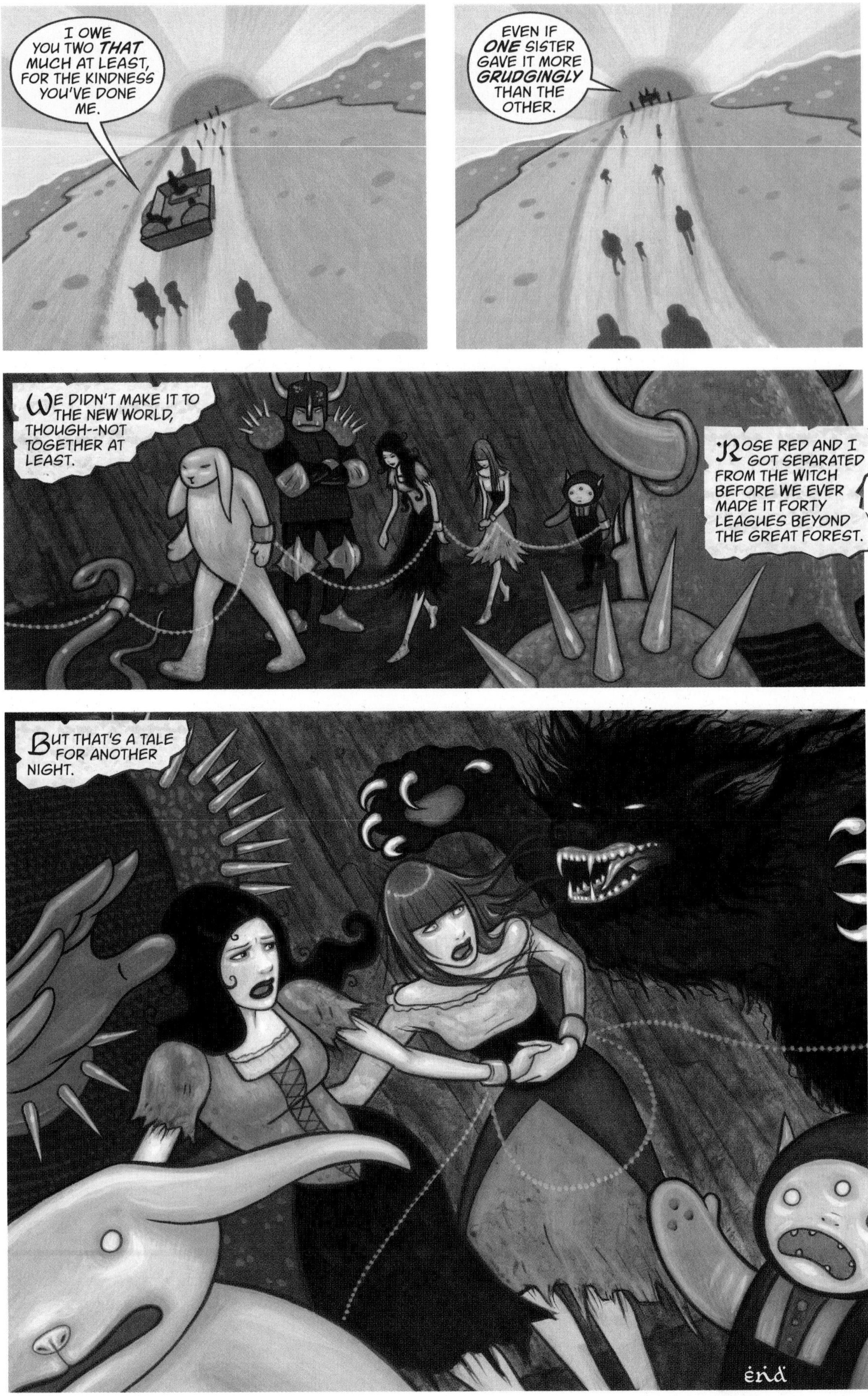
I OWE YOU TWO THAT MUCH AT LEAST, FOR THE KINDNESS YOU'VE DONE ME.
EVEN IF ONE SISTER GAVE IT MORE GRUDGINGLY THAN THE OTHER.
WE DIDN'T MAKE IT TO THE NEW WORLD, THOUGH--NOT TOGETHER AT LEAST.
ROSE RED AND I GOT SEPARATED FROM THE WITCH BEFORE WE EVER MADE IT FORTY LEAGUES BEYOND THE GREAT FOREST.
BUT THAT'S A TALE FOR ANOTHER NIGHT.
erid

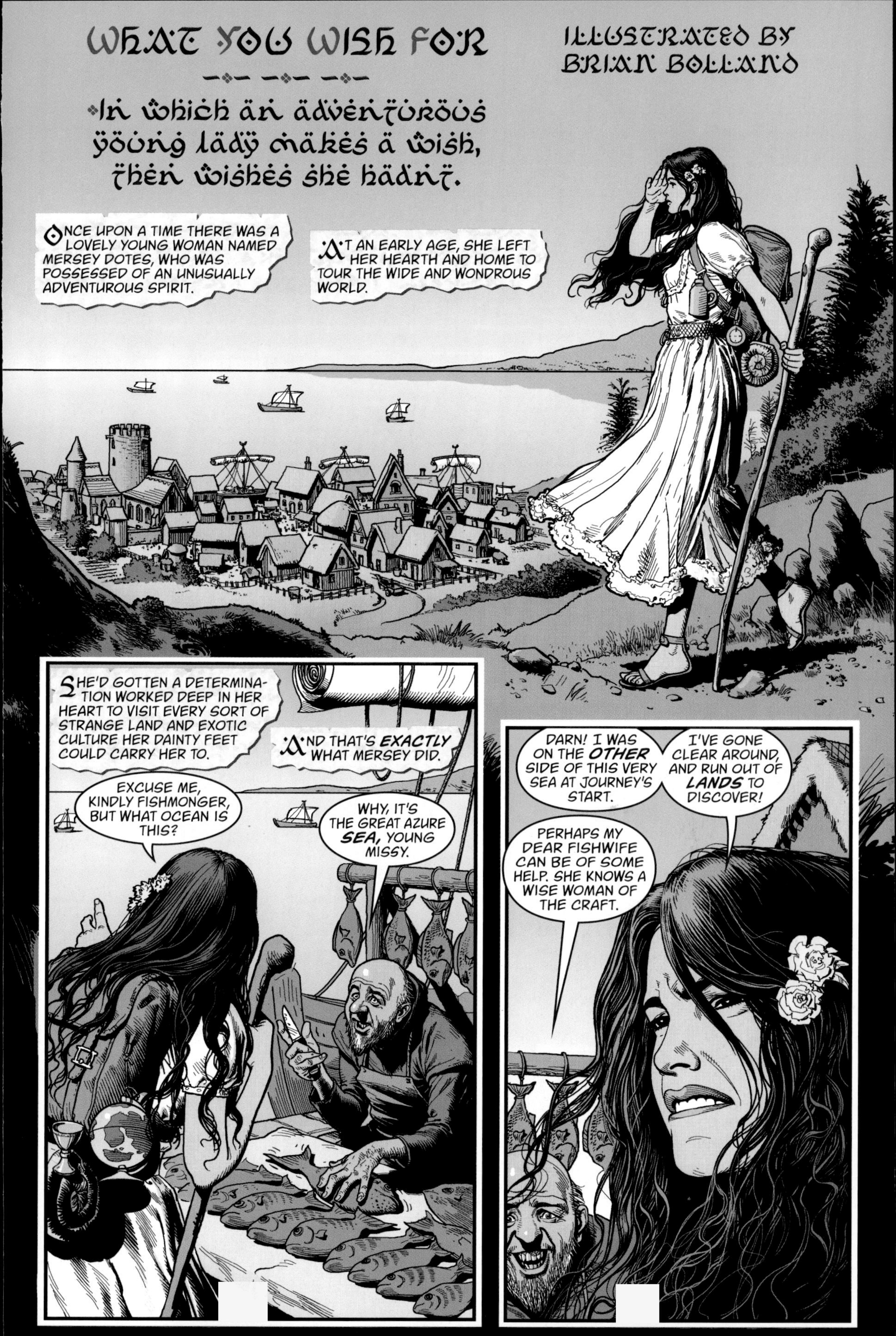
WHAT YOU WISH FOR
ILLUSTRATED BY BRIAN BOLLAND
In which an adventurous young lady makes a wish, then wishes she hadn't.
ONCE UPON A TIME THERE WAS A LOVELY YOUNG WOMAN NAMED MERSEY DOTES, WHO WAS POSSESSED OF AN UNUSUALLY ADVENTUROUS SPIRIT.
AT AN EARLY AGE, SHE LEFT HER HEARTH AND HOME TO TOUR THE WIDE AND WONDROUS WORLD.
SHE'D GOTTEN A DETERMINATION WORKED DEEP IN HER HEART TO VISIT EVERY SORT OF STRANGE LAND AND EXOTIC CULTURE HER DAINTY FEET COULD CARRY HER TO.
AND THAT'S EXACTLY WHAT MERSEY DID.
EXCUSE ME, KINDLY FISHMONGER, BUT WHAT OCEAN IS THIS?
WHY, IT'S THE GREAT AZURE SEA, YOUNG MISSY.
DARN! I WAS ON THE OTHER SIDE OF THIS VERY SEA AT JOURNEY'S START.
I'VE GONE CLEAR AROUND, AND RUN OUT OF LANDS TO DISCOVER!
PERHAPS MY DEAR FISHWIFE CAN BE OF SOME HELP. SHE KNOWS A WISE WOMAN OF THE CRAFT.

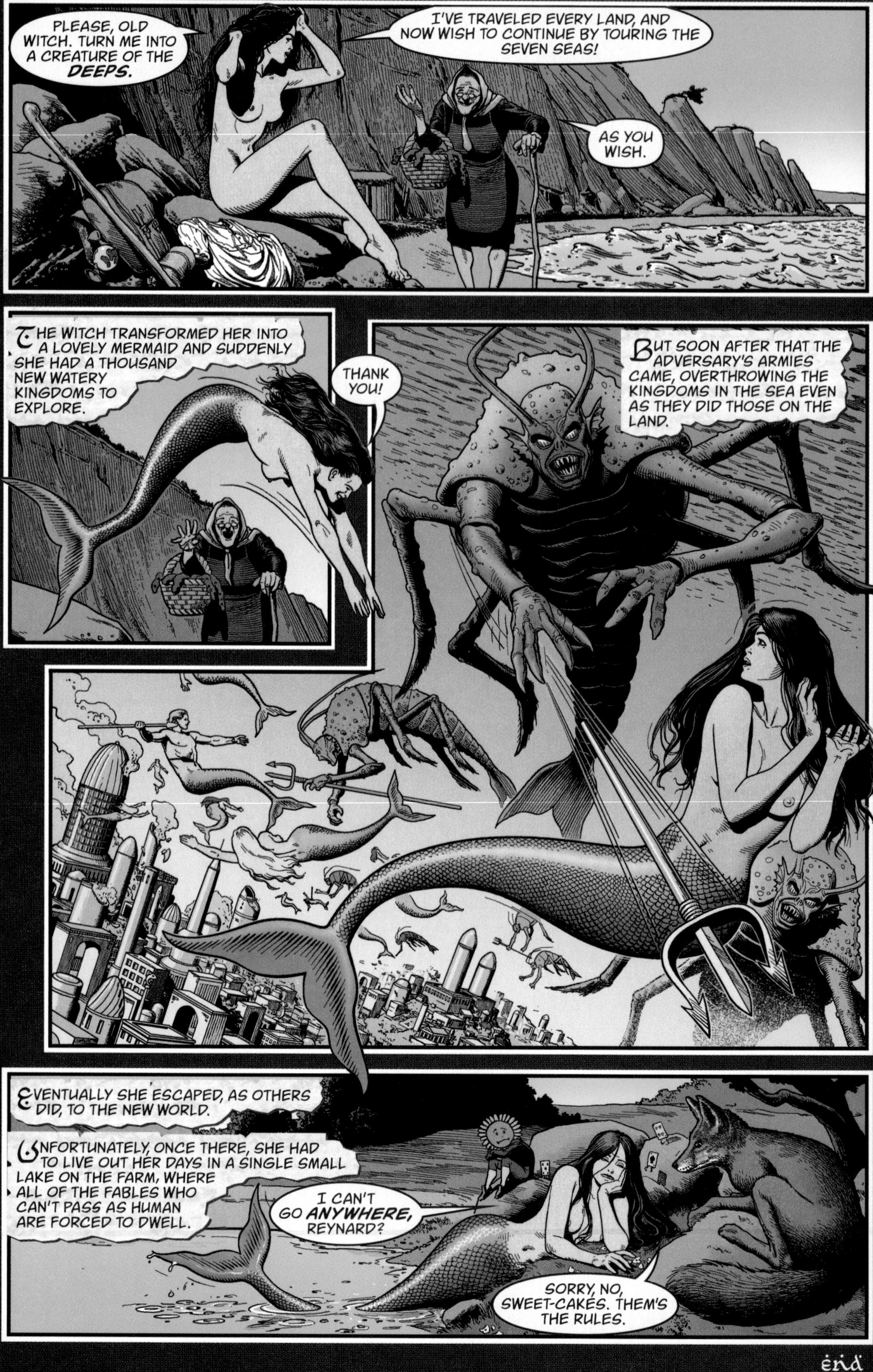
PLEASE, OLD WITCH. TURN ME INTO A CREATURE OF THE DEEPS.
I'VE TRAVELED EVERY LAND, AND NOW WISH TO CONTINUE BY TOURING THE SEVEN SEAS!
AS YOU WISH.
THE WITCH TRANSFORMED HER INTO A LOVELY MERMAID AND SUDDENLY SHE HAD A THOUSAND NEW WATERY KINGDOMS TO EXPLORE.
THANK YOU!
BUT SOON AFTER THAT THE ADVERSARY'S ARMIES CAME, OVERTHROWING THE KINGDOMS IN THE SEA EVEN AS THEY DID THOSE ON THE LAND.
EVENTUALLY SHE ESCAPED, AS OTHERS DID, TO THE NEW WORLD.
UNFORTUNATELY, ONCE THERE, SHE HAD TO LIVE OUT HER DAYS IN A SINGLE SMALL LAKE ON THE FARM, WHERE ALL OF THE FABLES WHO CAN'T PASS AS HUMAN ARE FORCED TO DWELL.
I CAN'T GO ANYWHERE, REYNARD?
SORRY, NO, SWEET-CAKES. THEM'S THE RULES.
end

FAIR DIVISION

In which an old king seeks refuge from the invaders in the company of a very odd collection of characters.

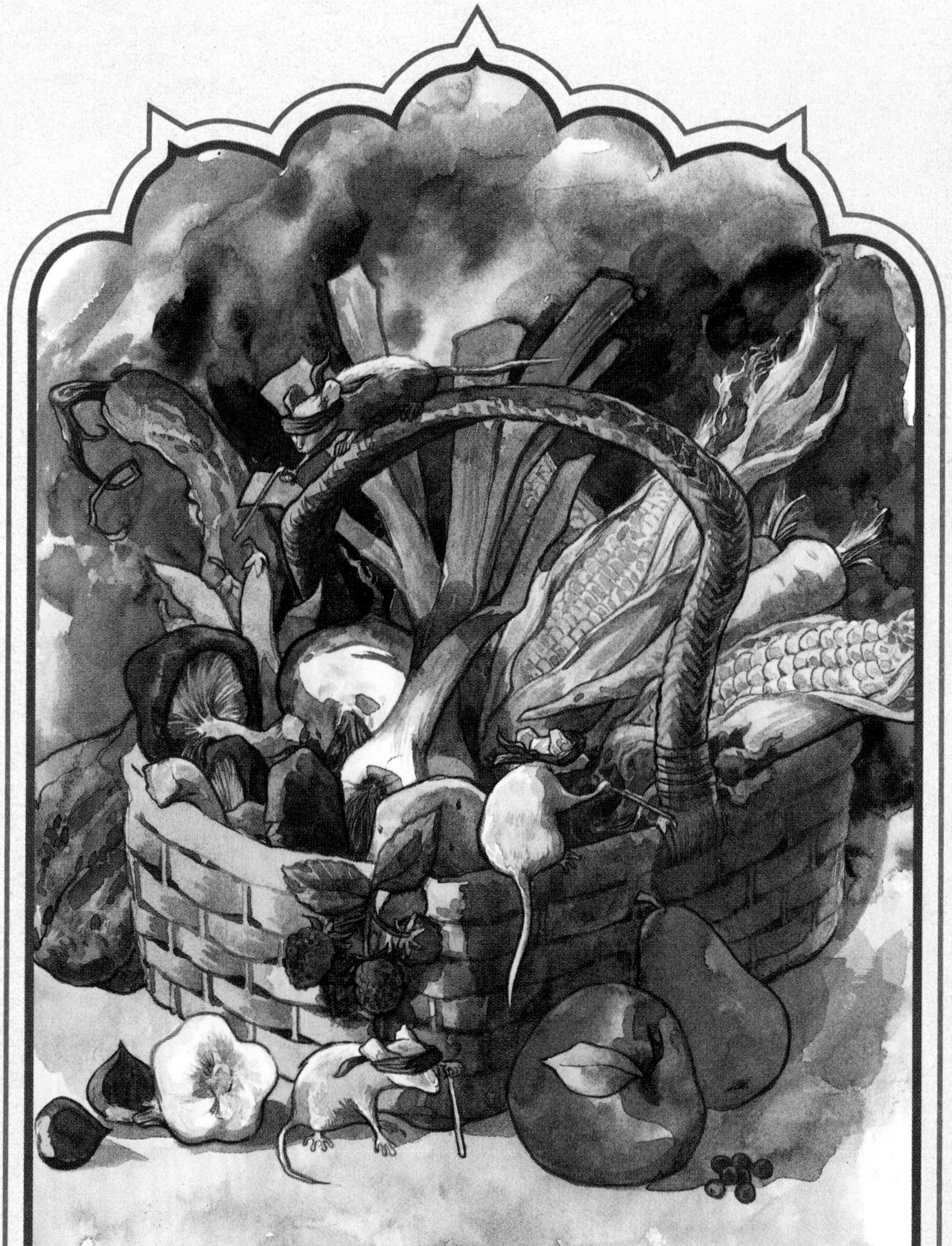

ILLUSTRATED BY JILL THOMPSON

OLD KING COLE WAS A VERY **LARGE** KING OF A VERY SMALL KINGDOM.

WHEN THE ADVERSARY'S FORCES CAME, IT TOOK LESS THAN A DAY TO OVERRUN IT, SENDING THE KING, HIS QUEEN, ONE OLD-MAID PRINCESS (WHOSE TWO YOUNGER SISTERS WERE LONG SINCE MARRIED OFF NICELY), ONE COUNT, TWO BARONS AND SEVENTEEN KNIGHTS OF THE REALM SCATTERING IN **EVERY** DIRECTION.

IN THE CONFUSION, KING COLE LOST TRACK OF HIS WIFE (AND JUST ABOUT EVERYONE ELSE, FOR THAT MATTER).

HE ENJOYED MANY A NARROW ESCAPE, AS THE INVADERS THUNDERED AND PILLAGED THROUGHOUT HIS LANDS.

Finally he thought to take shelter in an old, played-out tin mine that had long since been overtaken by forest.

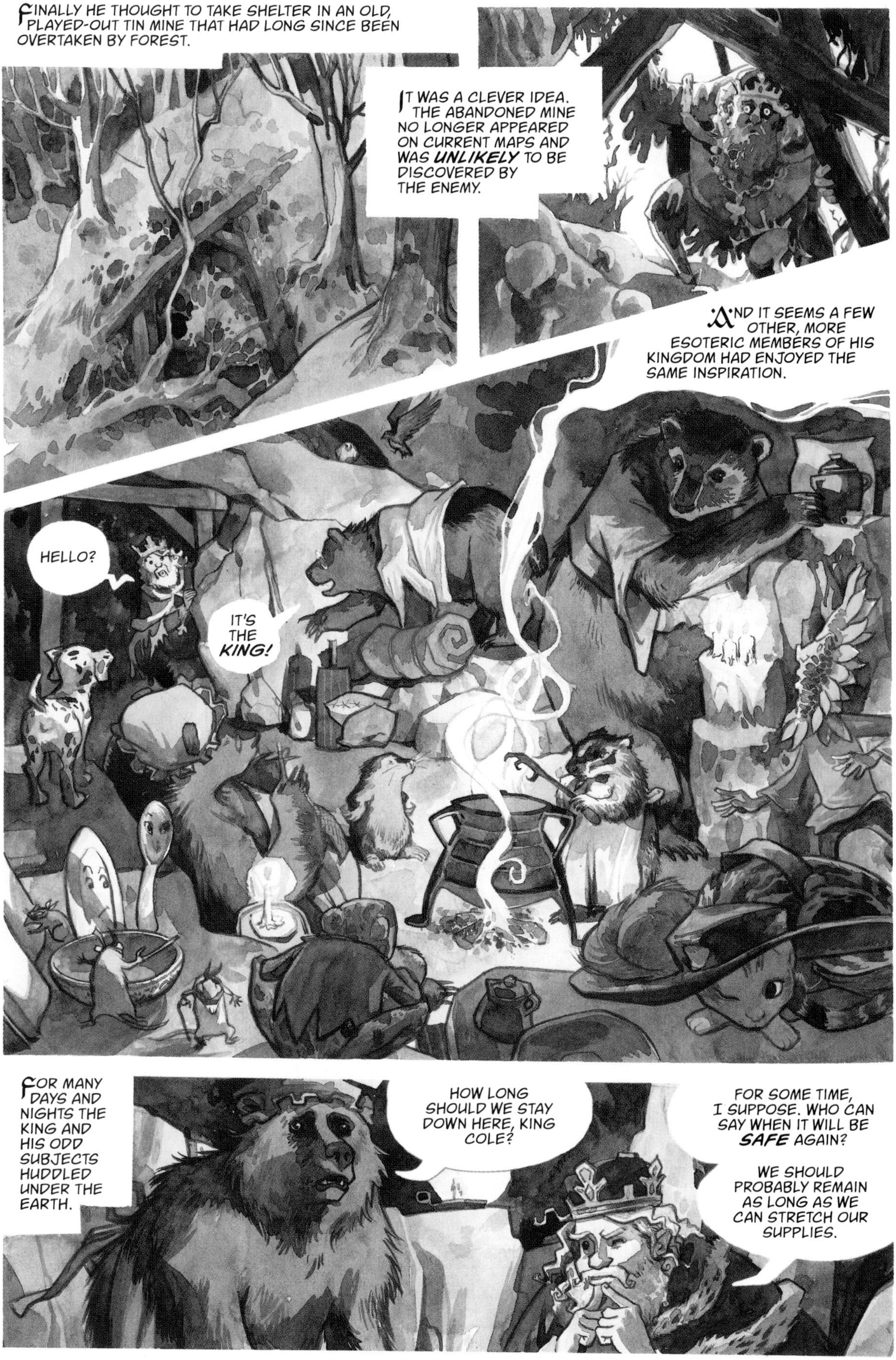
It was a clever idea. The abandoned mine no longer appeared on current maps and was *unlikely* to be discovered by the enemy.
And it seems a few other, more esoteric members of his kingdom had enjoyed the same inspiration.
Hello?
It's the *King!*
For many days and nights the King and his odd subjects huddled under the Earth.
How long should we stay down here, King Cole?
For some time, I suppose. Who can say when it will be *safe* again?
We should probably remain as long as we can stretch our supplies.

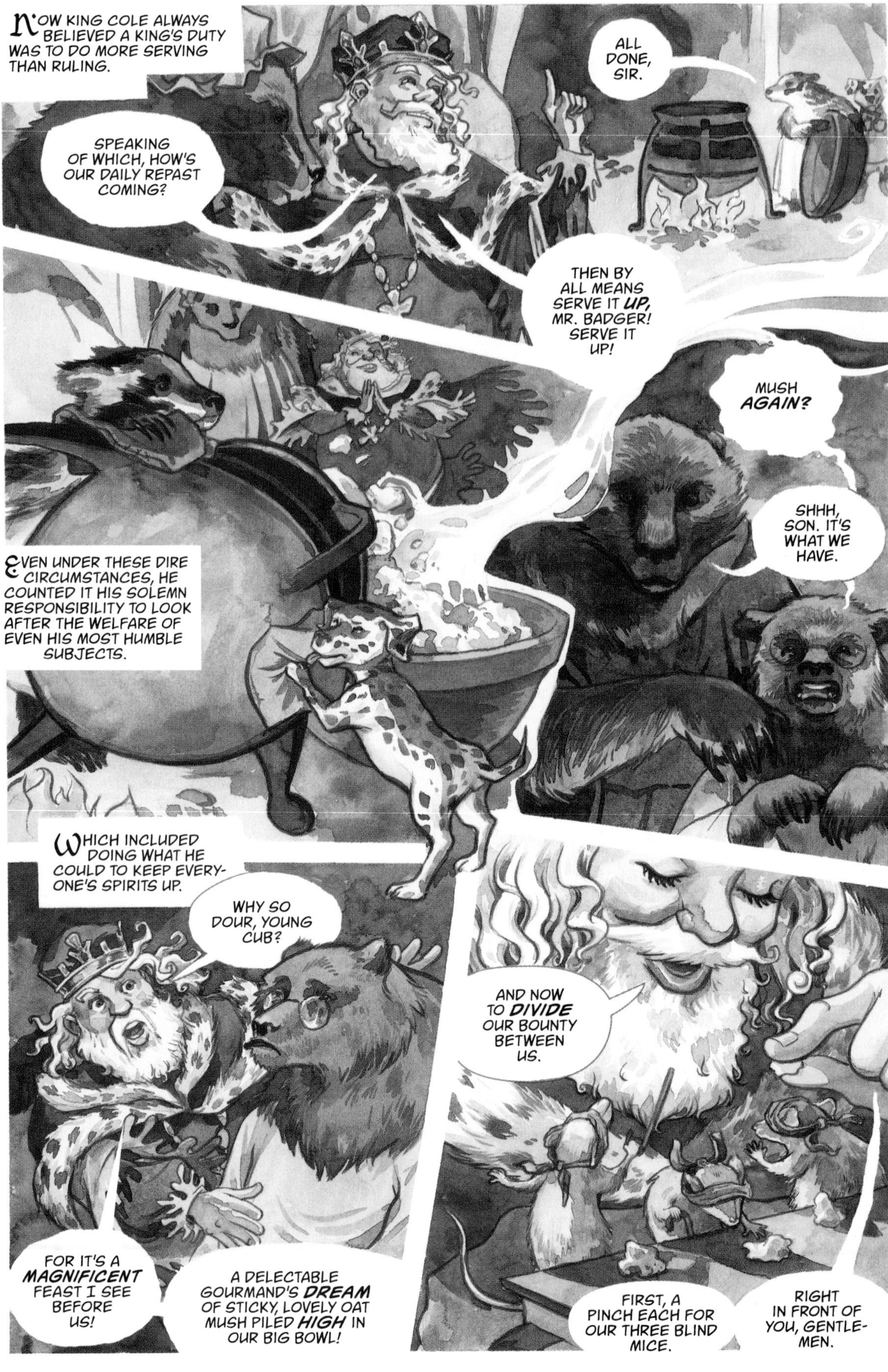
NOW KING COLE ALWAYS BELIEVED A KING'S DUTY WAS TO DO MORE SERVING THAN RULING.
SPEAKING OF WHICH, HOW'S OUR DAILY REPAST COMING?
ALL DONE, SIR.
THEN BY ALL MEANS SERVE IT UP, MR. BADGER! SERVE IT UP!
MUSH AGAIN?
SHHH, SON. IT'S WHAT WE HAVE.
EVEN UNDER THESE DIRE CIRCUMSTANCES, HE COUNTED IT HIS SOLEMN RESPONSIBILITY TO LOOK AFTER THE WELFARE OF EVEN HIS MOST HUMBLE SUBJECTS.
WHICH INCLUDED DOING WHAT HE COULD TO KEEP EVERY-ONE'S SPIRITS UP.
WHY SO DOUR, YOUNG CUB?
FOR IT'S A MAGNIFICENT FEAST I SEE BEFORE US!
A DELECTABLE GOURMAND'S DREAM OF STICKY, LOVELY OAT MUSH PILED HIGH IN OUR BIG BOWL!
AND NOW TO DIVIDE OUR BOUNTY BETWEEN US.
FIRST, A PINCH EACH FOR OUR THREE BLIND MICE.
RIGHT IN FRONT OF YOU, GENTLE-MEN.

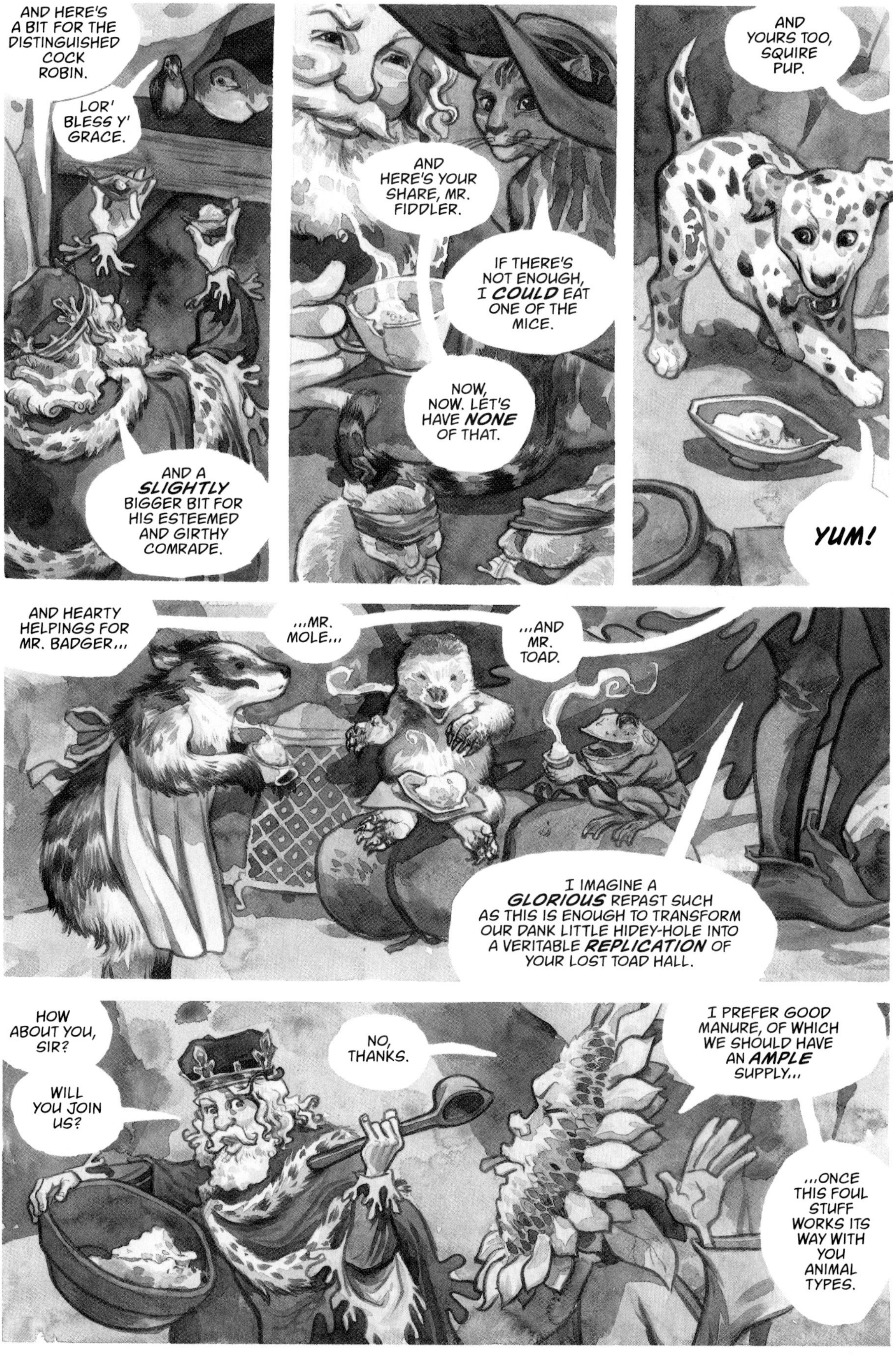
AND HERE'S A BIT FOR THE DISTINGUISHED COCK ROBIN.
LOR' BLESS Y' GRACE.
AND A SLIGHTLY BIGGER BIT FOR HIS ESTEEMED AND GIRTHY COMRADE.
AND HERE'S YOUR SHARE, MR. FIDDLER.
IF THERE'S NOT ENOUGH, I COULD EAT ONE OF THE MICE.
NOW, NOW. LET'S HAVE NONE OF THAT.
AND YOURS TOO, SQUIRE PUP.
YUM!
AND HEARTY HELPINGS FOR MR. BADGER...
...MR. MOLE...
...AND MR. TOAD.
I IMAGINE A GLORIOUS REPAST SUCH AS THIS IS ENOUGH TO TRANSFORM OUR DANK LITTLE HIDEY-HOLE INTO A VERITABLE REPLICATION OF YOUR LOST TOAD HALL.
HOW ABOUT YOU, SIR?
WILL YOU JOIN US?
NO, THANKS.
I PREFER GOOD MANURE, OF WHICH WE SHOULD HAVE AN AMPLE SUPPLY...
...ONCE THIS FOUL STUFF WORKS ITS WAY WITH YOU ANIMAL TYPES.

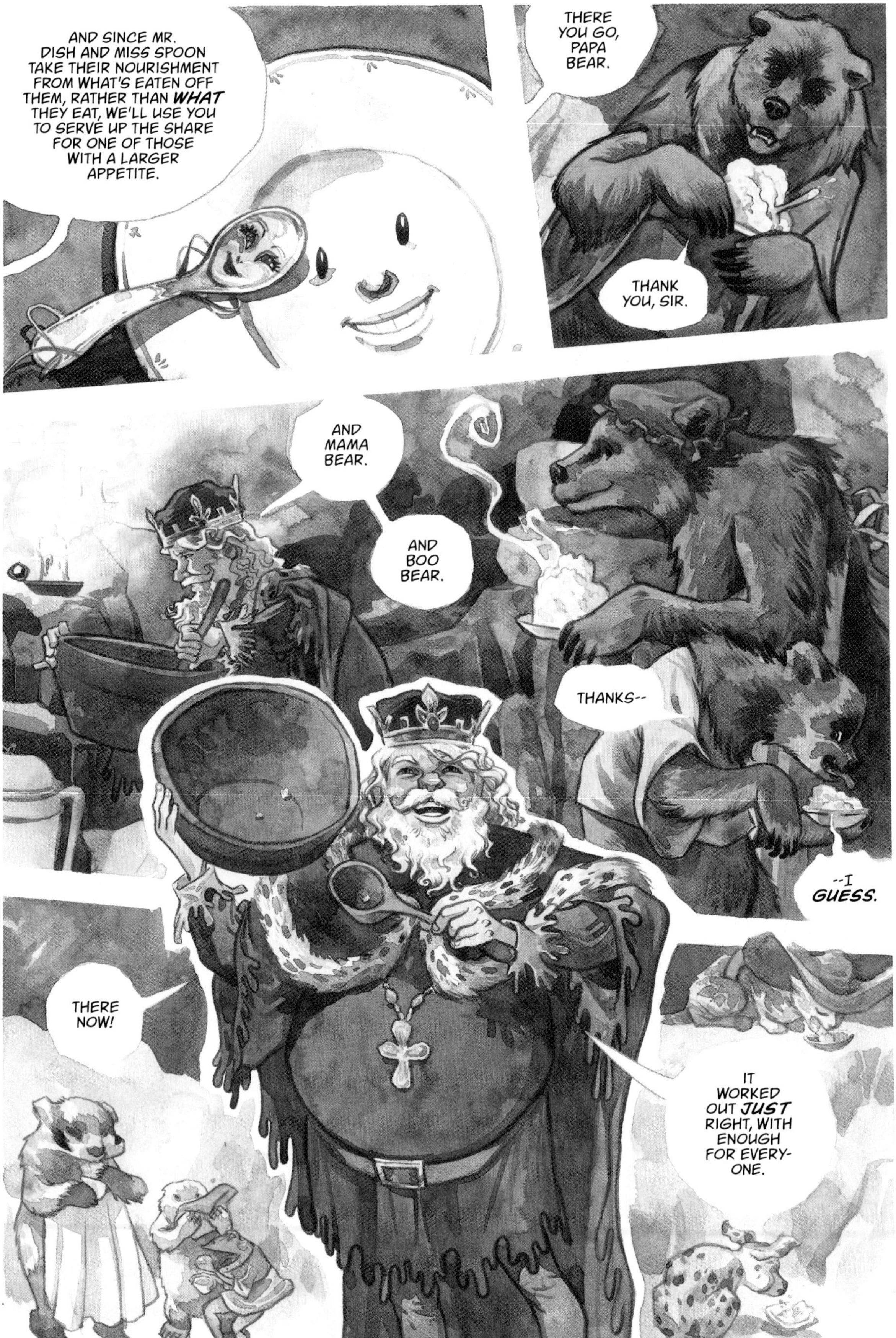
AND SINCE MR. DISH AND MISS SPOON TAKE THEIR NOURISHMENT FROM WHAT'S EATEN OFF THEM, RATHER THAN **WHAT** THEY EAT, WE'LL USE YOU TO SERVE UP THE SHARE FOR ONE OF THOSE WITH A LARGER APPETITE.
THERE YOU GO, PAPA BEAR.
THANK YOU, SIR.
AND MAMA BEAR.
AND BOO BEAR.
THANKS--
--I **GUESS**.
THERE NOW!
IT WORKED OUT **JUST** RIGHT, WITH ENOUGH FOR EVERY-ONE.

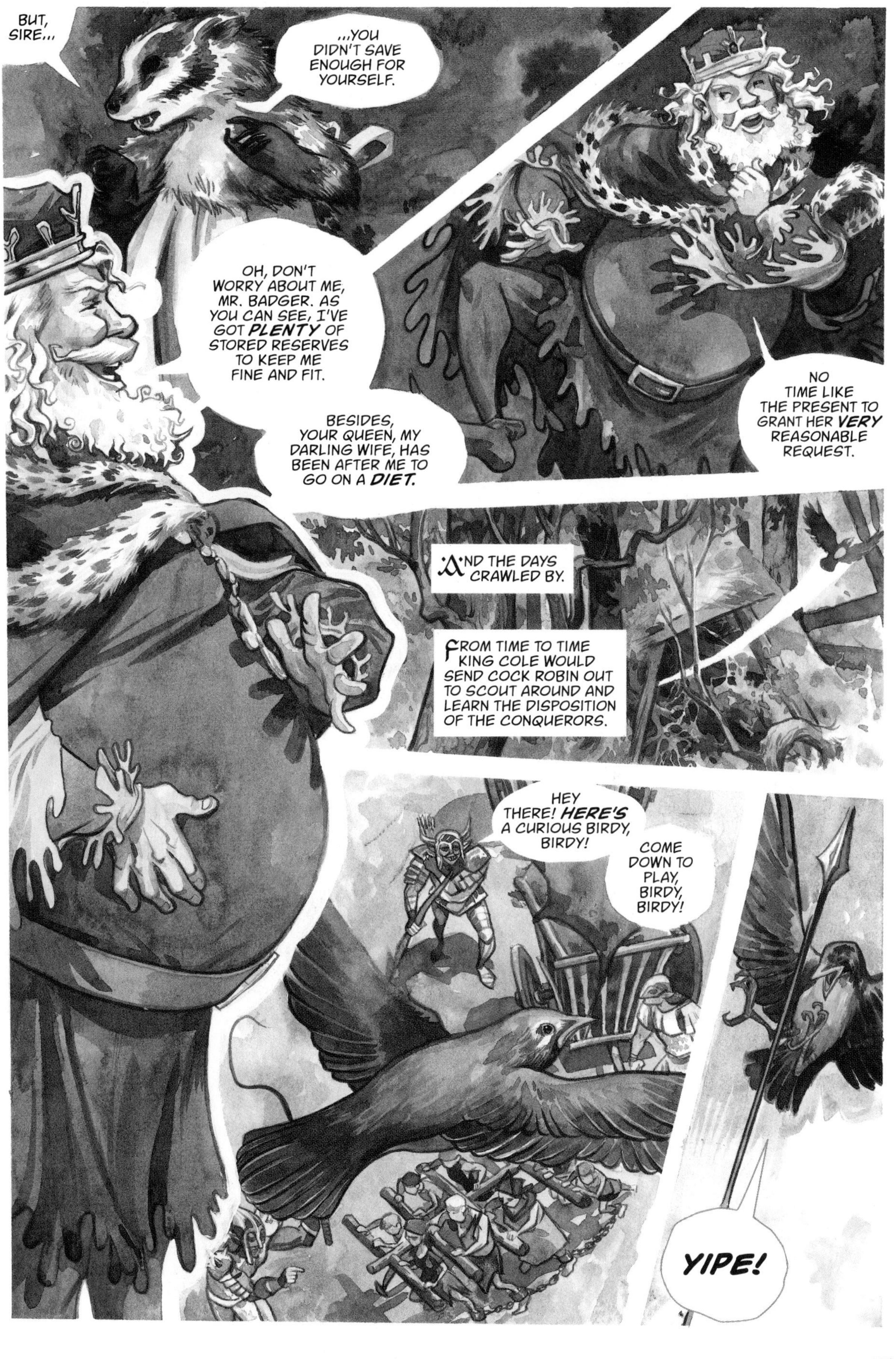
BUT, SIRE...
...YOU DIDN'T SAVE ENOUGH FOR YOURSELF.
OH, DON'T WORRY ABOUT ME, MR. BADGER. AS YOU CAN SEE, I'VE GOT PLENTY OF STORED RESERVES TO KEEP ME FINE AND FIT.
BESIDES, YOUR QUEEN, MY DARLING WIFE, HAS BEEN AFTER ME TO GO ON A DIET.
NO TIME LIKE THE PRESENT TO GRANT HER VERY REASONABLE REQUEST.
AND THE DAYS CRAWLED BY.
FROM TIME TO TIME KING COLE WOULD SEND COCK ROBIN OUT TO SCOUT AROUND AND LEARN THE DISPOSITION OF THE CONQUERORS.
HEY THERE! HERE'S A CURIOUS BIRDY, BIRDY!
COME DOWN TO PLAY, BIRDY, BIRDY!
YIPE!

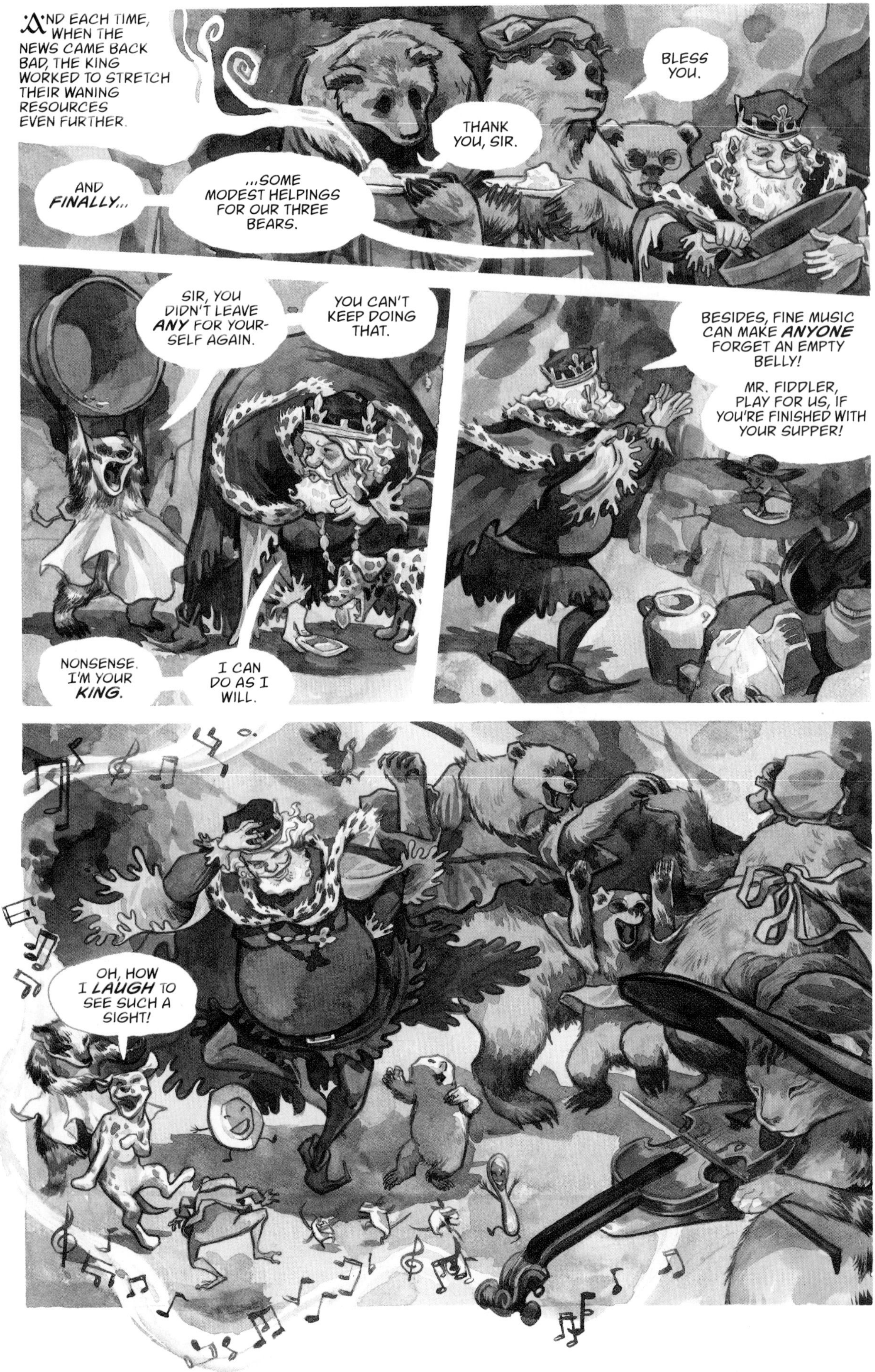

AND EACH TIME, WHEN THE NEWS CAME BACK BAD, THE KING WORKED TO STRETCH THEIR WANING RESOURCES EVEN FURTHER.
BLESS YOU.
THANK YOU, SIR.
AND FINALLY...
...SOME MODEST HELPINGS FOR OUR THREE BEARS.
SIR, YOU DIDN'T LEAVE ANY FOR YOURSELF AGAIN.
YOU CAN'T KEEP DOING THAT.
NONSENSE. I'M YOUR KING.
I CAN DO AS I WILL.
BESIDES, FINE MUSIC CAN MAKE ANYONE FORGET AN EMPTY BELLY!
MR. FIDDLER, PLAY FOR US, IF YOU'RE FINISHED WITH YOUR SUPPER!
OH, HOW I LAUGH TO SEE SUCH A SIGHT!

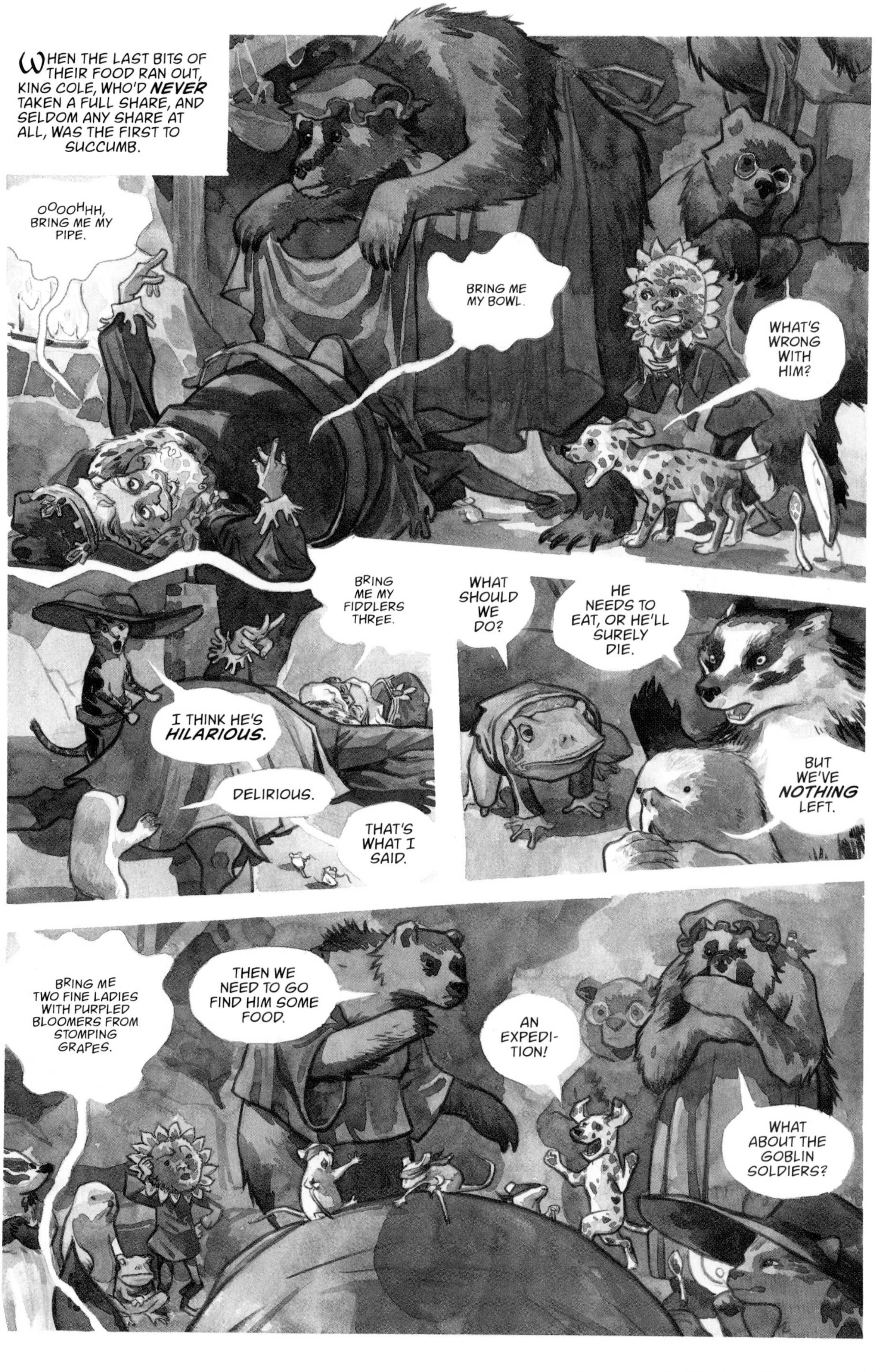
WHEN THE LAST BITS OF THEIR FOOD RAN OUT, KING COLE, WHO'D NEVER TAKEN A FULL SHARE, AND SELDOM ANY SHARE AT ALL, WAS THE FIRST TO SUCCUMB.
OOOOHHH, BRING ME MY PIPE.
BRING ME MY BOWL.
WHAT'S WRONG WITH HIM?
BRING ME MY FIDDLERS THREE.
I THINK HE'S HILARIOUS.
DELIRIOUS.
THAT'S WHAT I SAID.
WHAT SHOULD WE DO?
HE NEEDS TO EAT, OR HE'LL SURELY DIE.
BUT WE'VE NOTHING LEFT.
BRING ME TWO FINE LADIES WITH PURPLED BLOOMERS FROM STOMPING GRAPES.
THEN WE NEED TO GO FIND HIM SOME FOOD.
AN EXPEDITION!
WHAT ABOUT THE GOBLIN SOLDIERS?

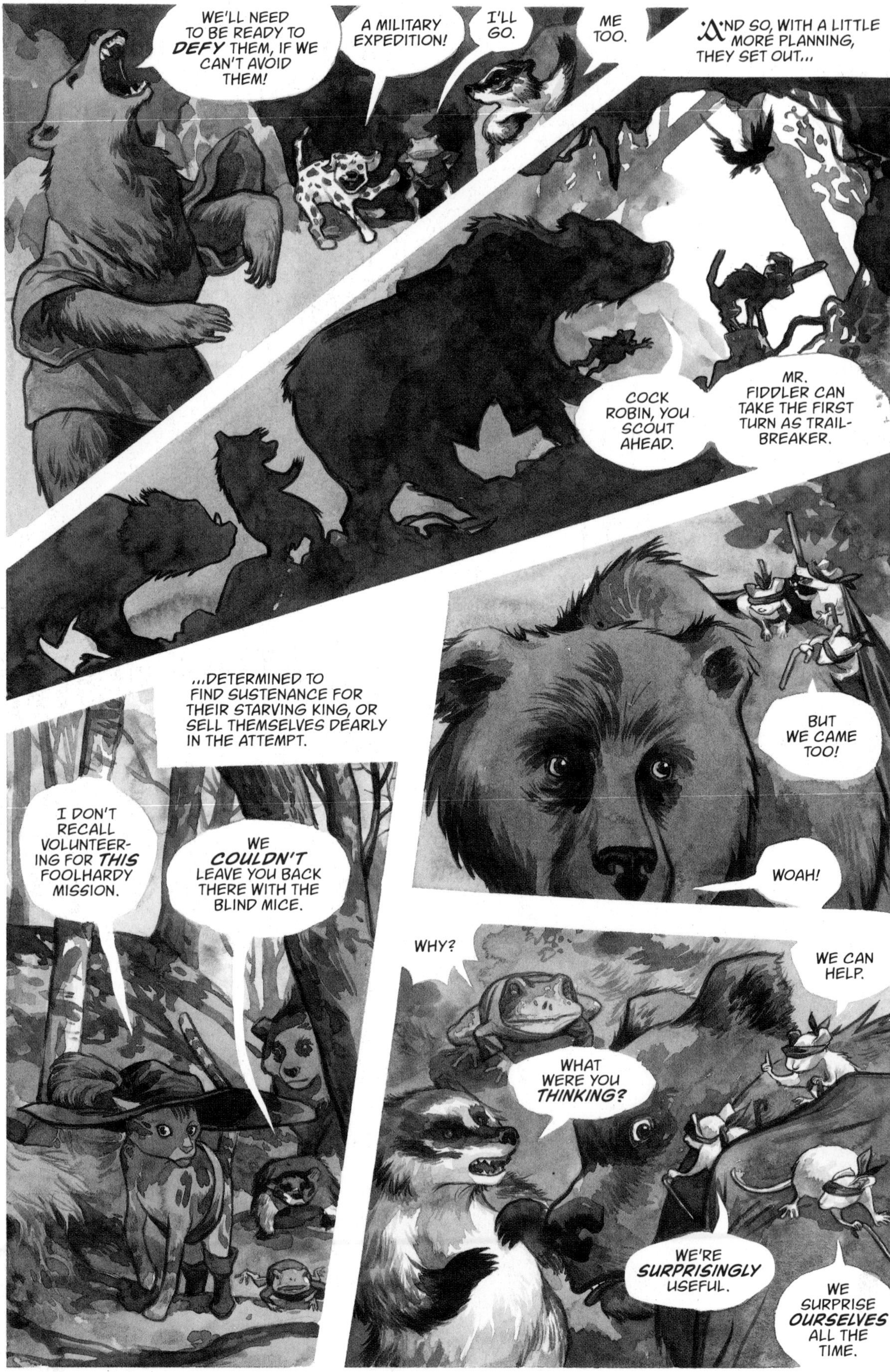
WE'LL NEED TO BE READY TO DEFY THEM, IF WE CAN'T AVOID THEM!
A MILITARY EXPEDITION!
I'LL GO.
ME TOO.
AND SO, WITH A LITTLE MORE PLANNING, THEY SET OUT...
COCK ROBIN, YOU SCOUT AHEAD.
MR. FIDDLER CAN TAKE THE FIRST TURN AS TRAIL-BREAKER.
...DETERMINED TO FIND SUSTENANCE FOR THEIR STARVING KING, OR SELL THEMSELVES DEARLY IN THE ATTEMPT.
BUT WE CAME TOO!
WOAH!
I DON'T RECALL VOLUNTEERING FOR THIS FOOLHARDY MISSION.
WE COULDN'T LEAVE YOU BACK THERE WITH THE BLIND MICE.
WHY?
WE CAN HELP.
WHAT WERE YOU THINKING?
WE'RE SURPRISINGLY USEFUL.
WE SURPRISE OURSELVES ALL THE TIME.

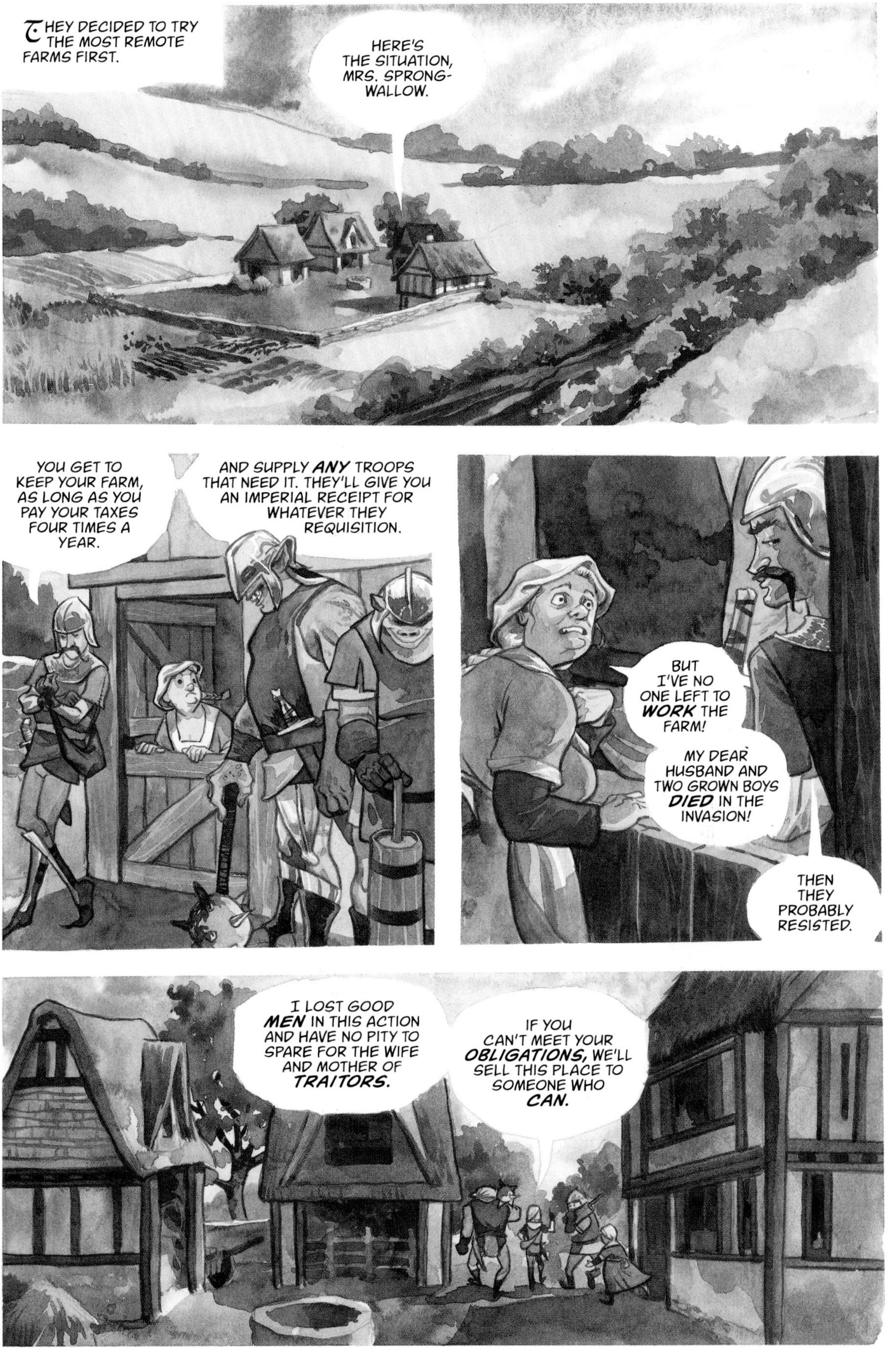
THEY DECIDED TO TRY THE MOST REMOTE FARMS FIRST.
HERE'S THE SITUATION, MRS. SPRONG-WALLOW.
YOU GET TO KEEP YOUR FARM, AS LONG AS YOU PAY YOUR TAXES FOUR TIMES A YEAR.
AND SUPPLY ANY TROOPS THAT NEED IT. THEY'LL GIVE YOU AN IMPERIAL RECEIPT FOR WHATEVER THEY REQUISITION.
BUT I'VE NO ONE LEFT TO WORK THE FARM!
MY DEAR HUSBAND AND TWO GROWN BOYS DIED IN THE INVASION!
THEN THEY PROBABLY RESISTED.
I LOST GOOD MEN IN THIS ACTION AND HAVE NO PITY TO SPARE FOR THE WIFE AND MOTHER OF TRAITORS.
IF YOU CAN'T MEET YOUR OBLIGATIONS, WE'LL SELL THIS PLACE TO SOMEONE WHO CAN.

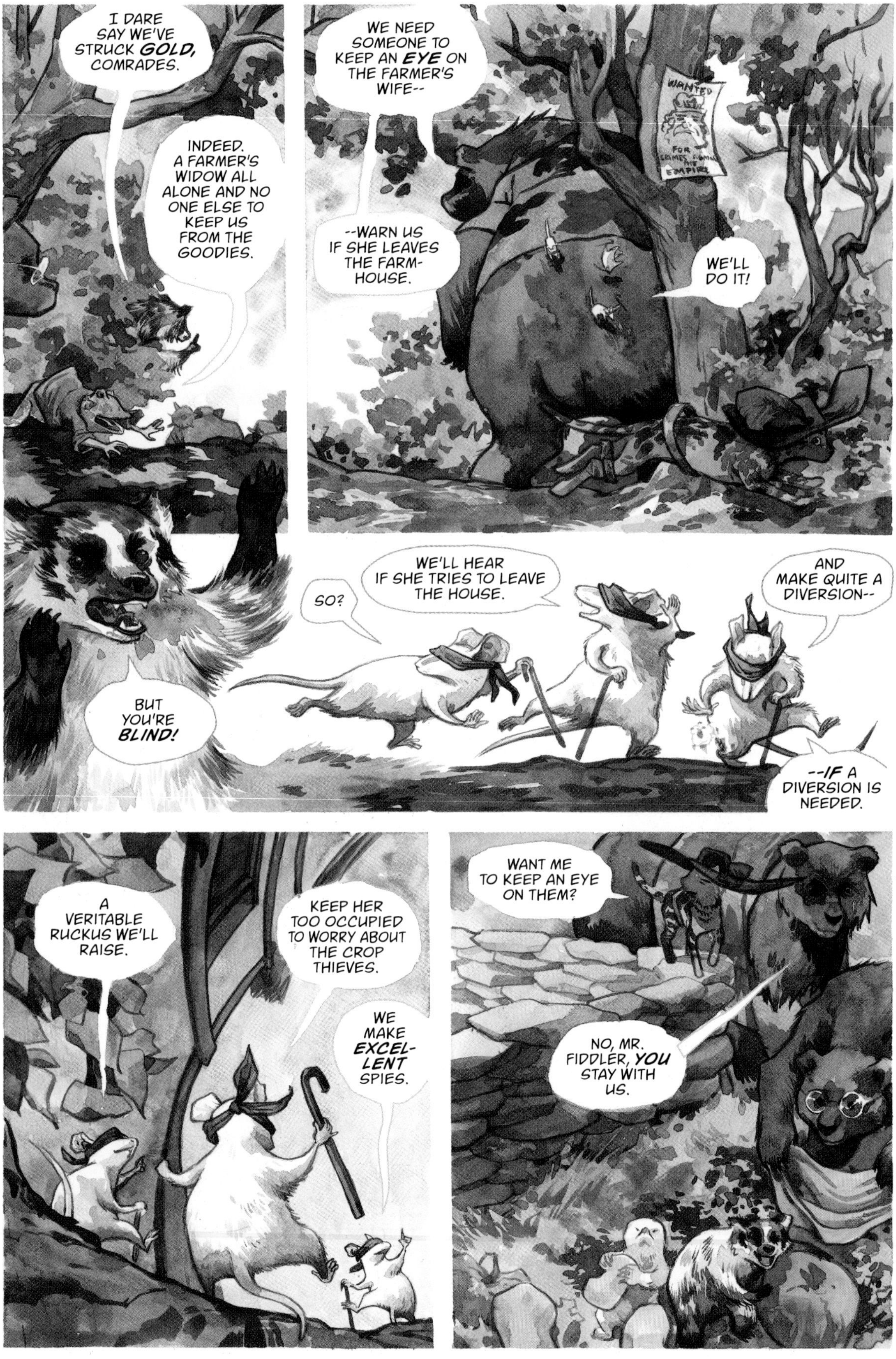
I DARE SAY WE'VE STRUCK **GOLD,** COMRADES.
INDEED. A FARMER'S WIDOW ALL ALONE AND NO ONE ELSE TO KEEP US FROM THE GOODIES.
WE NEED SOMEONE TO KEEP AN **EYE** ON THE FARMER'S WIFE--
--WARN US IF SHE LEAVES THE FARM-HOUSE.
WANTED
FOR CRIMES AGAINST THE EMPIRE
WE'LL DO IT!
BUT YOU'RE ***BLIND!***
SO?
WE'LL HEAR IF SHE TRIES TO LEAVE THE HOUSE.
AND MAKE QUITE A DIVERSION--
--IF A DIVERSION IS NEEDED.
A VERITABLE RUCKUS WE'LL RAISE.
KEEP HER TOO OCCUPIED TO WORRY ABOUT THE CROP THIEVES.
WE MAKE ***EXCEL-LENT*** SPIES.
WANT ME TO KEEP AN EYE ON THEM?
NO, MR. FIDDLER, ***YOU*** STAY WITH US.

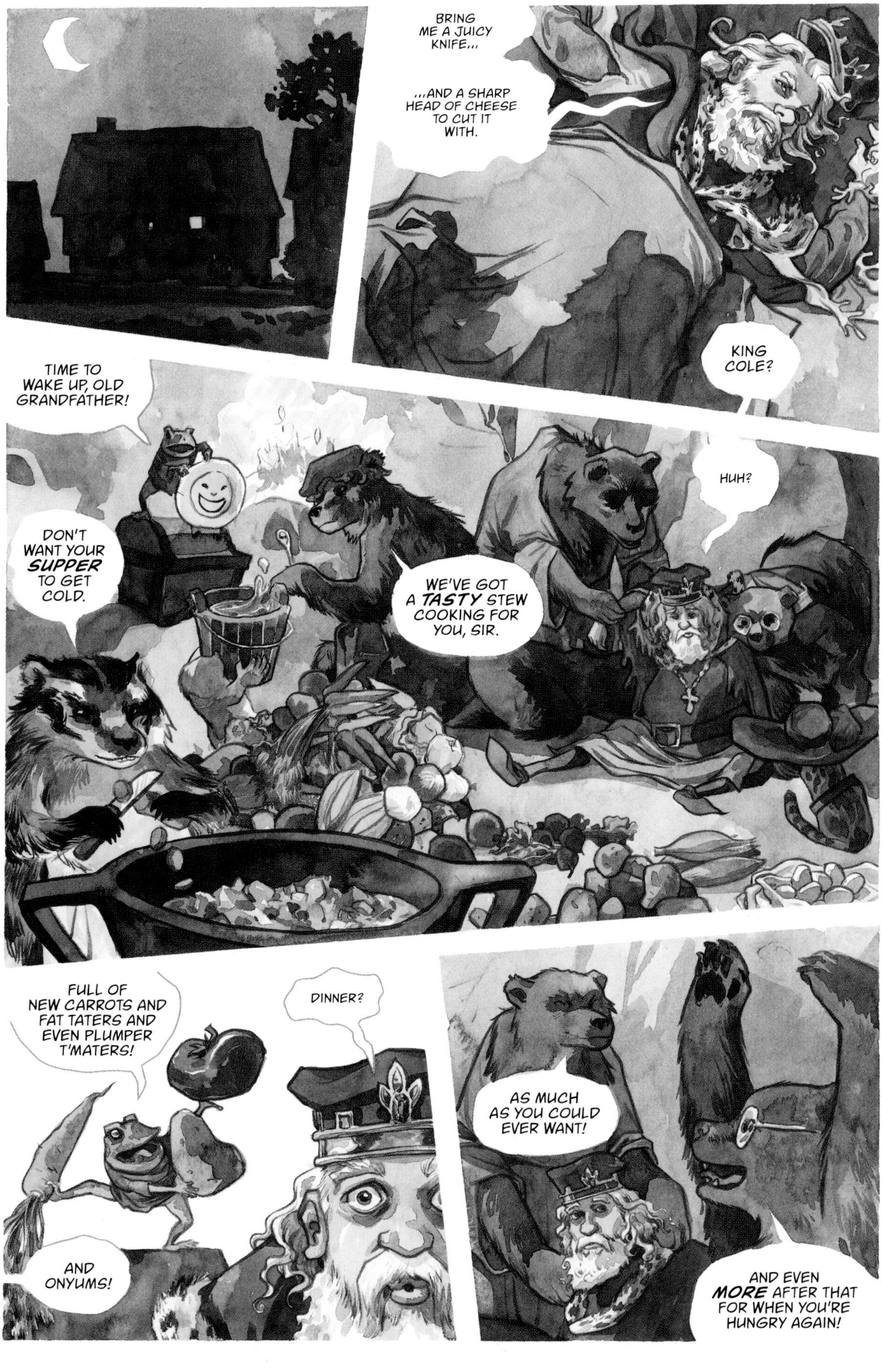
BRING ME A JUICY KNIFE...
...AND A SHARP HEAD OF CHEESE TO CUT IT WITH.
KING COLE?
TIME TO WAKE UP, OLD GRANDFATHER!
HUH?
DON'T WANT YOUR SUPPER TO GET COLD.
WE'VE GOT A TASTY STEW COOKING FOR YOU, SIR.
FULL OF NEW CARROTS AND FAT TATERS AND EVEN PLUMPER T'MATERS!
DINNER?
AND ONYUMS!
AS MUCH AS YOU COULD EVER WANT!
AND EVEN MORE AFTER THAT FOR WHEN YOU'RE HUNGRY AGAIN!

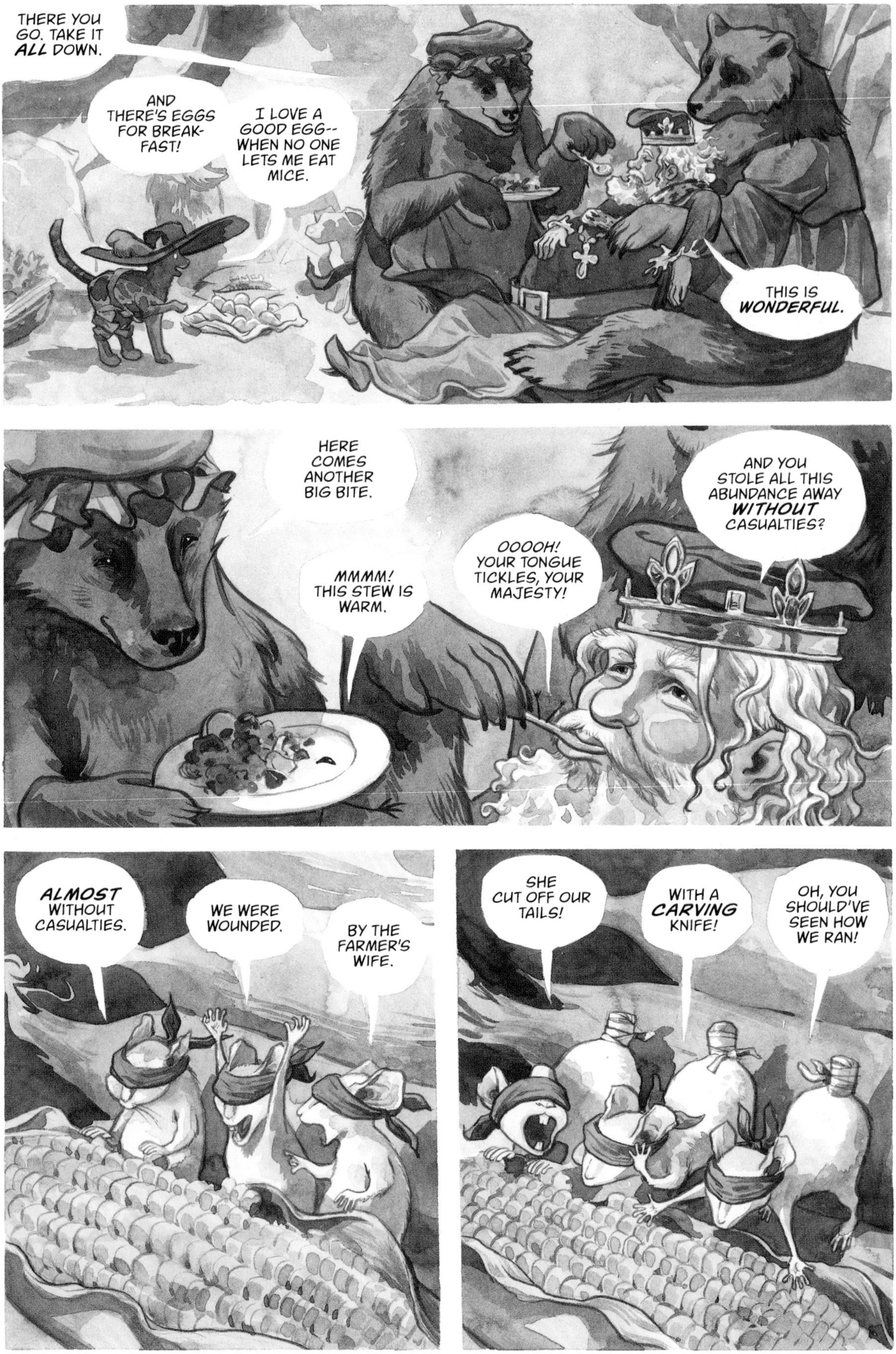
THERE YOU GO. TAKE IT ALL DOWN.
AND THERE'S EGGS FOR BREAK-FAST!
I LOVE A GOOD EGG-- WHEN NO ONE LETS ME EAT MICE.
THIS IS WONDERFUL.
HERE COMES ANOTHER BIG BITE.
AND YOU STOLE ALL THIS ABUNDANCE AWAY WITHOUT CASUALTIES?
MMMM! THIS STEW IS WARM.
OOOOH! YOUR TONGUE TICKLES, YOUR MAJESTY!
ALMOST WITHOUT CASUALTIES.
WE WERE WOUNDED.
BY THE FARMER'S WIFE.
SHE CUT OFF OUR TAILS!
WITH A CARVING KNIFE!
OH, YOU SHOULD'VE SEEN HOW WE RAN!

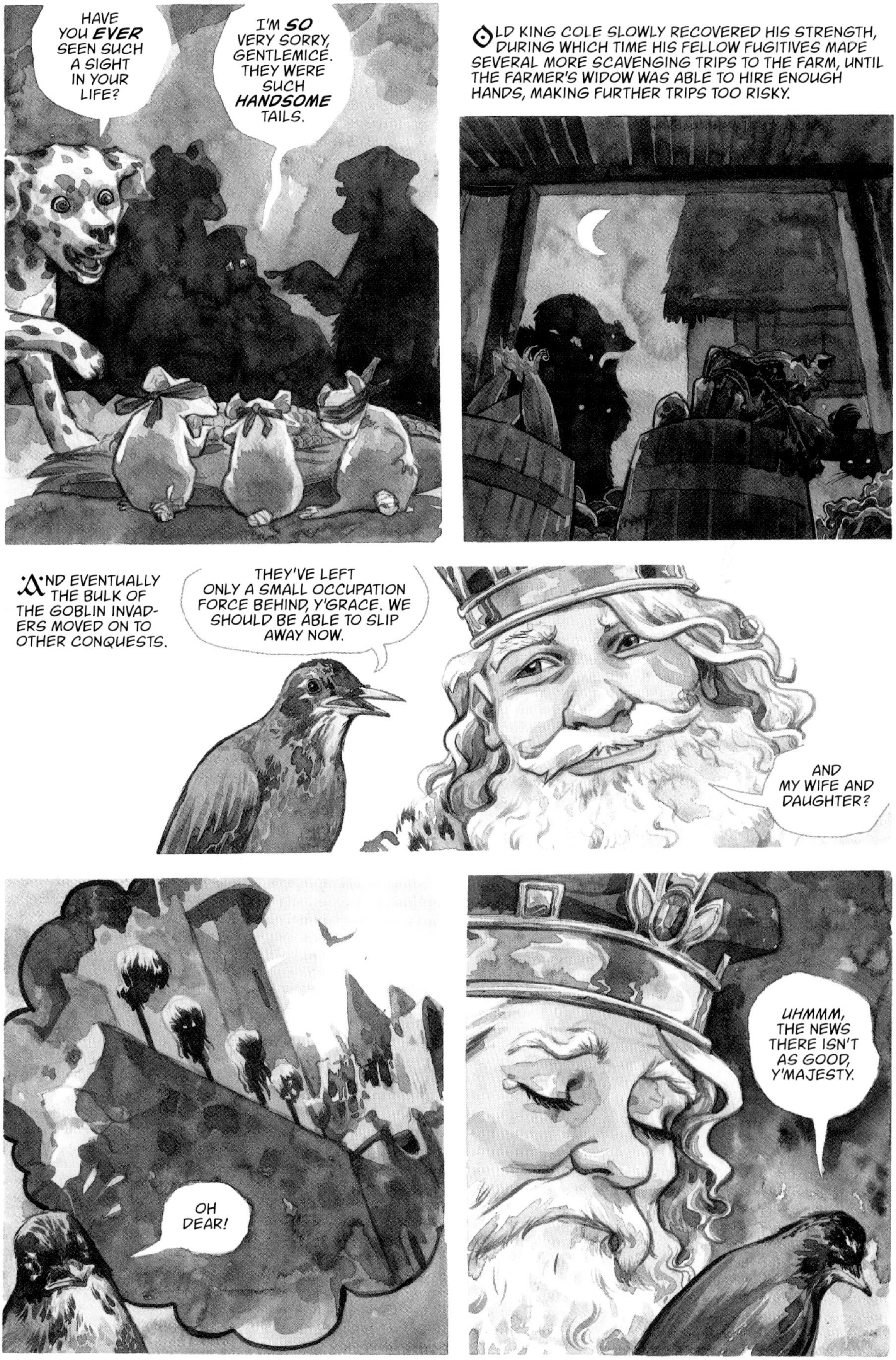
HAVE YOU EVER SEEN SUCH A SIGHT IN YOUR LIFE?
I'M SO VERY SORRY, GENTLEMICE. THEY WERE SUCH HANDSOME TAILS.
OLD KING COLE SLOWLY RECOVERED HIS STRENGTH, DURING WHICH TIME HIS FELLOW FUGITIVES MADE SEVERAL MORE SCAVENGING TRIPS TO THE FARM, UNTIL THE FARMER'S WIDOW WAS ABLE TO HIRE ENOUGH HANDS, MAKING FURTHER TRIPS TOO RISKY.
AND EVENTUALLY THE BULK OF THE GOBLIN INVADERS MOVED ON TO OTHER CONQUESTS.
THEY'VE LEFT ONLY A SMALL OCCUPATION FORCE BEHIND, Y'GRACE. WE SHOULD BE ABLE TO SLIP AWAY NOW.
AND MY WIFE AND DAUGHTER?
OH DEAR!
UHMMM, THE NEWS THERE ISN'T AS GOOD, Y'MAJESTY.

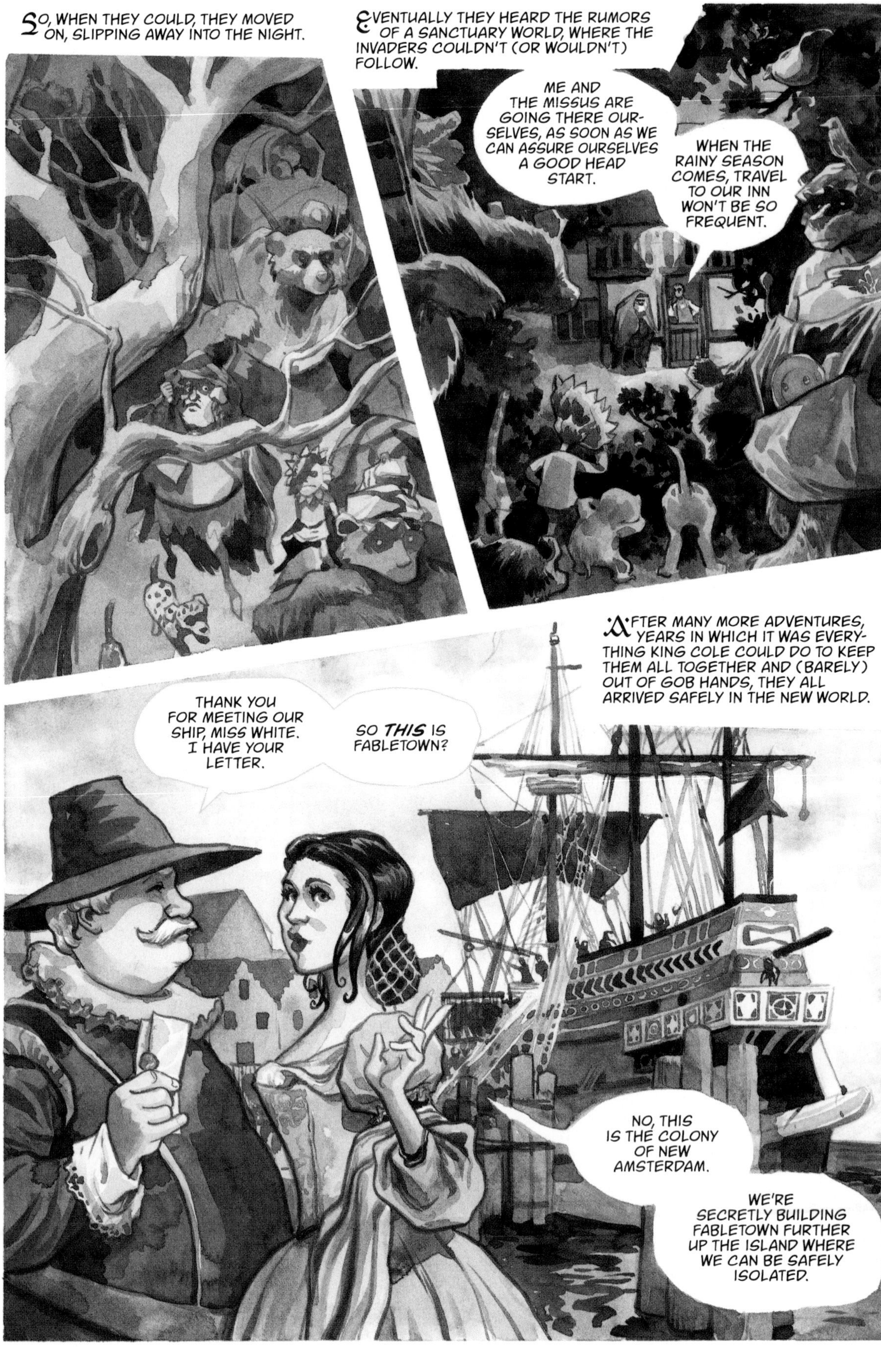
SO, WHEN THEY COULD, THEY MOVED ON, SLIPPING AWAY INTO THE NIGHT.
EVENTUALLY THEY HEARD THE RUMORS OF A SANCTUARY WORLD, WHERE THE INVADERS COULDN'T (OR WOULDN'T) FOLLOW.
ME AND THE MISSUS ARE GOING THERE OURSELVES, AS SOON AS WE CAN ASSURE OURSELVES A GOOD HEAD START.
WHEN THE RAINY SEASON COMES, TRAVEL TO OUR INN WON'T BE SO FREQUENT.
AFTER MANY MORE ADVENTURES, YEARS IN WHICH IT WAS EVERYTHING KING COLE COULD DO TO KEEP THEM ALL TOGETHER AND (BARELY) OUT OF GOB HANDS, THEY ALL ARRIVED SAFELY IN THE NEW WORLD.
THANK YOU FOR MEETING OUR SHIP, MISS WHITE. I HAVE YOUR LETTER.
SO *THIS* IS FABLETOWN?
NO, THIS IS THE COLONY OF NEW AMSTERDAM.
WE'RE SECRETLY BUILDING FABLETOWN FURTHER UP THE ISLAND WHERE WE CAN BE SAFELY ISOLATED.

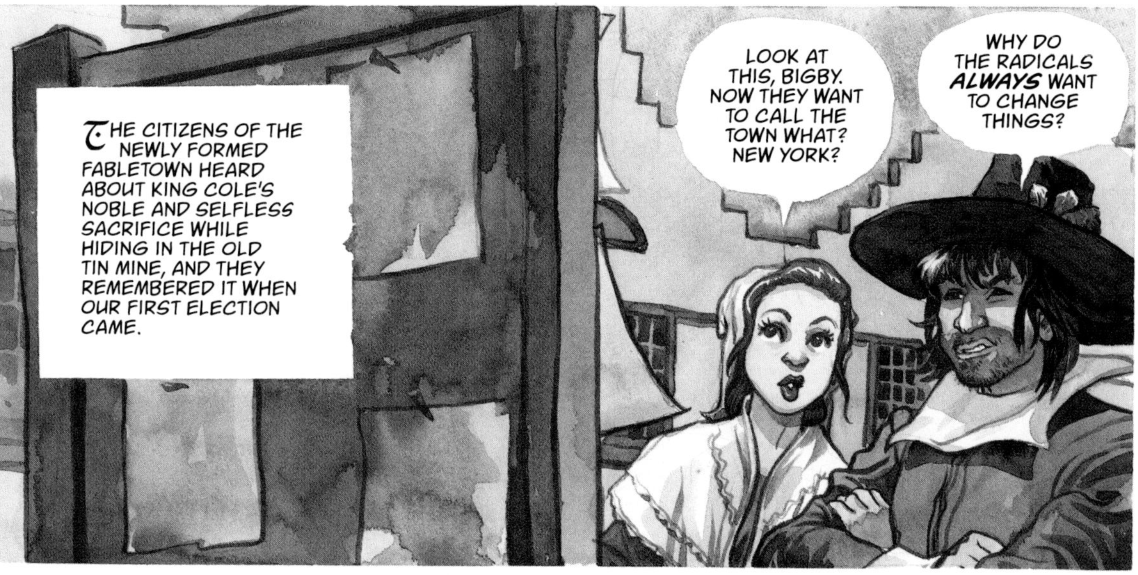
THE CITIZENS OF THE NEWLY FORMED FABLETOWN HEARD ABOUT KING COLE'S NOBLE AND SELFLESS SACRIFICE WHILE HIDING IN THE OLD TIN MINE, AND THEY REMEMBERED IT WHEN OUR FIRST ELECTION CAME.
LOOK AT THIS, BIGBY. NOW THEY WANT TO CALL THE TOWN WHAT? NEW YORK?
WHY DO THE RADICALS ***ALWAYS*** WANT TO CHANGE THINGS?

WE VOTED HIM, NEARLY UNANIMOUSLY, AS OUR VERY FIRST MAYOR.

AND HE'S BEEN SO TO THIS VERY DAY, UNIVERSALLY LOVED, UNTIL THE DAY HE SIGNED THE LAW FORMALLY BANISHING ***ALL*** NON-HUMAN FABLES TO THE FARM.

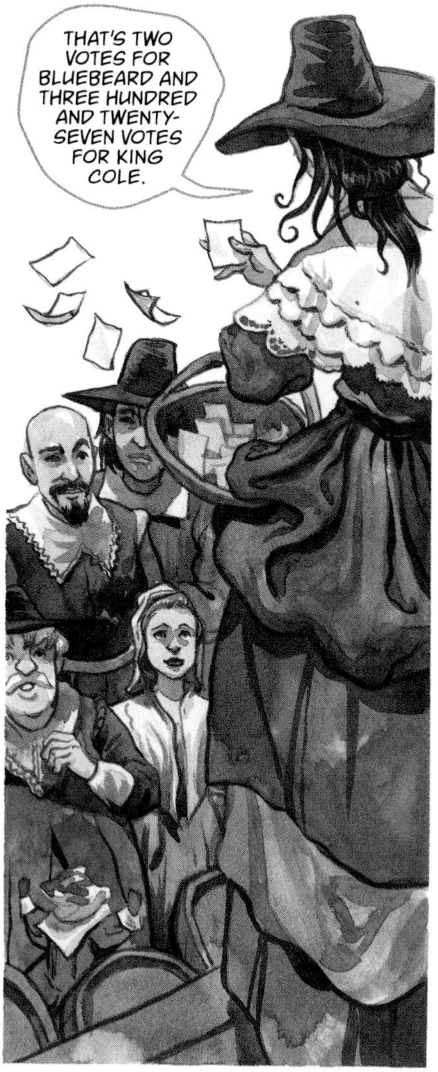
THAT'S TWO VOTES FOR BLUEBEARD AND THREE HUNDRED AND TWENTY-SEVEN VOTES FOR KING COLE.

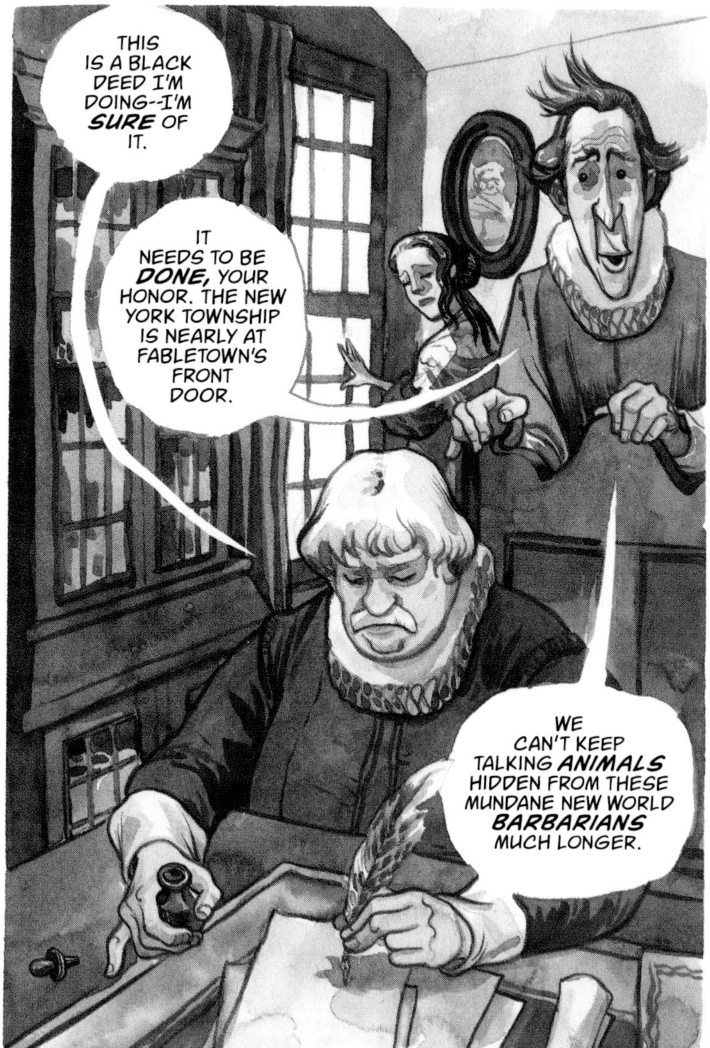
THIS IS A BLACK DEED I'M DOING--I'M ***SURE*** OF IT.
IT NEEDS TO BE ***DONE,*** YOUR HONOR. THE NEW YORK TOWNSHIP IS NEARLY AT FABLETOWN'S FRONT DOOR.
WE CAN'T KEEP TALKING ***ANIMALS*** HIDDEN FROM THESE MUNDANE NEW WORLD ***BARBARIANS*** MUCH LONGER.

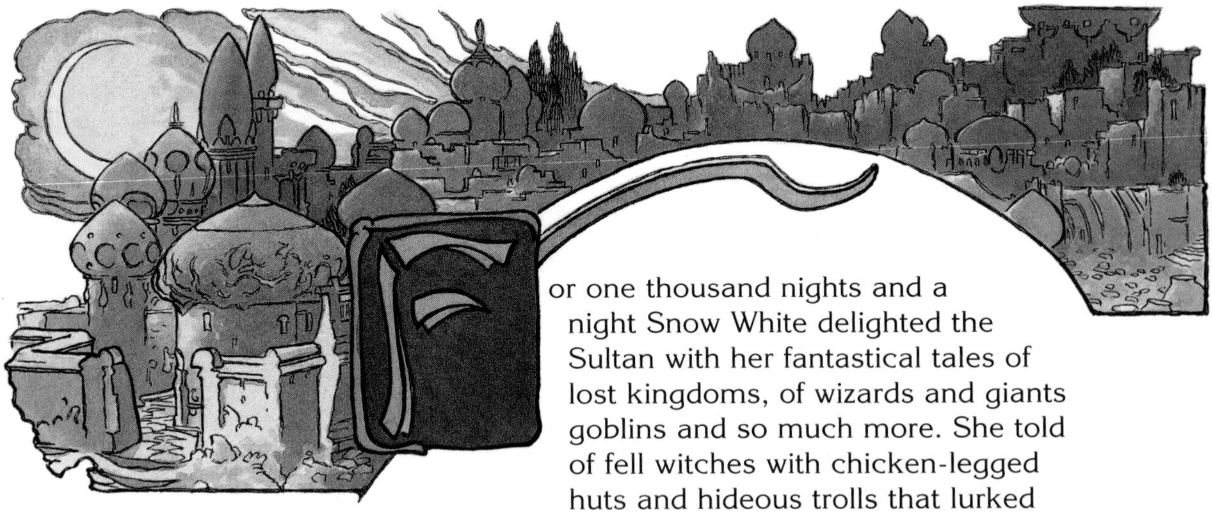

For one thousand nights and a night Snow White delighted the Sultan with her fantastical tales of lost kingdoms, of wizards and giants goblins and so much more. She told of fell witches with chicken-legged huts and hideous trolls that lurked under bridges. She bewildered his imagination with stories of lonely woodcarvers who carved living sons for themselves out of discarded branches, and daring boys who climbed giant beanstalks all the way into kingdoms in the clouds. Each night's tale concluded only when the morning's sun had begun its own climb into the blue sky, and each morning Snow promised, "I've another tale to tell you tonight, O King of the Time and Caliph of the Tide, if only you could put off my execution for one more day." And each time the Sultan agreed, yawning as he took himself alone to his carpet bed.

"Perhaps just for one more day, Snow," the Sultan would say, turning his sly smile away from her, so that she could not spy it.

But inevitably the evening came when Snow had to confess, "I'm sorry, O King of the Stars and Winds, but I've no more stories to tell. I've exhausted myself of giants and dragons and cursed princesses. I've quite simply run out. So finally, I suppose, I must face the grim sentence of death you've ordained for me."

We cannot know what Snow White expected the Sultan's reaction to be. Would he fly into a dark rage? Would he take up his scimitar and strike off her head that very instant? But, to her wonderment, King Shahryar did none of those things. Instead he immediately fell onto his knees before her and wept. And when he'd recovered, he kissed her hands and feet and cried, "O dearest Snow, in my heart I pardoned thee years ago, for that I found thee chaste, pure, ingenious and pious. Truly I'm exposed a fraud, for I've kept you here for nearly three years, letting you believe all the while that my doom still hung over you. But it was only because I loved your stories so much and was loath to miss any one of them. As you said on that long-ago first night, you're not one of my subjects and shouldn't be held to my mortal decrees. I release you, Snow, to return to your own world and community."

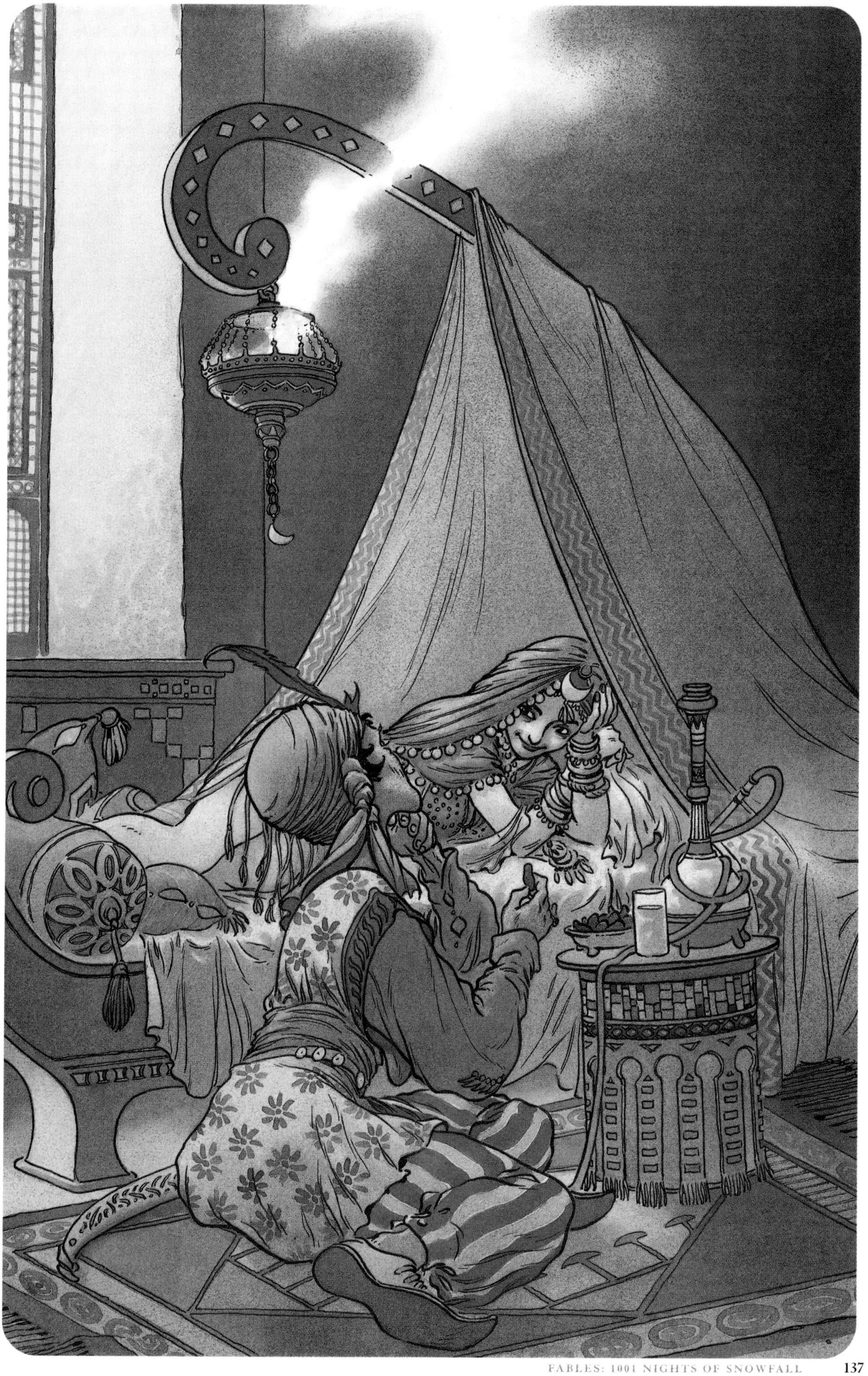

And the Sultan then decreed that there would be feasting and celebrations for the next three days, in his capital and throughout his vast domains. He gifted Snow White with presents of gold and alabaster, and horses white as Snow's pale skin and as black as a moonless night. They had saddles of gem-encrusted silver and carnelian, and there were other costly stuffs.

"I cannot make a military alliance with you, Snow," the Sultan told her, "without long days of prayer and pondering. For truly both your lands and those of The Adversary are of the Dar al Harb, which is to say, of the Domain of War, which one day may become part of the pan-caliphate, but not soon. But I owe you much, and so my gifts to you will include a host of magical and wondrous things, fair and rare, that they may prove helpful to you in your struggle against this infidel empire maker."

And so the Sultan increased her treasure with many wondrous things, fair and rare. There was a carpet that could fly through the very sky, and a clockwork tiger, and three and thirty clockwork warriors, and a stallion that could run over the top of the ocean's waves, even as over the solid earth.

There were a number of warlike jinnis and ifrits, each sealed into their bottles with the seal-ring of Lord Sulayman, son of David – may Allah accept the twain! Included were enchanted rings and lamps and other diverse things of miracle and wizardry.

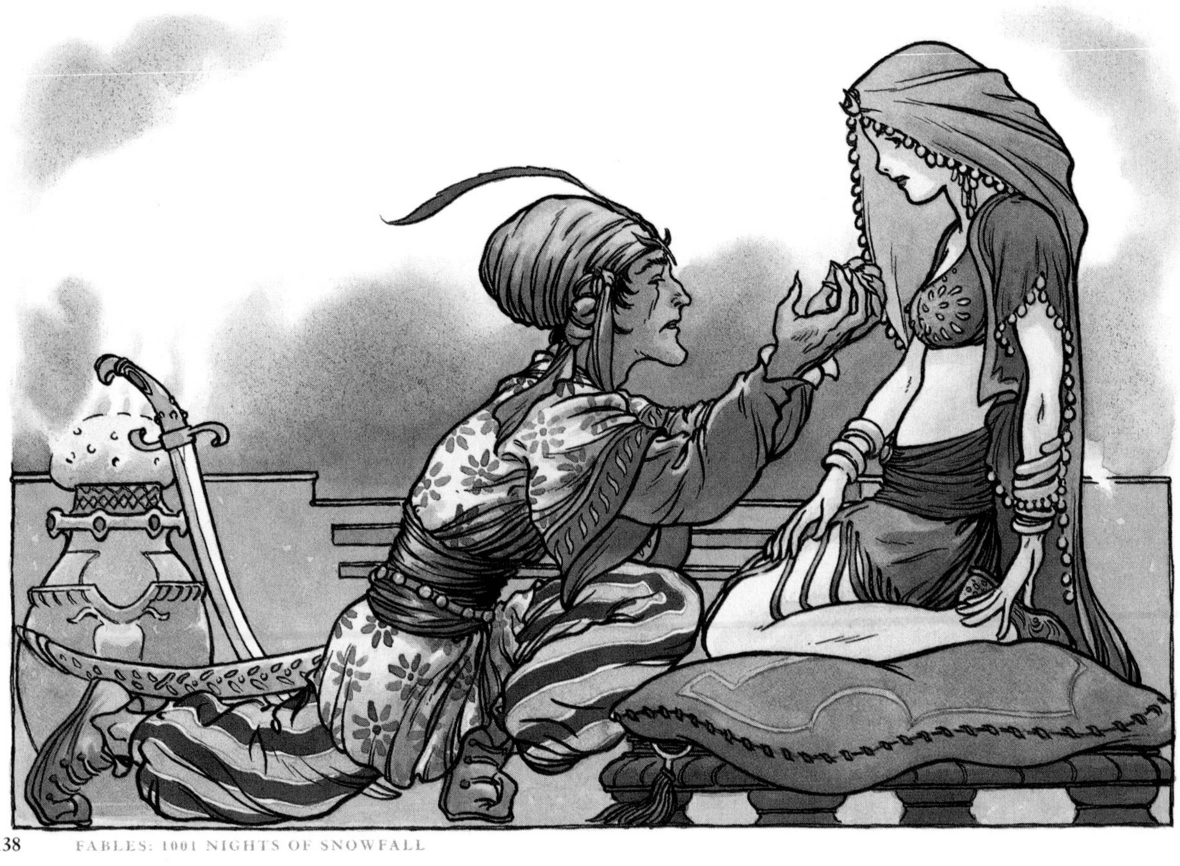

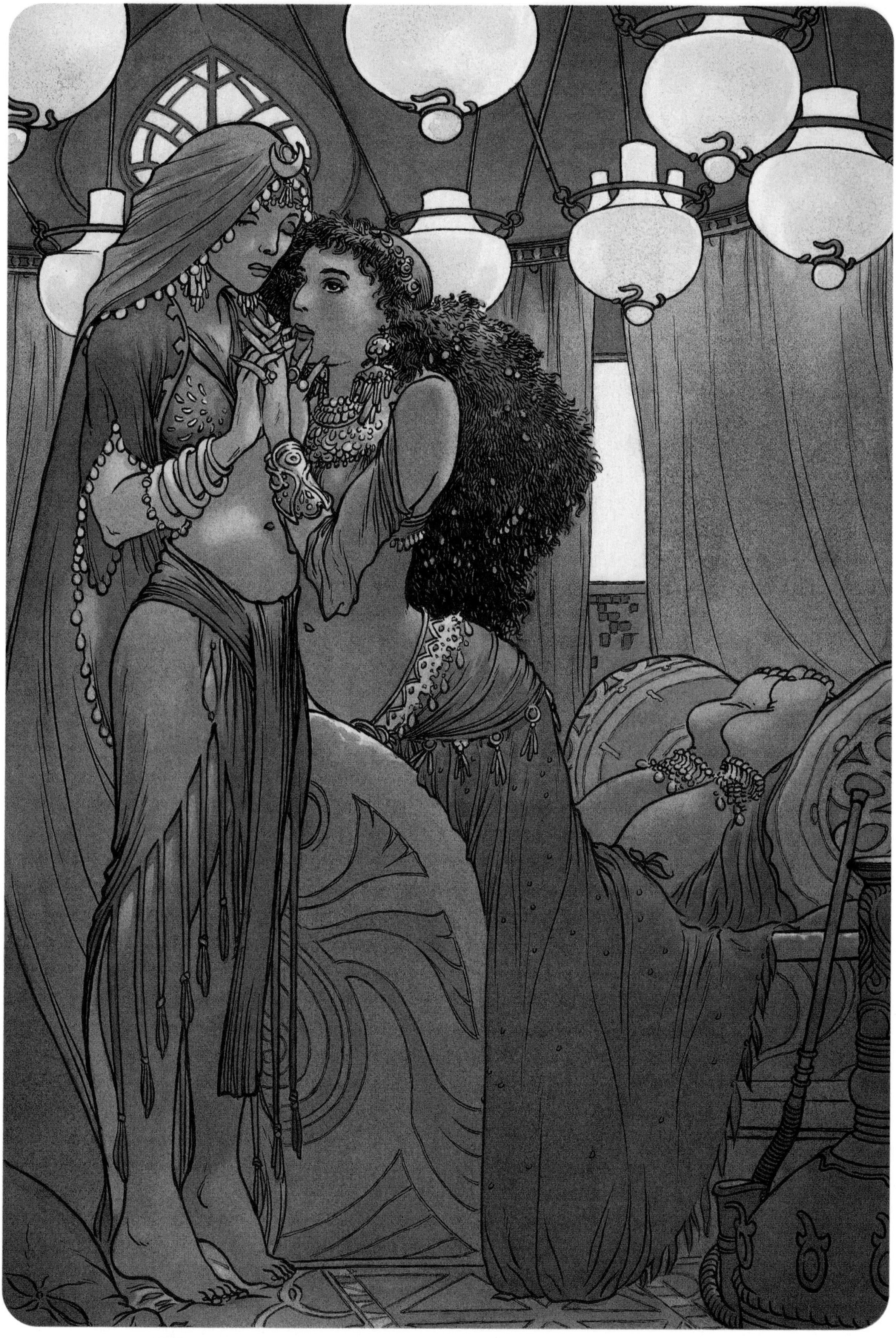

Then, on the night before Snow White was to take her leave, a woman came alone to her apartments.

She was anointed and scented with rose water and willow flower water and pods of musk and ambergris. Her dress was adorned with red gold and wrought with counterfeit presentments of birds and beasts, and her neck was encircled with a necklace of jewels of such price, in the like even Iskander rejoiced not. She was a woman, like Snow White, bright with exceeding fairness and grace and beauty, but where Snow was the rising sun, she was the somber twilight.

The woman presented Snow with her own gifts of splendid stuffs, and observed all of the courtly courtesies, saying, "I am Scheherazade, eldest daughter of the High Wazir. I have come to wish you well on your journey home and to thank you, honored lady, for these past three years."

"Why?" Snow asked.

"Because I was fated to be King Shahryar's bride on the night you instead went unto him. Now it is finally my turn to go unto him and be his bride of the night. But I've been dearly gifted with these three years, beyond what I could have hoped. I thank you for that much. May Allah bless your root and branch and increase your house with many sons."

"I"m truly sorry to hear that," Snow said. "But in truth, I suspect the Sultan's wrath may finally have dimmed."

"Do you believe so?"

"If not, would you like to know how I survived for a thousand nights and a night?"

"Oh, yes."

"He likes stories," Snow said.

BIOGRAPHIES

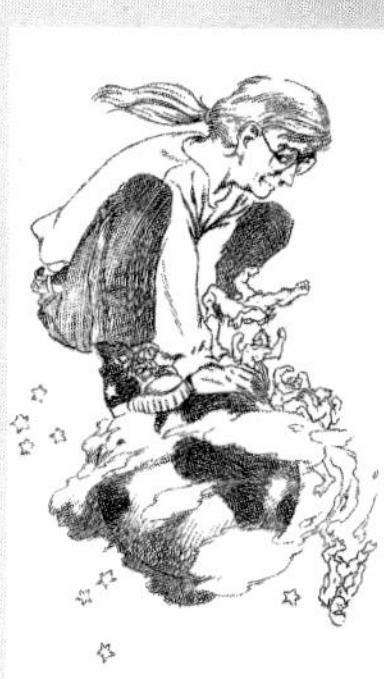

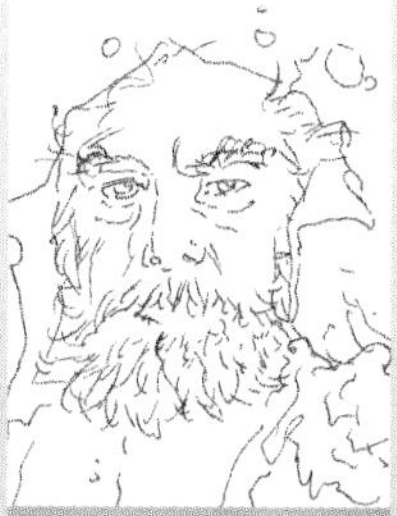

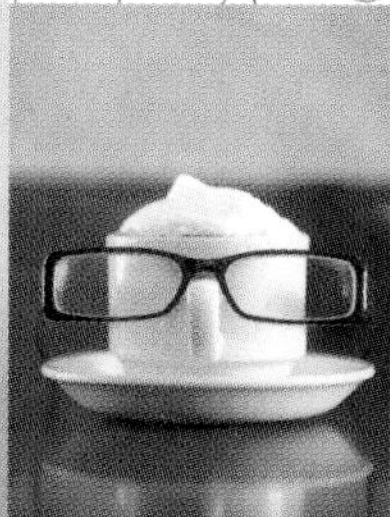

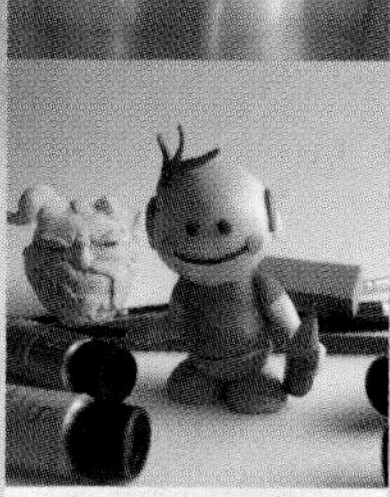

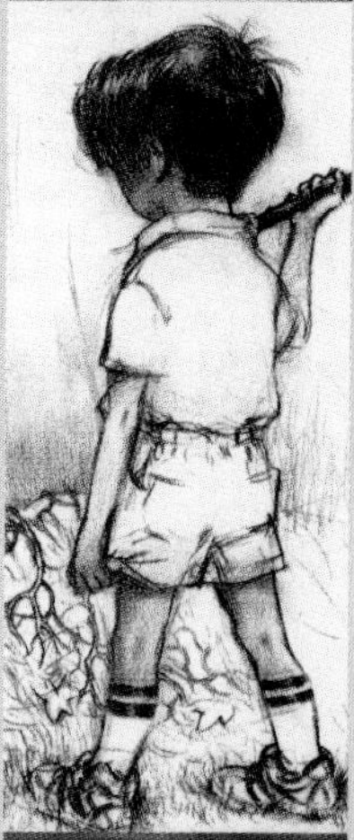

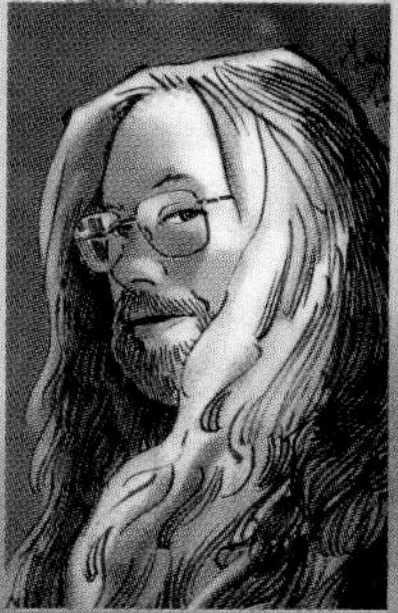

CHARLES VESS is the multiple award-winning illustrator of many stories and books, too many to list here. He's currently creating (with David Spence) a huge bronze sculpture based on *A Midsummer Night's Dream*, and painting a picture book called *Blueberry Girl* (HarperCollins), written by his frequent collaborator Neil Gaiman. He's also illustrating Susanna Clarke's short story collection *The Ladies of Grace Adieu* (Bloomsbury). The worst thing Charles ever did was to incite a bizarre and horrifying incident involving Santa's elves and Singer Sewing Machines, the details of which are thankfully unclear. All police reports have been purged.

MICHAEL Wm. KALUTA is the prolific illustrator of far too many covers for Vertigo Comics' *Lucifer* and *Books of Magic* series. He's also pretty proud of his illustrations for the 1994 J.R.R. Tolkien Calendar. Michael admits to appearing on and contributing to French television and seems unrepentant about it. Charges are pending.

JOHN BOLTON is the illustrator of *Switch* (DC Comics), written by Devin Grayson, *Harlequin Valentine*, written by Neil Gaiman, and he is working with Bob Zemeckis on character designs for the forthcoming movie *Beowulf*. John's worst deed involves nearly crashing a small plane into the French Alps before the actual designated pilot was able to wrest the controls back and save them all. John claims it was a simple mistake. For our own peace of mind we've decided to believe him.

MARK BUCKINGHAM is the most prolific illustrator of FABLES stories. He's also illustrated many other comic books, including *Miracleman: The Silver Age*, written by Neil Gaiman, and *Merv Pumpkinhead, Agent of D.R.E.A.M.*, written by Bill Willingham. His greatest accomplishment was marrying Irma. The worst thing he's ever done was destroying his parents' new kitchen while trying to wash his hands. He steadfastly maintains that it was no act of malice or vengeance, but he was merely innocently drunk and passed out mid-scrub, leaving the water running. He promises never to drink hard spirits anymore. We'll see. We'll see.

JAMES JEAN is the regular cover illustrator on all things *Fables*, including *Jack of Fables*. He designed Shaun White's snowboard, upon which Shaun won the Gold Medal at the 2006 Winter Olympics. James is also the author of *Process Recess*, a collection of his own work. James is a humble and soft-spoken fellow who claims never to have committed any heinous crimes. U.S. Marshal Task Force: Charlie X-217 has been formed to ferret out the truth.

MARK WHEATLEY is a writer and illustrator of more books than we can count, but he'd like to call attention to a few recent projects. With his co-writer Allan Gross he's producing and drawing a new comic book series, *Miles the Monster*, for Dover International Speedway who hosts two NASCAR races each year. He's also developing the Flash-animated graphic novel D in collaboration with filmmaker Robert Tinnell for Fangoria.com. Mark regularly writes and illustrates the comic book series *Frankenstein Mobster*. His dirtiest deed was in creating the fictional persona of Mark Wheatley to disguise his true identity from the world. We'd tell you who he really is, in the dark of night when the moon is high, but you'd tremble in your beds.

DEREK KIRK KIM is the writer/artist of the multi award-winning *Same Difference and Other Stories*. He is currently working on an as yet untitled graphic novel for First Second Books. Derek (God bless his tender young soul) actually believes the worst thing he's ever done was to be a single month over deadline for his story in this book. He's so wonderfully innocent, isn't he?

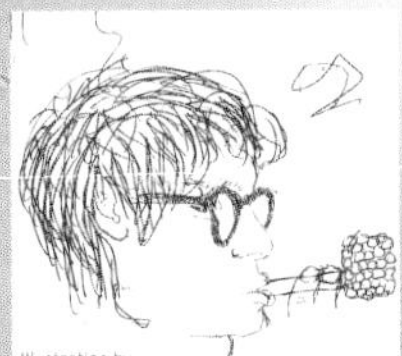
Illustration by Jason Shiga

TARA McPHERSON painted the covers for the four-issue series *Thessaly: Witch for Hire* (Vertigo), written by Bill Willingham. She's produced rock posters for bands such as Modest Mouse, The Strokes, and Death Cab for Cutie. She insists her worst crime ever was illustrating a sex-ed advice column for *Bikini Magazine*. We however know that she's hiding something dark and terrible. The investigation continues.

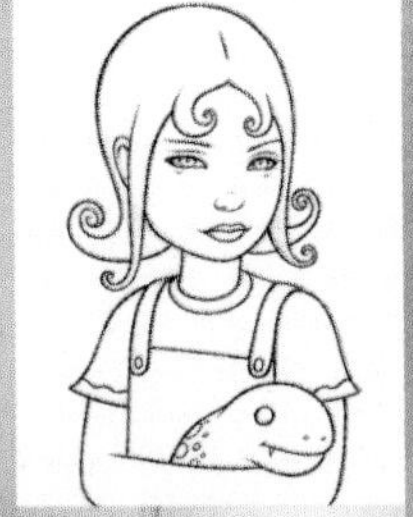

ESAO ANDREWS has done skateboard designs for Baker Skate-boards and is a contributor to the Meathaus comics series. The worst thing he's ever done was to shoot a nesting dove and then eat it in some sort of diabolical secret ritual, without ever telling his parents. Well, your parents know *now*, don't they, Esao?

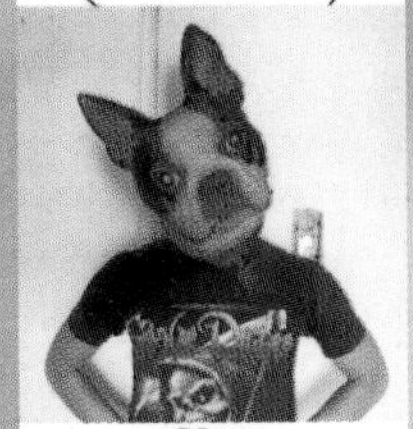

BRIAN BOLLAND has illustrated far too many Judge Dredd comic book stories. He's also the illustrator of *Mr. Mamoulian*, *The Actress and the Bishop*, and has illustrated hundreds of comic book covers. Once Brian scratched and dented a smart red sports car with his car door and drove away without telling anyone. As far as we know, his mad crime spree continues unabated.

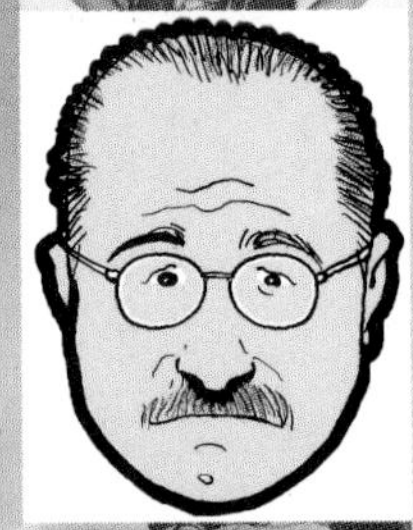

JILL THOMPSON has been writing and illustrating comics stories for many years. She's perhaps best known for her *Scary Godmother* tales and has recently illustrated the adventures of the coolest pack of dogs (and one occasional cat) in funnybook history. She once blew the metal door off her dear old grandmother's oven (and nearly blew up poor Granny's entire house with it). She claimed it was a simple accident with the gas, but further investigation revealed that she'd recently been reading the Hansel and Gretel story. Hmmmm.

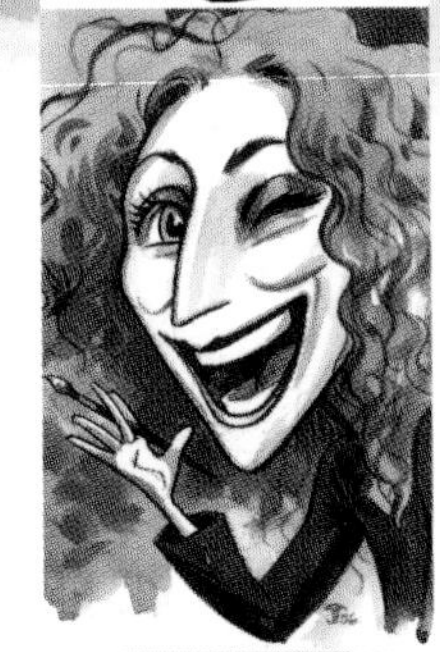

TODD KLEIN hasn't quite lettered every comic book ever published, but he's come close. He has, however, lettered every FABLES comic ever published, and we think that's just as impressive an accomplishment. Once in grade school he defaced the school's encyclopedia (by clipping out the *Superman* illustration to add to his collection) and then, under harsh grilling from the authorities, framed one of his neighbors. Todd has never paid for his crimes to this very day.

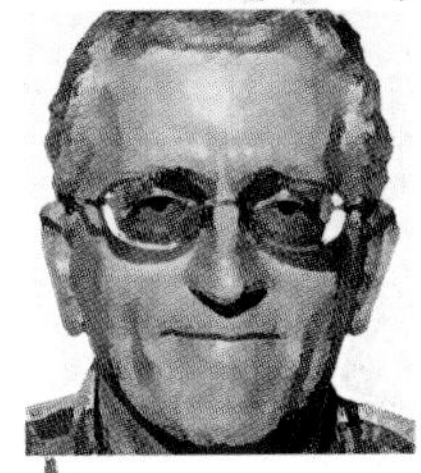

BILL WILLINGHAM has written *Fables*, *Proposition Player* and various other things for Vertigo Comics, *Robin* and *Shadowpact* for DC Comics, and other things besides. He was once arrested in Burlington, Wisconsin for overdue library books.

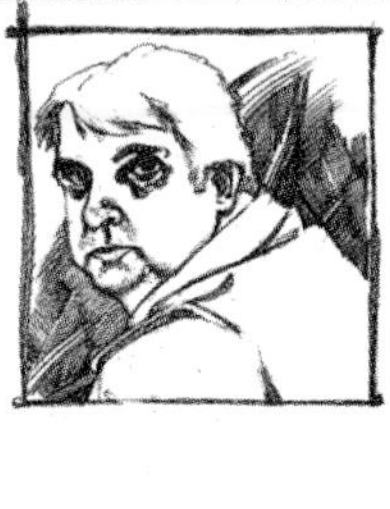

OTHER GRAPHIC NOVELS BY BILL WILLINGHAM

FABLES Vol. 1: LEGENDS IN EXILE
The immortal characters of popular fairy tales have been driven from their homelands and now live hidden among us, trying to cope with life in 21st-century Manhattan.

FABLES Vol. 2: ANIMAL FARM
Non-human Fable characters have found refuge in upstate New York on the farm, miles from mankind. But a conspiracy to free them from their perceived imprisonment may lead to a war that could wrest control of the Fables community away from Snow White.

FABLES Vol. 3: STORYBOOK LOVE
Love may be blooming between two of the most hard-bitten, no-nonsense Fables around. But are they destined for happiness – or a quick and untimely death?

**FABLES Vol. 4:
MARCH OF THE WOODEN SOLDIERS**
When Little Red Riding Hood suddenly walks through the gate between this world and the lost Fable Homelands, she's welcomed as a miraculous survivor by nearly everyone – everyone except her old nemesis, Bigby Wolf, who smells spying and subversion more than survival.

FABLES Vol. 5: THE MEAN SEASONS
This trade paperback features two tales of Bigby's exploits during World War II as well as "The Year After," which follows the aftermath of the Adversary's attempt to conquer Fabletown – including the birth of Snow White and Bigby's children!

FABLES Vol. 6: HOMELANDS
Boy Blue is on a mission of revenge as he uncovers the Adversary's true identity! Plus, the 2-part story of Jack's adventures in Hollywood, and the tale of Mowgli's return to Fabletown.

**FABLES Vol. 7:
ARABIAN NIGHTS (AND DAYS)**
Opening a new front in the struggle between the Fables and the Adversary, the worlds of the Arabian Fables are invaded – leading to an unprecedented diplomatic mission to Manhattan and a nasty case of culture shock.

OTHER BOOKS BY BILL WILLINGHAM:

**PROPOSITION PLAYER
Bill Willingham/Paul Guinan/Ron Randall**
When a professional Vegas poker player collects vouchers for the souls of a roomful of people as a bar prank, he's just anted up for a high-stakes game of celestial proportions.

**THE SANDMAN PRESENTS:
TALLER TALES
Bill Willingham/various**
A dazzling compendium of danger and hijinks from beyond the wall of sleep.

**THE SANDMAN PRESENTS:
THESSALY – WITCH FOR HIRE
Bill Willingham/Shawn McManus/
Andrew Pepoy**
Thessaly, the world's oldest, deadliest witch, becomes the unwitting partner in a monster-killing business with her ghostly, annoying and besotted sidekick Fetch.

And be sure to read the ongoing *Fables* monthly series, winner of seven Eisner Awards

All titles are suggested for mature readers.
Search the Graphic Novels section of VERTIGOCOMICS.COM
for art and information on all of our books.